AN IMMIGRANT'S STORY

AMERICA,
Land of My Dreams

ALPHA & ΩMEGA
HEALING ARTS

ADEL GOBRAN HANNA (KHOURI), MD

Copyrighted Material

America, Land of My Dreams: An Immigrant's Story

Copyright © 2024 by Adel G. Hanna, MD
All Rights Reserved.

No part of this publication may be reproduced, stored in a retrieval system or transmitted, in any form or by any means—electronic, mechanical, photocopying, recording, or otherwise—without prior written permission from the publisher, except for the inclusion of brief quotations in a review.

For information about this title or to order other books and/or electronic media, contact the publisher:

Alpha & Omega Healing Arts
PO Box 494
New Albany, OH 43054
alphaomegahealingarts.com
aloha@alphaomegahealingarts.com

ISBNs:
978-0-9960576-2-2 (softcover)
978-0-9960576-3-9 (eBook)

Library of Congress Control Number: 2024900274

Printed in the United States of America

Cover and Interior design: 1106 Design

All stories in this book are true. Some names of individuals in this book have been changed to protect their privacy.

AMERICA,
LAND OF MY DREAMS

*For Dad and his cherished memory,
and Mom whose faith and love live on.*

Gobran & Anna (Tikkabo): a union made in heaven.

*For their precious grandchildren,
my beloved children, AJ, Andre, and Abby.*

*"What is impossible with man
is possible with God."*

~Jesus
Luke 18:27 (NIV)

★ ★ ★
CONTENTS

Acknowledgments xi
Introduction: America, Land of My Dreams xv

PART ONE   DAD'S STORY. 1

Chapter 1   The Khouri Family: My Levantine Heritage 3
Chapter 2   Gabal Lebnan (Mount Lebanon):
             The Khouris' Ancestral Home? 7
Chapter 3   Gaza: Grandpa's Birthplace 13
Chapter 4   Egypt: The Khouris' New Home 17
Chapter 5   Al-Khouris' New Life and Challenges in Egypt 21
Chapter 6   Slavery and Racial Biases in Paradise 27
Chapter 7   Thriving in Egypt 33
Chapter 8   The Khouri Family's Riches to Rags Story:
             Life in Hayy El-Sakakini 53
Chapter 9   Egypt's Black-White Color Divide 57

PART TWO   MOM'S STORY 71

Chapter 10   Miraculous Birth and Early Childhood
             Separation in Africa's Highlands 73
Chapter 11   The Tearful Years of Young Childhood 85
Chapter 12   Mom's Farewell to Asmara: The Search
             for Italians and Britons 101

Chapter 13	The Journey: Crossing the Borders: Teseney to Kassala 115
Chapter 14	Crossing the Borders to Sudan: Walking to Kassala 121
Chapter 15	The Bus Trip to Khartoum: Mom and a Fake Husband 131
Chapter 16	Khartoum: Mom's New Home: The "Holy War" Against Britain and Ethiopia 139
Chapter 17	My Parents: A Black & White Love Story in Khartoum 151

PART THREE SUDAN 1960–1980: MY CHILDHOOD YEARS 167

Chapter 18	Life and Personal Tragedy in Sudan 169
Chapter 19	My School Days at a Catholic School in Muslim Sudan: Comboni College Khartoum aka CCK 181
Chapter 20	School Days, Civil War, and Political Unrest 197
Chapter 21	Finally Meeting Dad's Family in Egypt! 203
Chapter 22	The Day the Music Stopped in Sudan 209
Chapter 23	America: The Intriguing and Puzzling Land 213

PART FOUR FINALLY, AMERICA 223

Chapter 24	Coming to America: Fear and Divine Intervention . . . 225
Chapter 25	Undergraduate Years 233
Chapter 26	My Dad's Passing 259
Chapter 27	Medical School: The Journey 265

Afterword 279
Endnotes 283
References 295
About the Author 303
Index 305

* * *
ACKNOWLEDGMENTS

I LEFT THE WRITING of my acknowledgments page until the very end. I needed time to think and reflect on the many men and women who blessed, inspired, and encouraged me in my birth country of Sudan and America, my new home. This book that was completed as a manuscript over two decades ago, then revised to its present positive and well-researched form, was conceived, and birthed with God's help and the love and cheering of many. So, here's my humble attempt to thank those who blessed me and contributed their time, talents, and kindness to help me bring this fascinating story to life.

My first acknowledgment is to God. He gave me as a teenager in Sudan a seemingly impossible dream: to be a doctor in America. God helped me to accomplish it, and then helped me to write a story about it!

I am forever grateful to my mom, dad, their families, and ancestors in Africa and the Middle East. Their stories, challenges, trials, and tribulations have inspired me and will inspire many for years to come. This book tells their stories and the legacies many of them left behind. Thank you for your perseverance and faith.

My dad is now in heaven with my older brother George who died before I was born. I pray this book will honor your memories. Rest with God. I love you.

Mom, thank you for sharing with me your unbelievable life story, Dad's amazing story, and your fascinating life with him. Thank you for taking so many hours of your precious time to record on multiple cassette tapes all these stories that made this book possible.

AJ, Abby, and Andre', God is with you as you continue the good path of love, diligence, and faith. I am so grateful for your perseverance and accomplishments despite all the challenges. This book is a story about your roots and my gift to you. I am very proud of you.

Joesph, your compassion and caring are unparalleled. You're a true brother. You were a listening ear throughout the writing of the book. Thank you!

Anwar, your patience in afflictions and heart of brotherly compassion has always inspired me. Thank you, brother. This book is for you.

I am grateful to my sister and the rest of my siblings for all the childhood memories in Khartoum with Dad and Mom.

My Dad's parents and his siblings are long gone, and so are Mom's parents and siblings. Their memories and legacies live on. I am forever grateful for them. Rest in peace.

I am grateful to my cousin Hany who kindly shared some of Dad's, and his siblings' stories that enriched this book. My aunt, Rose, Dad's favorite sibling, is now in heaven with him. She warmly welcomed me, Mom, and my siblings, when we met her for the first time in Cairo. I will always be grateful for that.

Thank you to Abraham and Michelle, Berhane and Hannah, Selvie, Ruth, Veronica and William, Abraham and his family, Joe and his family, Hewit, Zimam, Scott and Kathleen, and the one and only Amony for the years of supporting me with your genuine caring and encouragement. I am grateful to you for encouraging me to finish this book. Selvie, thank you for your prayers!

I want to acknowledge Magid, Aaron, Bushra, Nouga, Reem, "Angels & Disciples" small church group, and Samir for sharing, caring, and helping me to grow in my faith. Thank you for your prayers and for standing by me.

Thank you to my editor Wendy who cared for this project and blessed me with her vast knowledge and creative editing skills. I also thank Ronda and Michele from 1106 Design. They created an amazing front cover and interior design for my book, but more importantly, they cared for me, and my dream to finish this project. Thank you!

A special shout-out and appreciation to two groups that I consider America's finest!

The first group is composed of passionate young male and female students, the hope and the future of America, who encouraged my dream of finishing this book and inspired me with their big dreams. Thank you to Nicole, Max, Vera, Sania, Cynthia, Tori, Isabella, Jenna, Jessica, Ashley, Annika, McKenna, Erik, Sydney, Chloe, and Sophia.

The second group reminds me of the kind American men and women of all backgrounds, races, colors, and ethnicities who once encouraged me as a young student from Sudan to pursue my dream of becoming a doctor in America. They varied in age, some recent graduates who just started new jobs and others with much more years of experience and maturity. They were always generous with their time, kindness, and words of encouragement to the young ones around them and me as I pursued my dream to finish this book. My gratitude to Hanna, Tawonia, Adam, Dr. W, Dr. G, Abigail, Renee, Monica, Laura, Angie, Sharon, Kenisha, Gretchen K, AP, Rena, Sharon, Matt, John, Elliot, Tizita, Gina, Ann, and Allen. Abigail, you're a blessing to everyone!

There are so many people to thank and acknowledge but not enough space on this page to list them all. My deepest appreciation to those who are not listed here, but who touched my life with their kindness, love, and encouragement. To all the readers who will be touched and blessed by the true stories in this book, I say sincerely: Thank you for taking the time to read this book, and I pray that it will be a source of hope, healing, and inspiration to you.

Finally, and importantly, I would like to mention and acknowledge the so many fond memories of Sudan where I was born. Sudan and the Sudanese people from the North, South, East, and West, Christians, Muslims, and Jews made Mom and Dad feel at home. Khartoum was my beautiful childhood home. I am grateful to my home country Sudan and to my Sudanese friends of all religions. Our Christian family had many Muslim friends who genuinely cared for us. Civil wars, including the April 2023 war that transformed my home city of Khartoum into a war zone with ruined buildings, killed lives and turned millions of proud Sudanese into refugees. Some of the stories in this book tell of the past political and religious wars that had befallen my parents' ancestral homes, and Sudan. It was that old religious extremism that gradually showed itself again in Sudan, divided the country, ignited wars, and sent the country's innocent: Christians, Muslims, and Jews away from their homes. I pray that a new Sudan will emerge where religion, color, race, and ethnicity will never separate its kind and generous people.

★ ★ ★
INTRODUCTION
AMERICA, LAND OF MY DREAMS

I WAS BORN IN AL-MANSHIA, a lush suburb of Khartoum, the capital city of the Northeastern African country of Sudan. That was my home until I left in 1980 to pursue a dream in America. At the age of thirteen, I found a book in a book fair in Khartoum about an American missionary doctor; it changed the course of my life. I was fully convinced after reading it that God's purpose for my life was to be a doctor in America. And so, I left Sudan soon after finishing high school to go to Indiana, the only state in America with which I was acquainted. Michael Jackson and The Jackson 5's hit song "Goin' Back to Indiana" (written by The Corporation) was all that I needed to choose an undergraduate college there. And so, equipped with an impossible dream, my bell-bottom blue jeans, and a big Afro like Michael's, I went to America.

My life and that of my parents and grandparents have all been rooted in cities adjacent to the River Nile. I grew up in a beautiful home just a short walking distance from the waters of the Blue Nile, which originates in the Highlands of Ethiopia, Mom's birthplace. A few miles from my childhood home, the Blue Nile flows to Khartoum where it merges with the White Nile to form the great River Nile. From there it flows northward through the dry desert sands of Egypt forming the fertile Nile delta near Dad's birthplace of Al-Zagazig, Egypt. The River Nile, the world's longest river, eventually spills its waters into the Mediterranean Sea, ending its long journey.

Along its path, the River Nile witnessed wars, religious strife, slavery, and colonization. But it also brought life—sustaining water and food to various generations. My parents lived through the storms of religious strife, wars, and foreign colonization in its vicinity. But still, Mom and Dad's thirst and hunger were satisfied, and their lives prospered by God's blessing of the River Nile. Their stories began in colonized Africa. They lived at a time in Africa's history when society openly treated Black people as being inferior to whites. Dad's white skin color during the era of the Europeans' colonization of Egypt, Sudan, and Ethiopia ensured him privileges and rights that Mom could only dream of.

But against all odds and contrary to society's norms, Dad and Mom got married. He was fascinated by her black skin color, but most important, by her beautiful character. Dad, a man of strong Christian faith, did not view his white color as a ticket to a higher status in Anglo-Egyptian colonized Sudan. They met and fell in love in Khartoum. He was a white gentleman who came from Egypt's high society but chose to break his society's standards when he fell in love and decided to marry Mom. Apart from their mutual love, dreams of a better life, and belief in Jesus Christ, they had nothing else in common. They came from different worlds. Dad, a university-educated white man of Levantine heritage, and Mom, a dark-skinned woman from Ethiopia's Highlands without any formal education, did not even speak each other's languages.

Mom worked all her childhood life to support her family. A trusted friend of a friend smuggled her through the perilous borders of Sudan as a teenager. Her dream was to find a job as a live-in babysitter or a domestic help with an English family in Khartoum to help feed her family back home. Dad, on the other hand, was in his mid-thirties when he flew on a luxurious commercial flight from Cairo to Khartoum. King Farouk of

Egypt sent Dad, a devoted skillful Christian architect with a big dream, with a few Egyptian architects, to build the famed King Farouk Mosque in Khartoum! The two met miraculously in the late 1940s in Khartoum—a city where firm ethnicity, color, and racial barriers existed.

His life with Mom and the love that united them against all odds and societal prejudices became my inspiration in life and throughout my immigrant journey in America. They were a Black-and-white couple in Anglo-Egyptian-colonized Sudan where long-held biases, prejudices, religious conflicts, foreign control, and colonization seem to all coalesce in one geographic location.

Like my parents and ancestors before them, I left my birthplace with a God-given dream and hope for a better life. Mom and Dad's immigrant journey in Sudan as a biracial couple made their hopes and dreams harder to attain, but they believed, remained focused, and persevered. Their relationship, hopes, and dreams that once looked impossible to accomplish became possible with God's help. That is what they believed as immigrants, and they lived to see their dreams come true. They encouraged my dream to be a doctor in America, a mission that seemed impossible because they simply believed that with God all things are possible. They were right. With God's help, I became a doctor in America, Land of My Dreams!

As an immigrant, I joined a long tradition of people who come from every corner of the world to America. Millions came here to escape wars, religious persecution, and are in pursuit of financial stability, peace, and laws that offer human rights and freedom of expression. People who live in nations where they experience biases because of their beliefs, opinions, skin color, race, gender, or economic and social status do not have the luxury of such laws. It is easy for us to take these laws that protect our peace, rights, and freedom for granted. But my list of blessings will always include the fantastic opportunity to live in America where there is such peace and freedom in a world where global wars and conflicts are always raging.

My immigrant journey has shown me the obvious: America is not perfect, just like none of us is. But America is way better than many other places in the world. That is why millions came to America in the past and countless others want to come to this land of dreams. I am thankful for my parents and their ancestors' pioneering spirit that made them emigrate from one nation to another in pursuit of religious freedom and a better life for themselves and their children. It was that same pioneering spirit that brought me to America.

It has been decades since I first came to America. It still feels as if it were just yesterday when I swam in the waters of the great River Nile with my Boy Scout troops. Memories like those from the old country, sweet or sad ones, occasionally fill my heart as it does to other immigrants who left their childhood homes. Yet, I consider myself blessed and privileged to live in America.

In this book, you will encounter the heart of an immigrant as you read my parents' and my own stories. You will experience the emotional toll and challenges of loneliness, biases, prejudice, and colorism, and how not to let any of the above bury your dream. And more important, these stories will inspire you to never give up on a good dream in your heart that will bless you and others but instead to dare to believe that with God nothing is impossible.

As a thirteen-year-old teenager in Sudan with nothing but a dream, I never envisioned that one day I would hear my children, first-generation Americans, sing in their school's choir a favorite American song, "God Bless America," and recite proudly the Pledge of Allegiance. The last line of the song—"God bless America, my home sweet home"—often makes me pause a little. America is my children's home, but gratefully it is my home sweet home too.

PART ONE
DAD'S STORY
★ ★ ★

CHAPTER 1

THE KHOURI FAMILY: MY LEVANTINE HERITAGE

AL-KHOURI IS MY FAMILY'S NAME. "'Khouri' (also spelled as 'Khoury') is an Arabic surname that is unique to Christians in the Middle East. The term *Khoury* means "priest" in Arabic. It derives from the Latin word *curia*. It is often given as a last name to a new priest or minister, replacing the old one, and to the children of the married priest and their descendants."[1] ("Al-" roughly means "from" or "the.")

Naturally, Dad's surname of Khouri described the family's long ancestral Christian heritage and its priesthood lineage.

Dad often told me and my siblings about his Khouri ancestral priestly heritage, which dates back to Jesus's days and the early Church. He guessed that his Khouri family's heritage goes all the way to the Apostle Paul! If that was a true story told and retold by one generation to another, or a way to make us proud of our Christian heritage, I will never know. As I grew older, my parents taught me that it was not any lineage to a remarkable figure, such as the Apostle Paul, that would get me to heaven. I needed Jesus and not Paul to go to heaven.

Khouri was my last name until I went to America to start pursuing my dream to be a doctor. So, leaving Sudan did not only mean leaving my childhood home in the beautiful suburb of Al-Manshia, but it also meant leaving my family's name behind. A hasty government clerk in Khartoum decided to drop my family name "Khouri" from my Sudanese passport. There was no space in the passport to print my whole name, Adel Gobran Hanna Khouri. He stopped at the name Hanna and handed me the passport. With that, the Khouri family name suddenly vanished from my heritage at least on paper, and Hanna, my grandfather's name, became my new last name in America.

How did my dad's ancestors stay faithful to their Christian calling as priests and ministers amid centuries of Muslim conquests and rule? That thought always intrigued me. These conquests date back to the first invasion of the Levant (Al-Sham) by the Rashidun caliph in the seventh century. The word "Levant" (which is French for "rising") originally referred to "the East" or "Mediterranean lands east of Italy." The term referred to the rising of the sun in the east, or the point where the sun rises.[2] Historically, it comprises "the region along the eastern Mediterranean shores, roughly corresponding to modern-day Israel, Jordan, Lebanon, Syria, and certain adjacent areas."[3]

Numerous Islamic conquests followed, and the region remained under Islamic control after the defeat of the crusaders who tried unsuccessfully to reclaim Jerusalem and the surrounding region. With the Islamization of a large part of the Christian population and the migration of Muslims from surrounding areas (mainly Egypt), the Christian population began to decline gradually.

My Khouri Christian ancestors lived through those invasions and obviously chose to not abandon their faith in Jesus Christ. Not only that, but they continued their calling as priests and minsters promoting their Christian faith even as Islam spread in the Levant. Whatever economic hardships or persecution they endured throughout the centuries, they still managed to pass the baton of their Christian faith to my grandfather Hanna, Dad, and the rest of the family. But things must have taken a turn for the worst for the Khouri family in 1865 prompting them to head southwest to Egypt in search of a better life.

In the late nineteenth century and beyond, millions of Christians, including the Khouri family, particularly in Lebanon, decided to do the same. They left in large numbers to greener and safer pastures in Egypt, Europe, and the United States. Following the migration to various regions of the world, the "Khouri" name

> ... acquired different variants in different countries and is also uncommonly spelled as El Khoury, Elcure, Elkhori, Elkouri, Kouri, Couri, Koury, Coury, Kourie, Koory, Koorey, Kuri, Khuri, Khury, Kury, Curi, Cury, Coorey, Courey, Korey, Kory, Corey, Chory, Correy, and in Latin America as Kure, Cure, Correa, Juri, Jury, Cura, Jure, Eljure, Aljure or Alcuri.[4]

CHAPTER 2

GABAL LEBNAN (MOUNT LEBANON): THE KHOURIS' ANCESTRAL HOME?

DAD BELIEVED THAT HIS AL-KHOURI ANCESTORS had originally moved from Mount Lebanon before settling down in the Gaza region. The towering mountain range of Mount Lebanon runs parallel to the Mediterranean Sea in the country of Lebanon, with an average elevation of over 8,200 feet and a peak of 10,131 feet.[5] The Old Testament mentions the Mount of Lebanon and the cedar of Lebanon trees that are known for their high-quality wood. It is also the birthplace of the famous Christian Lebanese author Gibran Khalil Gibran (January 6, 1883–April 10, 1931).[6]

Gibran (commonly spelled as Gobran), the author of the best-selling book *The Prophet* and other notable works of art and literature, shared with my dad the name Gobran. I still remember Dad's collection of Gibran's books in Arabic. *"Are Gibran and Dad related?"* I often wondered.

War and Migration

A series of tragic events in the Mount of Lebanon culminated in the massacres of Lebanese Christians in 1860. Did my great-grandfather move his young family to the ancient city of Gaza on the eastern side of the Mediterranean Sea after that bloodletting? This question is hard to answer given the absence of family records from that era. If the family did move during those turbulent days, the coastal city of Gaza, found about fifty miles from Jerusalem, with its pleasant temperatures and rich history must have intrigued the Khouri family. Gaza, Cairo, and other cities in the world must have been a haven for the Christian Lebanese of that era. Makdisi and Fawaz (1994, cited in Mansel 2011) wrote about that tragedy:

> In May 1860, at a time of economic protests by Maronite peasants against Druze landlords, Druze began to attack Maronites in the mountains, as they had in 1840. Another Levantine catastrophe was imminent. Random murders turned into massacres sparing neither age [nor] sex. The Druze made up in ferocity for what they lacked in numbers, cutting up Christians like firewood. Seventeen members of the Shihab dynasty alone were killed. Finally, one Druze chronicler wrote, 'They set fire to all the villages and farms in the district, and left them like smouldering lava whose ashes the wind carried into the air, and thus the vast district became desolate wasteland, where only the crows croak and the owls hoot.'[7]

Akardi and Fawaz (cited in Mansel 2011) report: "Around 15,000 died in Mount Lebanon. Two hundred villages were destroyed; there were 100,000 refugees. Many Christians fled to Alexandria, strengthening the Syrian community there."[8]

The Debbas Archives, Beirut, Journal of Madame de Perthuis (1860, cited in Mansel 2011) captured the events through the eyes of the wife of a Frenchman businessman, the Comte de Perthuis, who was living in Beirut:

> From her windows, with incomparable views of mountains and the sea, she could see Christian villages burning in the distance.

Gabal Lebnan (Mount Lebanon): The Khouris' Ancestral Home?

Her servants were in agonies of fear for their families. 'All night you can hear the sound of firing in the distance.' Druze believed there was a Christian insurrection committee in Beirut, backed by the French consul. News arrived of Druze destroying Christian villages, going from house to house with torches. Christian refugees flooded into the city and camped in the foreign consulates. Druze women compensated for their inability to fight in person by encouraging, or shaming, the men into further atrocities.[9]

Meanwhile, 130 miles away from Mount Lebanon in the city of Damascus, Syria, more Christians were massacred. Fawaz (cited in Mansel 2011) detailed that event:

> Bloodshed spread to Damascus. At the time of the Greek uprising in 1821, Damascus Muslims had protected local Christians from the Sultan's order to kill or 'humble' them. By July 1860 they resented Christians' growing prosperity and use of foreign trade and consulates to promote it: Muslims in the provinces, unlike the Ottoman government in the capital, had few foreign friends. Christians were beginning to be regarded as traitors and a danger to the Empire. Even a Greek Catholic chronicler called Mikhail Mishaqa complained that 'ignorant,' 'humble' Christians had begun to behave with 'insolence' as equals of 'exalted' Muslims. Muslims massacred local Christians and sacked their houses. The Christian quarter in Damascus became a corpse-strewn mass of rubble; around 5,000 died.[10]

Christians Escaping the Levant and the Ottoman Empire

Life in the 1800s and the first few decades of the 1900s was hard and full of risks for Christians like my dad's Al-Khouri family. They lived as minorities in Lebanon, Syria, and other cities in the Levant under the control of the Ottoman Empire. The news to the Christians of the Levant, including my dad's ancestors, at times was very grim. They were cognizant of the plight of other Christians in the cities of the Levant that surrounded them. Immigration to safer and more peaceful places in the world where they could practice their faith must have been on everyone's mind. History records various massacres in the region including one that occurred in 1822 in the Greek city of Chios. Aksan, David Brewer, Consular Reports (cited in Mansel 2011) record a mass execution that occurred in that city located six hundred miles away from Mount Lebanon:

> On 25 March 1822, a fleet from the rival island of Samos with 1,500 soldiers landed in Chios and began to kill Turks. The Greek massacre was answered, on the orders of Mahmud 11 . . . by a massive countermassacre. On 11 April Turkish troops, some in a state of near mutiny, landed and massacred or burnt alive as many as 25,000 Chiots, including hospital inmates, and enslaved 50,000 others, mainly women and children (including a future grand vizier, Ibrahim Edhem)—causing a fall in price due to a glut of slaves on the market. . . . The population of Chios sank from 120,000 to around 25,000. The Rev. Robert Walsh, chaplain of the British Ambassador Lord Strangford, found the city stinking of death, human, and animal. There was no one in the streets. The elegant stone villas had been pillaged. 'Among the rubbish lay skulls, arms, and half-consumed bodies amid paper, books and broken furniture.' 'Weltering' bodies resembled 'heaps of rags. Glass cases in monastery antechambers on Chios still display victims' skulls and bones to the curious visitor.[11]

What exactly happened in Chios in 1822 will always be open for historians to discuss or dispute. But intense fear must have gripped the

Khouris and other Christians of the region as they heard reports of the Mount Lebanon and Damascus massacres of 1860 that claimed the lives of thousands of Christians, preceded by the 1822 tragedy in the city of Chios. That must have been enough of a driving force for Christians of the Levant including Armenians, Greeks, and Dad's family to emigrate to safer havens. Al-Khouris' decision to eventually immigrate from the Levant region was timely and lifesaving. Things just got worse for those who remained in Mount Lebanon and the Levant regions following the 1860 massacres in Mount Lebanon and Damascus. Historical records report that an estimated five hundred thousand people died of starvation in Mount Lebanon during the Ottoman Empire's control from 1915–1918.

"One third of the population died in the largely forgotten famine of Mount Lebanon. A devastating confluence of political and environmental factors lead to the deaths of 200,000 men, women and children in the region."[12]

A Ray of Hope in the Darkness

Yet, even during that period of darkness and shortly after the 1860 bloodshed in Lebanon, an American missionary, Daniel Bliss, helped found in 1866 the American University of Beirut which was originally named the Syrian Protestant College.[13]

With Jesus's words of *"That they may have life and have it more abundantly"* as its motto, it became a source of hope at a bleak time for Christians and Muslims of the region. The university, including its school of medicine, hospital, pharmacy, and nursing school, helped thousands including those reeling from the long-lasting shock of the 1860 massacre. It also played a positive role during the 1915–1918 Great Famine of Mount.[14]

The famous author Gibran Khalil Gibran dedicated a poem "Dead Are My People" in memory of those who perished in the famine that claimed over 200,000.[15] Sadly, for Lebanon, that tragic history repeated itself. In 1975 religious civil war between Muslim and Christians lasted over 15 years killing an estimated 120,000 of its citizens.

Beirut, known to Dad as "Switzerland of the Middle East," was again in ruins after its civil war. Many of its Christian, Jewish, and moderate Muslim citizens began a new wave of immigration to other nations of the world.

For my Al-Khouri ancestors, staying alive and finding a safe haven in which to practice their Christian faith was all that they hoped for. They eventually settled down in Gaza close to Jesus's birthplace. The city, a trading hub inhabited by Levantines, Arabs, Greeks, and countless other nationalities throughout the centuries, became their home. In 1865 the Al-Khouri family emigrated to Egypt, land of the ancient Pharaohs, pyramids, and the River Nile. They were again in search of a safer place to practice their Christian faith, a better place for their children, and to be prosperous.

CHAPTER 3

GAZA: GRANDPA'S BIRTHPLACE

THERE ARE NO RECORDS of when my dad's family and early ancestors established themselves in the port city of Gaza in present-day Palestine. But what is certain is my grandfather's birth in 1862. That was the time when the Ottoman Turks Muslim Empire ruled over Ard Al-Sham (the Levant region which included Lebanon, Syria, Israel, and Palestine among others). For generations, Gaza became home to the Khouri family and to other Christians from various regions including Lebanon and Syria.

Throughout history, several powers, including ancient Egyptians, Greeks, Romans, Turks, and British among others, invaded and ruled the city because of its strategic location on the eastern coast of the Mediterranean Sea and proximity to Jerusalem. "The known history of Gaza spans 4,000 years. It was ruled, destroyed, and repopulated by various dynasties, empires, and peoples."[16]

Historically, the Bible mentions Gaza as the place where the stories of Samson, David, and Goliath took place. It was where Phillip, the Apostle of Jesus, met "an Ethiopian eunuch, an important official in charge of all the treasury of the Kandake (which means 'queen of the Ethiopians')" (Acts 8: 26–39 NIV).

Filiu & King describe the allure of Gaza to many throughout the centuries:

> Travelers who have visited Gaza over the centuries have often remarked on the fecundity of its vegetation and the diversity of its agriculture, both of which are the products of its underground waters and the gentle nature of the prevailing climate. The Gaza Valley (Wadi Ghazza), which runs down into the sea to the south of the modern city, offers a welcome refuge to migrant birds and small animals; the coolness and shade of this coastal oasis contrast with the dusty tracks nearby that lead toward the Negev. Gaza is the endpoint of the Levant coastline, the last haven before the inhospitable desert. Mastery of Gaza has, therefore, been a keen issue in the rivalry between the powers that have established themselves in the Nile Valley and the Middle East. Whereas it was impossible to conquer Egypt from the eastern Mediterranean without relying on Gaza, Gaza was also an indispensable bridgehead for any invasion of the Levant from Sinai. As a result, ownership of Gaza has been transferred from one empire to another.[17]

The Khouri family's peaceful dwelling in Gaza did not last long. Wars and diseases soon began to disturb their peace and security. King wrote about those turbulent days:

> The Bubonic Plague struck again in 1839 and the city stagnated, as it lacked political and economic stability. In 1840, Egyptian and Ottoman troops battled outside of Gaza, with the Ottomans emerging victorious, effectively ending Egyptian rule over Palestine. The battles brought about more death and destruction, just barely after the city began to recover from the plague.[18]

The Egyptians rule over Gaza ended with the Ottoman invasion in the 1840s. My great-grandfather was a young man at a time when the political and religious turmoil was sweeping Gaza and surrounding areas. It was under the Turkish Muslim rule when the devout Christian Khouri family decided to immigrate to Egypt in 1865. The British and French influence on neighboring Egypt, coupled with the higher demand for Egyptian cotton during the American civil war, offered them new opportunities for religious freedom and economic prosperity. Eventually, my three-year-old grandpa Hanna left his childhood home in Gaza and immigrated with the family in search of a safer and more prosperous life in Egypt.

CHAPTER 4

EGYPT: THE KHOURIS' NEW HOME

Egypt, land of the ancient pharaohs, is a densely populated country located in the northeastern part of Africa. It shares the Mediterranean Sea on its northern borders with Europe. On its eastern border there is the Red Sea (Al Bahr Al-Ahmar), Israel, and Gaza, where the Khouris migrated from, on its northeastern border. It shares border with Libya on the west, and Sudan, where my parents first met and I was born, on the south. Given the Khouri family's generational commitment to their faith in Jesus Christ as priests and ministers, Egypt with its rich biblical history must have captivated them. For the first time, they were in the land of Joseph, who was sold as a slave by his jealous brothers to Egyptian masters, and Moses, whom God led to free the Israelites from Pharaoh's slavery.

The Al-Khouris' step of faith to immigrate to Egypt in pursuit of economic prosperity, peace, and freedom to practice their faith turned out to be a wise one. In Egypt, they were able to financially prosper and to preserve their Christian heritage and pass it on to the future generations including my siblings and me. The Khouri family found hope as new immigrants in Egypt as doors of opportunities began to open for them. A short distance away from their new home in Al-Zagazig, another family—Mary, Joseph, and the baby Jesus—had lived about two thousand years prior in Masr Al-Gadima (Old Cairo). Dad's immigrant family might have found inspiration and hope from the holy family who fled from the Holy Land to escape King Herod's sword in pursuit of safety and security. They were in good company!

Egypt: The Gift of the Nile

Throughout history, Egypt, watered by the life-sustaining River Nile, became home not only to the baby Jesus, Mary, and Joseph, but also to millions of people. The ancient Egyptian proverb: "Once you drink from the Nile, you are destined to return" seems very befitting as invaders, various ancient civilizations, and colonizers kept on coming back for generations.

Herodotus, the ancient Greek historian, appropriately called Egypt "the gift of the Nile."[19] Without the River Nile, Egypt's more than one hundred million inhabitants would not survive. Its ancient civilizations, including the pharaohs who built the pyramids and the Sphinx, could not have existed without its waters. It has transformed Egypt for centuries into an oasis in the desert inhabited by the world's most well-known ancient civilizations.

According to the United Nations Development Programme:

> About 95 percent of Egyptians live along the Nile—on less than 5 percent of Egypt's territory making the Nile Valley one of the world's most densely populated areas, especially in greater Cairo, Alexandria, and other major cities in the Nile Delta.[20]

For centuries, the over four-thousand-miles-long river, considered the longest in the world, had traveled through the arid desert. It never stopped flowing. That fascinating body of water was where the Old Testament prophet Moses floated, as a newborn baby, in a basket before Pharaoh's daughter rescued him. It was in Pharaoh's palace near the River Nile, that Moses grew up, and eventually heeded God's call to lead the Israelites out of their captivity in Egypt.

The Nile creates along its long barren path fertile lands, including the Nile Valley Delta Region where grain, rice, cotton, and date palms grow. The city of Al-Zagazig in the eastern part of this fertile Delta became the Khouri family's new home and Dad's birthplace. It always fascinates me to think how deep-rooted and entrenched my life and the lives of my parents and ancestors were in the Nile. Mom was born and grew up in the Highlands of Tigray, Ethiopia, where the Blue Nile originates. Dad was born a short distance away from the River Nile before the end of its journey in the Mediterranean Sea.

My own childhood home was just a short walk to the bank of the Blue Nile! A few miles away from my home in Al-Manshia, the Blue Nile merges with the White Nile, the second tributary of the Nile, in Khartoum forming the Great River Nile. The two rivers merge in the vicinity of the presidential palace in Khartoum, the place where an Islamic military leader called Al-Mahdi killed British General Charles George Gordon in 1895. This ancient river blessed my ancestors, brought life to many generations, and witnessed wars and death along its path.[21]

CHAPTER 5

AL-KHOURIS' NEW LIFE AND CHALLENGES IN EGYPT

The year was 1865 when my three-year-old grandpa Hanna first arrived with his family in Al- Zagazig. They immigrated to Egypt during a peaceful and prosperous time in Egypt's history. The construction of the Suez Canal (1859–1869) was actively underway sixty-five miles away from their new home. The country they settled in was loosely associated with the Ottoman Empire and aspiring to be independent from Turkish rule. It was a hub for refugees from neighboring Levant countries and wide-eyed groups of tourists from Europe and America.

But Egypt's prosperity did not last long as the country amassed debts with the building of the Suez Canal and other modernization projects. This gradually led to the takeover of the country by the British in 1882 after scoring a victory in the battle ground of Tel-el-Kebir about an hour and half from the new Khouri home in Al-Zagazig. Egypt became a British protectorate in 1914.[22]

After the British takeover, Egypt continued as a monarchy with nominal ruling by the Khedives (governors or viceroys). There were still freedom and great opportunities for the family to practice their Christian faith and prosper. They stayed put in Al-Zagazig and called Egypt home.

Levantines in Al-Zagazig, Egypt

Al-Zagazig is located fifty miles from the capital, Cairo. Muhammad Ali Pasha, the founder of modern Egypt, founded the city in 1830. Ancient pharaohs, Greco-Roman archaeological sites and antiquities around the city, as well as Cairo with its modern vibrancy not far away, all attracted the Khouri family. The establishment of the railroad system in the mid-1800s provided new opportunities for independent businesses to flourish. It also allowed Dad's family to easily travel to Cairo and enjoy its coffee shops, theaters, and cultural environment. But assimilating as Levantines in Egypt's culture proved to be not as easy.

Fahmy describes the challenges that "non-Egyptians," like Dad's immigrant family, initially faced:

> The perceived differences between a native Egyptian (ibn al-balad, or literally "son of the country") and the foreign (khawaga) "other" were often strengthened by the deliberate portrayals of this dynamic in colloquial culture ... contrasting the habits, demeanor, and, most important, the accent of the native Egyptian urbanites with those considered "foreign" was often dramatized in the latest jokes, in the cartoons and dialogues of the satirical press, and later in the theatrical sketches and plays of the developing comedic theater. Many of these cultural productions emphasized the accented non-Egyptian pronunciations of Syrian, Sudanese, Greek English, and other foreign residents and contrasted them with the fluency of a native Egyptian. . . .[23]

The Khouri family must have initially felt stereotyped because of their accents and Levantine origin. But soon, they assimilated, their children adapted the Egyptian accent, and they considered themselves

Egyptians. That same pattern could be seen in other immigrant families of that era. Fahmy states:

Many of the sons and daughters of the thousands of Levantines, Maltese, Italian, and Greek immigrants were so thoroughly integrated culturally and linguistically into Egyptian society that they considered themselves de facto Egyptians. During the first-third of the twentieth century, these mutamassirun (Egyptianized foreigners) fully participated in Egyptian culture and economic life; some were fervent Egyptian Nationalists, and in the 1920s many acquired Egyptian citizenship.[24]

Egypt offered an excellent opportunity for the Khouri family to educate their children and to remain committed to their faith. It became their permanent home, and they were determined to accomplish their dreams and to prosper in Al-Zagazig.

Music and Culture in Nineteenth- and Early-Twentieth-Century Egypt

Grandpa Hanna lived with his family a short distance away from the Arab world's most cultural and artistic cities, Cairo. Before Starbucks became widespread in the United States, there were coffee shops on the street corners of almost every city. There, the customers rested, read Egyptian newspapers, smoked shisha, and listened to phonograph records of Egypt's best singers.

Those coffee houses became places where *azjals* (colloquial poems) were recited, and the recorded music of Egypt's famous singers such as Munīra Al-Mahdiyya, Umm Kulthum, and Sayyed Darwish were regularly played.[25]

The Khouri family were right in the middle of it all. They enjoyed the strong Arabic coffee, the music of the Middle East's most famous female singer Umm Kulthum (also known as Kaowkabat Al-Sharq Al-Awsat or "the planet of the Middle East"), and Cairo's rich cultural scene. There was no shortage of entertainment in Egypt in the late 1800s, and most definitely in the early 1900s with the rapid spread of recorded music. The music and artistic culture of Cairo delighted and influenced the Khouri family soon after their arrival in Egypt.

Years later in Sudan, where Dad eventually immigrated to, he never missed listening to Umm Kulthum's live concerts, broadcast from Egypt, on our family radio. Her mesmerizing vocal style and powerful voice reminded Dad of his past pleasant days in Egypt. His love of music included classical and opera music such as Giuseppe Verdi's opera "Aida," which premiered in Cairo in 1871, as well as soprano Maria Callas, and classical composers like Beethoven and others. The new economic prosperity that the Khouris experienced in Al-Zagazig gave Dad and his siblings the opportunity to experience the best of Cairo's rich eastern and western composers' classical music. Dad relived those childhood and early adulthood cherished memories as he listened to the voice of Maria Callas and Umm Kulthum in our family home in Sudan.

Religious Tensions in Their New Home, Egypt

When my three-year-old grandfather arrived in Egypt, Islam was the predominant religion with Egyptian Coptic Christians composing about 10 percent of the population. Historically, Christianity started in Egypt by Mark, the Apostle of Jesus Christ, in AD 33. It gradually spread throughout the country becoming the predominant faith until the Arab Muslim invasion in AD 642. In about two hundred years, Islam became the dominant religion in Egypt and the Christian Coptic Egyptians became a minority. Gradually, Arabic and Islam replaced the Greek and Coptic languages, as well as Christianity in Egypt

My grandfather and his family felt safe enough in Egypt to practice their Christian faith. The period of the last few decades of the nineteenth century, and the early decades of the twentieth century was a suitable time for the Khouri family to be there. The influx of Christian immigrants to Egypt, and the European influence, especially Great Britain, on the country offered them a layer of security. As devout Christians in a Muslim majority country, they needed that assurance of religious freedom to freely practice their faith.

In 1865, my great-grandfather saw Egypt as a land of dreams, religious freedom, and opportunities and he moved his family there. Over eight decades later, Dad saw Sudan as his land of dreams and immigrated there. In the 1980s, it was my turn to pursue my own path and move to America, Land of My Dreams. Dad's grandparents were able to pass the baton of their Christian faith to my grandfather in Al-Zagazig. He passed it in turn to Dad and his siblings.

But Egypt's quiet and peaceful religious scene of the last decades of the nineteenth century gradually transitioned into religious tensions. Intolerance against Copts and other Christians escalated in the early twentieth century. On February 20, 1910, two years before Dad was born, tensions between Christians and Muslims peaked with the assassination of the Christian Prime Minister, Butrus Ghali. The Copts believed at the time that his murder was religiously motivated.[26]

Graham mentions a Muslim cleric named Abd-al-Aziz Jawish who in 1909 accused the Coptic prime minister of being a traitor before his assassination.

> Jawish, who would soon be released from prison, continued his attacks on Butrus Ghali, vilifying him as a traitor to the nation, while expanding his attacks on the entire Coptic Egyptian community, accusing them of collaboration with the British.[27]

Religious tensions heated up as a tug-of-war between the forces of modernization in Egypt and those who wanted to follow a traditional Islamic path leading to the Sharia law intensified before and following World War I. A well-known theatrical comedy at the time that hinted at this religious tension was "*Dukul al-Hamam Mish Zay Khuruguh*," which translates to "entering the Turkish bath is easier than exiting it." The play was meant to warn the public that starting the path to strict Islamic laws is easier to start but harder to exit from.[28]

According to Fahmy, the comedy "was an indigenous social critique of traditional Egyptian society . . ." that attempted to "reveal some of the flaws of the sharia courts especially when it comes to personal status laws."[29]

I heard that Arabic proverb, which was also the name of that comedy, hundreds of times throughout my adolescent life. Dad often invoked that proverb *"Dukul al-Hamam Mish Zay Khuruguh"* whenever I or my siblings wanted to embark on one of our silly childish plans, or before choosing to do something that could potentially harm us. The words of the proverb echoed in the old *"Dukul al-Hamam Mish Zay Khuruguh"* comedy turned out to be prophetic. Decades later, thousands of Christians, Jews, other minorities, and moderate Muslims migrated to America and the West when their home countries enforced strict versions of the Sharia Laws. Sudan, where my parents met and where I was born, was one of those countries.

On December 18, 1914, when Dad was about two years old, Egypt became a British protectorate after England removed the Ottoman empire's control over the country. Under Britain's rule, my grandfather, Dad, and his siblings experienced a sense of security even as the undercurrent of religious tensions against westernization and Christians in Egypt was gradually increasing. In the late 1940s, Dad decided to immigrate to Sudan. He felt his Christian faith subjected him to religious biases that hindered his career dreams in Egypt. And so, he left like his own ancestors, hoping to start a new page elsewhere.

CHAPTER 6

SLAVERY AND RACIAL BIASES IN PARADISE

In EGYPT, THE WHITE KHOURI FAMILY experienced something that they must have never seen before in their old city of birth. They found out about the grim reality of slavery of Black and dark-skinned non-Muslim men, women, and children in their new paradise. Egypt's proximity to Sudan transformed Cairo into a major slavery marketplace in the 1800s: "over the course of the eighteenth and nineteenth centuries as many as 722,000 Africans were forcibly brought to Egypt by all routes, including the Red Sea, some of whom transited Egypt to other Ottoman provinces."[30]

The Khouri family came to Egypt of their own accord as free people. But that was not the case for the majority of the Black and dark-skinned men and women they saw there. Those were slaves, ex-slaves, or their descendants. Grievously, men, and sometimes women, with money and power kept those powerless victims as their property. Slave traders captured men, women, and children from Sudan, Ethiopia, and various parts of West Africa and sold them to the Ottoman Empire, Egyptian citizens who could afford it, and other Middle Eastern countries. In Egypt, people with financial means and authority used them in manual, domestic labor, as soldiers, or as concubines in palaces with the harem that included white Circassian women, or as sexual slaves and prostitutes.[31]

In 1865, the year of the family's arrival in Egypt, which coincided with the year America passed the thirteenth amendment to abolish slavery, there was a significant increase in Egypt's slave trade. There was a high demand for Egyptian cotton during that time which, in turn, amplified the slave trade.

> For most of the nineteenth century, the majority of slaves imported into Egypt were women. Overall, there was a steady decline in the number of male slaves imported until the worldwide cotton boom that accompanied the American Civil war from 1861–65. Nearly all of the slaves were destined for domestic servitude in middle- and upper-class households. During the cotton boom, however, many more people in the lower classes were able to afford slaves to assist with agricultural work.[32]

The sight of slaves and the selling and buying of humans must have been a shock to their deep-rooted Christian beliefs.

About two decades after the Khouri family made Al-Zagazig their permanent home, the British introduced laws to stop the slavery trade. Cuno (as cited in *Slavery in Egypt*) reports:

> The Anglo-Egyptian Slave Trade Convention or Anglo-Egyptian Convention for the Abolition of Slavery in 1877 officially banned the slave trade to Sudan, thus formally putting an end on the import of slaves from Sudan. Sudan was at this time the main import of male slaves to Egypt. This ban was followed in 1884 by a ban on the import of white women; this law was directed against the import of white women (mainly from Caucasus and usually Circassians), which were the preferred choice for harem

concubines among the Egyptian upper class. The import of male slaves from Sudan as soldiers, civil service and eunuchs, as well as the import of female slaves from Caucasus as harem women were the two main sources of slave import to Egypt, thus these laws were, at least on paper, major blows on Slavery in Egypt. Slavery itself was not banned, only the import of slaves.[33]

It was only in 1904, eight years before Dad was born, that slavery ended. "In 1904, the British consul general in Cairo was able to report that slavery had been completely eliminated in Egypt."[34]

Meanwhile, the British who occupied Egypt and made it their policy to abolish slavery in Sudan and Egypt in the late 1800s, showed their own biases against Levantines like the Khouri family. Mak explains one of the possible reasons Britons kept their children from public schools:

> It seems that many Britons in Egypt, particularly those from the upper and middle classes, did not want their children educated with other ethnic groups, especially from the Levant, out of fear that their children's educational standards would be threatened by the inclusion of what was seen as inferior 'oriental races.' Other reasons also existed.[35]

Thankfully, goodness still prevailed amid the senseless biases. Christian missionaries who established schools and clinics to help the less fortunate in Egypt reached out to the Egyptians and sought their friendship.[36]

Meanwhile, the British Anti-Slavery Society, which was originally started in 1839 by a Quaker to fight global slavery, played a significant role to combat slavery in Egypt.[37] The British Anti-Slavery Society "helped establish a home for freed slave women in Cairo in 1884 and appointed Mrs. Crewe as headmistress" to help "female slaves freed by police or who fled their masters. . . ."[38]

As a young man, my grandfather was close to the center of action in Cairo. There, British authorities, abolitionists, and American missionaries were in a never-ending battle with slave traders. Author Beth Baron describes how these battles and challenges played in 1887 in the lives of twelve African girls. The British authorities freed the girls and brought them to a Boarding School run by American Presbyterian missionaries near Cairo. Their journey and life experiences after freedom offer glimpses of the pain endured by the freed slaves in the weaning years of the institution of Egyptian slavery.[39]

With the history and background of slavery in Egypt, it followed that racial biases and prejudice affected various aspects of society including the entertainment industry.

Fahmy remarks:

> "The Nubians and Sudanese were arguably the most maligned outsider group; they were mercilessly stereotyped for cheap laughs by most forms of Egyptian mass culture. Fitting this mold were Qishta's sketches "al-Barbari wa al-Haj Sayyidu" (the Nubian and Haj Sayyid) and "Hikayit al-'Abid al-Talata" (The story of the three Black slaves). Four of the twelve recorded comedic sketches of Ahmad Fahim al-Far available in the Egyptian national Library collection stereotypically satirize Nubians and Sub-Saharan Africans."[40]

Given the racially charged environment in Cairo and how society viewed dark-skinned and Black people, it was an irony of ironies that Dad decided decades later to immigrate to Sudan (the name means "land of the Blacks" in Arabic), fall in love, and marry Mom—a beautiful dark-skinned Tigrayan woman. His contemporary society's biased view of Black people as slaves and inferior did not sway him. Thankfully, Dad remained committed to the foundational Christian belief passed to him from his parents that God created everyone equal, unique, and in His image.

The destructive power and the degrading nature of racial discrimination that Dad witnessed growing up shaped him into a very protective father. In Sudan where I grew up, he made sure to keep Mom, my siblings and me away from any of his white Levantine friends, acquaintances, and even family until he made sure that we would not face any discrimination.

Witnessing as a young man the racial biases of his society and its culture toward people of Mom's skin color made him vigilant and cautious. He was determined to shield us and protect our young hearts and minds from the toxic effects of any stereotyping, racial discrimination, and colorism. Dad's efforts proved to be successful. I grew up seeing my skin color and mixed ethnicity as unique, beautiful, and never inferior. Years later in America, as I embarked on my own immigrant journey, I needed every bit of that solid foundation that Dad and Mom planted in me.

CHAPTER 7

THRIVING IN EGYPT

Economically, Egypt provided a chance for my grandpa and his family to grow and prosper. The American Civil War of 1865 launched cotton production in Al-Zagazig and their prosperity propelled as the region became one of the largest producers of cotton in Egypt. The family worked hard, started a gold and jewelry business, and prospered from it. The excellent opportunity of a high demand for gold in the region with well-paid British soldiers and other wealthy clientele helped them amass a great fortune.

My grandfather Hanna started his career goals with humble beginnings. He began his work life as a young "donkey boy." That gig, which was the older version of being a taxi driver or an Uber driver, meant offering tourists and locals a ride for a set price. Old pictures from the 1800s show donkeys "parked" outside the famous Shepherd Hotel in Cairo waiting for a paying rider. That job offered him a wonderful opportunity to meet interesting people and get paid. It was on one of those bumpy donkey rides that he met my paternal grandmother, who was one of his regular passengers. He fell in love with her during one of those routine paid donkey rides. Her parents hired him at the time to regularly take her to school.

Grandpa Hanna's humble beginnings as a "donkey boy" became a "rags to riches" story as he gradually became a talented and well-respected goldsmith in Egypt. He accomplished being a well-known expert in his trade and, in turn, gained tremendous fame, respect in the region, and legendary fortunes. He became known not just for his wealth but for his extravagant generosity and his yearly Christmas parties that became a tradition in his Al-Zagazig community.

"Families from the surrounding neighborhoods were invited and treated with champagne bottles and a gold coin," Dad recalled years later.

The family's wealth in their adopted home, Egypt, afforded a luxurious life including expensive private education, trips, and abundance of possessions. But more important, life in secular Egypt in the late 1800s and early 1900s provided them with general political stability and the religious freedom they were hoping for. They loved their new home, Egypt.

Dad's Childhood Memories

Dad was born in Al-Zagazig in 1912, one of eighteen children! Ten of his siblings died at an early age, as was common in that era, with only nine of them still alive by the time his dad died in 1932. Nestled an hour away from Cairo, Al-Zagazig was the only childhood home he ever knew. Egypt was his home. As an immigrant family, he and his siblings grew up, as far as I could tell, without uncles, aunts, or extended blood relatives. My siblings and I grew up the same way. We had no uncles, aunts, or blood relatives around us in Sudan when Dad and Mom married and grew their family decades later.

The Al-Khouri beautiful family home was about fifty miles from Cairo's ancient mosques with their towering minarets and churches dating to early Christianity. During his visits to Cairo as a child, my father walked with fascination in its crowded streets and bazaars. He could hear the *muezzin*'s call to Muslim prayers blasting from the tall minarets as veiled women, Bedouins, tourists, and fellahin bought cold drinks, coffee, watermelon, and antiques from vendors and sellers lining the hot Cairo streets. Growing up in the most fertile land of the Nile Delta offered him interesting natural sights and sounds. He was fascinated by the fellahin watering their cotton, rice, wheat, and fruits fields with hardened oxen and other ancient methods passed on from one generation to another.

Growing up as rich *Shaouam* (Levants) in Al-Zagazig, Dad and his siblings found in Egypt a comfortable and luxurious childhood. That lifestyle continued until the family fortune gradually dissipated after the passing of Grandpa Hanna. Dad never forgot his childhood home, and the beautiful memories he experienced there. He frequently shared with Mom stories from those cherished Christmas parties, including the golden coins his dad gave away to the children and the champagne bottles he gave his neighbors every Christmas.

Decades later in Sudan, he built a lavish home in the suburb of Al-Manshia, a few blocks away from the Blue Nile, and recreated those happy days. My childhood Christmas parties in our Al-Manshia home were memorable events that the surrounding neighbors looked forward to. There was live music, colorful festival of lights, delicious food to feed an army, and his favorite Christmas childhood game *"L' Ebat Al fanagean"* (game of the China teacups).

My siblings and I got to play the same game he and his siblings played decades before. Dad would give us a signal to walk slowly around our dining room table where he placed China teacups turned upside down. He would then suddenly clap his hands as we walked round the table, just like his own dad did in their Al-Zagazig home, signaling us to stop. He would then tell us to claim whatever he and Mom put under the upside-down teacups: candy, chocolates, or coins. There were no golden coins though.

Dad's Early Childhood During World War I

Dad was born during the reign of Egypt's Abbas II Helmi Pasha, the last Ottoman viceroy (ruler) who ruled Egypt. At the onset of WWI, the

British replaced the viceroy who sided with Germany with one of their preferred rulers, continued their control of Egypt and the Suez Canal, and made the country a British Protectorate. My dad's early childhood years were peaceful and quiet until the Great War began.

The war that started when he was two years old ushered with it a large influx of WWI soldiers from the British Empire, refugees from Southern Europe escaping the war, food shortages, and famine. The economic hardships that included steep increases in prices of food and goods, shortages of essentials such as kerosene and gasoline, in addition to wartime rationing.

I wonder how Dad and the rest of the Khouri family survived physically and emotionally those turbulent days. The raging battles were at the Suez Canal only a few hours away from them! In his book, *The British in Egypt*, Mak describes how Cairo, Alexandria, and other Egyptian cities received thousands of troops with war injuries.

> "...about 90,000 British soldiers from the Gallipolis campaign arrived and were treated in hospitals and makeshift hospitals, while thousand others from England and other commonwealth countries were awaiting their deployment to the battlefields."[41]

It must have been frightening to Dad and his family to see their Egyptian paradise transforming right before their eyes into a war zone. But even amid the war, Cairo still offered places for respite and rest to the soldiers who flooded the region. One such place that offered entertaining programs was the Young Men's Christian Association (YMCA) in a historical district called Zeitoun in Cairo.

According to the *Egyptian Gazette*:

> Perhaps the most prominent club established and frequented by the British troops was the Cairo Soldiers' Recreation Club,

run by the YMCA in Ezbekiyya. It provided them with a venue for boxing matches, cinematograph shows, hockey games on a skating rink, concerts, and lectures frequently given by a well-known preacher named Oswald Chambers.[42]

The Al-Azbakiya YMCA and the Zeitoun district, one hour drive from the Khouri family's home, was where the renowned well-known Scottish evangelist Oswald Chambers (1874–1917) regularly talked and preached to WWI war-bound soldiers.

His wife eventually published his inspirational talks and sermons after his death as a devotional, "My Utmost for His Highest." It became the best-selling Christian devotional of all time. The YMCA, which Dad joined years later as a young adult, became a place for soldiers about to fight in the Great War to meet, have clean fun and entertainment, and to listen to Oswald Chambers. Sadly, Oswald Chambers—who was the YMCA chaplain in Cairo—died at the age of forty-three on November 15, 1917, due to complications following an appendectomy and was buried in Cairo.[43]

Meanwhile, at Dad's hometown of Al-Zagazig, less than two hours away from the war front of the Suez Canal, the war was too close for comfort. Due to its proximity to the raging battlefields of 1915 where German and Ottoman forces attacked, Al-Zagazig had an Advance Ordnance Depot. A battalion known as the 32nd (Imperial Service) Brigade, part of the British Indian Army, defended the military installation during the war.[44]

Fortunately, the British spared Dad's older siblings and most Egyptians from joining the British army's military campaign. Nevertheless, the extension of WWI to Egypt, particularly the Suez Canal, brought misery and profound consequences to Egyptians in general, and to Christian minorities. The declaration of the Turkish Sultan of *jihad* (holy war) on November 14, 1914, was very unsettling to Christians in Egypt, including Dad's family.

> "The Ottoman Sultan Mehmed V, in his role as Caliph, along with his Sheikh-ul-Islam, issued a call for *jihad* against the Allied powers of Britain, France, Russia, Serbia, and Montenegro. Muslims living within those states (and their overseas empires) were encouraged to rise up against their Christian oppressors, and the Persians were encouraged to join the fight."[45]

As the war persisted, so did the economic hardships that rich and poor Egyptians began to endure. Salim noted:

> "Shortages of most essentials from grain and meat to clothing and paper were commonplace. Unemployment and inflation were rampant as prices soared. The economic hardships were felt across class lines...."[46]

Thankfully, Dad and the rest of the family were able to weather the storms of those days together. They remained financially secure and were able to survive the waves of crime and mayhem that wars often bring. Mercifully for them, Germany and the Ottoman empire failed to capture the Suez Canal, their main objective, and lost the Great War. The fear of the Turkish Sultan's *jihad* war against the British and "Christian oppressors" ended to their relief and that of Egypt's Christian minority.

After WWI ended, there was a palpable rise in Egypt's nationalist movement, led by its leader Saad Zaghlul, and an increasing resentment of the British. Riots and demonstrations filled the streets of Cairo especially after the British detained the popular nationalist leader. The British eventually released Saad Zaghlul and granted Egypt independence in February 1922. Great Britain continued to retain control of the country after the declaration of independence including "... Egypt's defense and foreign policy, the security of the Suez Canal, the governing of Sudan, and protection of foreign interests and inhabitants in Egypt...."[47]

Post WWI Egypt: Life and Historical Discoveries

But despite the onslaught of WWI, and the risk of jihad and religious tensions, the Khouri family made it. They stayed committed to their Christian faith, continued their economic prosperity, and remained generous with their wealth. The war did not stop them or other fun-loving Egyptians from enjoying their favorite pastimes and ancient Egyptian traditions. One of those ancient traditions that marks the beginning of the spring is *"Sham El-Nessim Day,"* which means "sniffing of the breeze." For generations, Egyptians—regardless of their religion—have always celebrated this day with picnics, colored eggs, and salted fish on Coptic Orthodox Easter Monday.[48]

Decades later after Dad immigrated to Sudan, he continued to celebrate *"Sham El-Nessim."* The day, which Sudanese celebrate as well, became one of our most favorite family traditions. On that day, we would wake up early in the morning and drive our car, with everyone in the neighborhood driving their own food-loaded cars, for an enjoyable day of fun and picnicking along the bank of the Nile. Just like Dad's own family in Egypt decades earlier, we colored boiled eggs, ate *'feseekh,'* (salted, flavored, and aged fish), and celebrated together the blessings of life regardless of the turmoil that often surrounded us.

The years following the Great War were full of discoveries and adventures. Dad was only ten years old when Howard Carter and Lord Carnarvon discovered in 1922 the tomb of King Tutankhamun in the Valley of the Kings in Southern Egypt. The decade after WWI was particularly full of fun, traveling, and adventures for Dad. He visited historical sites, vacationed, swam in the Mediterranean, excelled in school, and took lots of pictures. But Dad was not the only one fascinated by Egypt and its ancient history. European and American tourists came in the nineteenth and early twentieth centuries in droves drawn by the allure of the Giza pyramids, Sphinx, and the Nile.

One of the visitors to the Church of *Abu Serga (St. Sergius)*, believed to be the site where the Holy Family stayed in Egypt, was the writer Robert Hichens. Hichens described in *The Spell of Egypt* his awe of the Church the first time he saw it:

> "When it opened, I left behind me the world I know, the world that belongs to us today with its animation, its impedes, its flashing changes, its sweeping "hurry and go." I stepped at once into surely some mouldering centuries long hidden in the dark womb of the past."[49]

His words echoed those of renowned travel writer Bayard Taylor of *The New York Times* who traveled to Egypt in the 1850s. In his book *A Journey to Central Africa*, he shared his impression of the serenity and quietness he found as he traveled on a Nile trip in Egypt. As his *felucca* cruised the Nile passing by many villages under the spectacular sunset, he remarked, *"In America we live too fast and work too hard,' I thought shall I not know what rest is, once before I die.'"*[50]

To the Khouri family, Egypt was just as fascinating despite the Great War that they just survived. Al-Zagazig was a place where they did not live too fast and where they could slow down to rest. Interestingly, Bayard Taylor wrote his *statement "In America we live too fast and work too hard"* over 170 years ago!

With the advent of the internet, smartphones, social media, and long hours of work, life in America and heavily populated cities like Cairo has become a rat race and unrecognizable to people like Bayard Taylor, Robert Hichens, and Dad. They all likely cherished a slow trip in a *felucca* on the tranquil water of the Nile as they watched the sunset. Thankfully, such a trip is still possible today, but not without a text message or a social media interruption.

Surviving WWII in Egypt

Dad was a twenty-seven-year-old practicing architect at the onset of the Second World War in 1939. He completed his university education at the prestigious Royal School of Engineering in Cairo at the top of his class about three years before the war.

In 1942 when Dad was thirty years old, one of the most crucial battles of WWII was raging in El-Alamein about three hours away from the Khouri family's new apartment in Cairo. The decisive battles of El-Alamein, an Egyptian city on the Mediterranean coastline, were between the "Desert Fox"—Field Marshal Rommel—with his German army and Britain's Lieutenant-General Montgomery's Eighth Army.[51]

Winston Churchill, who was in Cairo in August 1942, considered El-Alamein battles as a make or break. He believed Britain's victories in those crucial battles were the first stage of failure of Hitler's military expansion dreams. In a November 10, 1942, speech about El-Alamein he said, "This is not the end. It is not even the beginning of the end. But it is, perhaps, the end of the beginning."[52]

To Sir Winston Leonard Spencer-Churchill, El-Alamein was a main turning point in the Second World War. He wrote, "It might almost be said, before Alamein we never had a victory, after Alamein we never had a defeat."[53]

WWII did not only bring political and economic uncertainties to Dad and his family, but it brought also the fear of religious turmoil and instability. Egyptian nationalists wanted to end Britain's control of Egypt. In addition, the organization of Al-Ikhwan Al-Muslimin (Muslim Brotherhood), an Islamic organization founded in 1928 that aimed to impose Islamic law, rose in power, and became more militant. Demonstrations and protests in Cairo increased in number and violence.[54]

The increase of riots, anti-Western sentiments, and the rise of the Muslim Brotherhood made Egypt feel less safe and secure for Christians like Dad. He felt strongly that the religious intolerance of some in society had affected his promotions. He believed his career goals were hindered because of his Christian family name. Eventually, he decided it was wiser and safer to immigrate to Sudan to pursue his goals and dreams.

Surviving Young Adulthood & Sibling Rivalries in Egypt

Having two world wars at Dad's backyard was not the only problem Dad had to worry about. Family feuds and siblings' rivalries related to the family wealth after my grandfather's death was another war he had to deal with. The impact of that war was long-lasting and left him with lifetime consequences that surpassed the combined effects of Egypt's wars and political upheavals.

My grandparents had a total of eighteen children, with many dying at an early age as was common during that era. They loved their children and provided them with a warm and luxurious home in Al-Zagazig. The phenomenal success of my grandfather's business as a goldsmith afforded the family with the privileges of a high socioeconomic status and an envied lifestyle among Egypt's elites. Grandpa Hanna strongly believed in the value of education. He considered educating his children was a greater and long-lasting legacy than leaving them with wealth and money after his passing. To his credit, he used his riches to provide his children with the best available elementary and higher education in Egypt and France.

Dad's Feuding Older Brothers

Life was not easy for Dad after the death of his father in 1932 in Al-Zagazig. Following the death of my grandfather, Dad's two older brothers squandered the vast family wealth. My grandfather entrusted them with the family business before he died but they wasted it, leaving Dad without enough money to pay for his school tuition and other needs. Yet, he still managed to complete his education.

Decades later in Sudan, he recalled in vivid details the deep distress and agony of those days. They felt more wounding and painful than any of his WWII memories.

> "Mousa and Ibrahim lost all the family money. They spent it on drinking and women. I had to repeatedly ask for money from my other university-educated brothers who had jobs. I did not get what I needed from them. That was why I had to walk two miles every day to my university, and only had two suits to wear for the entire year."

But one of the most painful memories of those days was when his older and most favorite brother George did not allow him to temporarily stay with him and his French-educated Levantine wife in their luxury apartment. Dad was extremely sick with dysentery and took the train to his brother's home, hoping that his brother, a physician, and his wife would take care of him. Sadly, his brother's wife told him to leave the house as she feared he would get someone infected. George did not insist that he should stay and that hurt Dad's feelings. He did not know where to go.

Dad suffered most probably from what is known as amebiasis, a disease caused by a parasite found in areas of contaminated Nile Delta waters. It affected his colon, causing him a lifetime of intestinal problems for which he sought specialized care all his life. But even worse than the long-lasting amebiasis was the lifelong hurtful memory of those days when he was not welcomed by his brother when he most needed it.

George studied medicine at the renowned university La Sorbonne in Paris. He became a renowned physician in the early decades of the 1900s and practiced medicine in Cairo's famous and historical Emad Al-Din Street. His practice was in a district considered to be the art and music center of Egypt. Theaters, cinemas, night clubs, and casinos frequented by Egypt's famous singers and entertainers of that period filled the street.

George was the private physician of a few of the country's well-known names including one of Egypt's most famous belly dancers.

Mousa, the second oldest son, did not want to pursue higher education and wanted instead to help Grandpa Hanna run his gold business. That was a good decision at the time but eventually turned out to be a big mistake. Dad's brother Ibrahim, younger than Mousa, contracted typhoid and chose not to pursue higher education, opting instead to stay mostly at home and dabble in carpentry. Those were the two brothers who squandered the family wealth. They both decided to forgo higher education and wanted to help their father with the family business. He, in turn, trusted them with the family wealth and the business before he died. Decades later, at our family home in Sudan, Dad often shared how they ruined the family gold business entrusted to them.

Soon after Grandpa Hanna's death, Mousa and Ibrahim lost both the family home and business. The repercussions of their actions affected every member of the Khouri family and changed forever my dad's view of money and wealth. The loss of the family wealth by his older brothers and the ensuing family disputes shaped his thinking about money. He saw how money and possessions can lead to family feuds and can break up the whole family.

Dad did not see any good that would come from amassing fortunes and leaving it to his children after passing. He believed in having just enough money to have a comfortable life, activities for the children, and yearly vacations. The negative effects of losing his family wealth and siblings' disputes in Egypt taught him to never let that trauma repeat itself in our own family in Sudan. After grandpa's death and the loss of the family home in Al-Zagazig, my grandmother and the rest of the family moved to an apartment in Cairo located in the Hayy El-Sakakini district.

Dad's brother Edward was younger than Ibrahim and Mousa. Grandpa Hanna paid for his medical education and supported his dream of being a physician. He became a very skilled surgeon in Al-Zagazig in addition to being a violinist and a painter. Dad recalled how hard Edward was working as he rushed from one operation to another to make money. Restoring the great wealth and good name of the Khouri family seemed to lie heavy on Edward's heart. His dream was to build a fancy and lavish high-rise building in Al-Zagazig. He held tightly to his money to accomplish his dream.

Edward's pursuit of money and wealth while refusing to help financially after grandpa's death became a contentious issue between him and Dad. My grandmother, paralyzed at the time, was dependent on her children's financial support for her living expenses. Dad became increasingly upset that Edward would come to the family's Hayy El-Sakakini apartment after performing multiple surgeries with a suitcase full of money but was refusing to help. One day, Edward entered the apartment with his cash-filled suitcase and again refused to contribute to his mom's home needs. Dad became enraged and decided to act.

"Edward came to the apartment after a day of doing surgeries. His suitcase was full of money. He was not paying for Mom's financial needs, and I was upset. When he refused to pay, I took the suitcase and threw it from the balcony. The money scattered on the street," recalled Dad decades later.

Dad was a kind and compassionate man. He felt deep love and empathy for his Protestant Christian mother who lost her husband and had a disability because of a stroke. The squandering of the family wealth by her older sons, the early death of a few of her children, the emotional pain of never seeing one of her daughters who became a nun, and the nervous breakdown of another daughter whose fiancé abandoned her before her wedding was too much to bear. Edward's refusal to help their mom financially greatly troubled Dad, especially given what she had endured. She was known for her deep Christian faith. The foundation of Christianity was the legacy that she and my grandfather planted in Dad even as the Khouris' wealth vanished.

About two decades following that incident with Edward, Dad became a renowned and prosperous architect in the country of Sudan. He chose to forgive Edward and his other brothers, and he supported them financially for the rest of their lives. His brother Edward continued to do well as a well-known surgeon and invested his money in building his magnificent building in Al-Zagazig. He called the high-rise building with marble walls and other luxuries his own version of Al-Sakakini Pasha Palace, "the Edward Building." Dad's tough stand with his brother Edward must have worked well. Their relationship matured, and Dad with his growing success and wealth in Sudan confided to Mom years later that he was sending money to his surgeon brother Edward to finish the construction of his dream, the Edward Building.

The impressive building in Al-Zagazig, now old and in need of maintenance, is still standing. It outlived Edward, much like El-Sakakini Pasha Palace, located a short distance from their apartment, and the great pyramids that have outlived their dreamers and wealthy builders. Edward died young in his mid- to late-forties from either a heart disease (as Dad and Mom thought) or a tetanus infection, as my Egyptian cousin once said. Over five decades later, the same cousin immigrated to Canada and became a skilled surgeon. He recalled seeing an Egyptian patient in Canada whose surgeon was Dad's brother Edward!

Yousef, one of my dad's older brothers, finished his civil engineering university degree when the family wealth was still available. He excelled early in his career as a civil engineer in Cairo, including a stint at the Suez Canal where he built the El Ferdan swing bridge probably during, or right after, the Second World War. Years later as an accomplished architect in Sudan, Dad shared with Mom in Sudan how he decided to fly to Italy to bring Yousef's daughter, his beloved niece, to Egypt. Her dad, my father's brother Yousef, left her indefinitely in Italy with her maternal Italian relatives and went to Syria in pursuit of some of his personal interests.

Dad, whose heart of caring and tenderness developed from experiencing the pain of his older siblings' rejection and behavior, felt his niece's anguish and fervent hope to leave Italy. He took her with him to Egypt to the safety and love of her paternal family's care before returning to Sudan. Dad's niece eventually immigrated to North America where she became a college professor. She was eternally grateful to Dad's act of kindness. And that was Dad. His caring and generosity to his family and to strangers of all races and colors never changed throughout his life. He really cared.

Dad's Sisters: Challenges & Vulnerability

Dad deeply cared for his mom and sisters. After his dad's death, he shouldered the burden and responsibility of caring for them. His sisters were Matilda, Odelle, Isabelle, and Rose. Growing up a girl and navigating life as a woman in the early decades of the 1900s was not easy. The death of the patriarch of the family, Grandpa Hanna, compounded by the loss of wealth and status, increased their sense of burden and vulnerability.

Matilda was her dad's favorite daughter. Her decision to become a nun hit him extremely hard. In the convent, she cut all her ties to the outside world including her dad and the rest of the family. Sadly, her decision to die to the world might have led to Grandpa's early death. The deep sadness of never seeing her again might have hastened his death.

Odelle, on the other hand, married a Christian man and had four children, including Fouad who immigrated to America and became a hematologist on the East Coast and died there. Another son, Kameel, an accomplished pianist, and accountant, was Dad's only blood relative able to visit Sudan and meet Mom, me, and my siblings. He was friendly, pleasant, humorous, and without an ounce of prejudice in him. He admired Mom's patience and often remarked about how she supported Dad. Kameel followed the Khouri family's generational traditions of immigrating in pursuit of a better life. He immigrated to Canada where he unexpectedly died after a major surgery.

Isabelle's story is sad. She was madly in love with a man who became her fiancé. She was preparing for the marriage and filled with joy and excitement when he suddenly canceled the engagement before the wedding day. She was heartbroken. To young women in a traditional society where being married is a major milestone that was a devastating blow to her tender heart that she never recovered from. She lived until her death at the age of sixty in the family's Hay El-Sakakini apartment, still grieving the loss of her love. She left behind cloth and wedding items embroidered with her ex-fiancé's name for a wedding day that never happened.

Another one of Dad's sisters that he mentioned to Mom was also one of his dad's favorite children. He sent her to study in France, but sadly she died unexpectedly. Grandpa was grief stricken, and that contributed to his decision to leave his gold family business to Mousa and Ibrahim. They mismanaged it and wasted all the money on "women and drinking," as Dad often said.

And finally, there was Rose, Dad's youngest and most favorite sibling. The death of her dad, Hanna, brought major changes in her life. That included the interruption of her private school education at the costly Notre Dame School For Girls. She married an Egyptian Coptic Christian, and years after my siblings and I were born in Sudan, Dad introduced us and Mom to her and to her welcoming family. And true to the long-held Al-Khouri family traditions, Rose's older son immigrated to California in search of a better life and became a successful businessman. My other cousin, her younger son, immigrated to Canada where he became a skillful ENT specialist. Years later, my path crossed in North America with the younger cousin. He graciously contributed invaluable information about Dad's siblings that filled a few gaps in the Khouri family life story.

Rose died in Egypt, but not before Dad fulfilled his dream of introducing Mom and my siblings to his favorite sister, her husband, and our cousins in Egypt. He accomplished his mission well. Despite the periods of rejection and unkindness witnessed by Dad from his older siblings, he forgave them. And as he built name, fame, and fortune decades later in the country of Sudan, he supported all his siblings financially. He regularly sent his brother Mousa money to pay for his apartment and continued to do that until Mousa's death. He loved everyone in his blood family and remained loyal to them until the very end.

Dad (second row, first on the right) as a teenager in the 1920s.

Young Dad (second from the left), his parents, and siblings at a picnic.

Dad and his brother wearing one of his tailored suits in late 1930s.

Dad.

Thriving in Egypt \ 51

Dad, and the palm trees, in one of his cool suits in the early 1940s.

Dad in Italy approximately in late 1950s.

Dad in a resort in Port Said, Egypt, in the 1930s recuperating from severe dysentery.

Dad on one of his European trips in the 1950s.

Grandpa Hanna in late 1920s.

Grandpa Hanna Obituary in an Egyptian newspaper. He died on Sunday, June 26, 1932. Retrieved from the Library of Congress archives.

CHAPTER 8

THE KHOURI FAMILY'S RICHES TO RAGS STORY: LIFE IN HAYY EL-SAKAKINI

THE LOSS OF THE AL-KHOURI FAMILY HOME was a major tragedy eclipsed only by the death of Grandpa Hanna. Fortunately for them, they had enough money to invest in an apartment in the historical district of El-Sakakini. The family home apartment, which eventually became their new home, was close to El-Sakakini Pasha Palace, a historical landmark in Cairo.

The fifty-room opulent palace, built in 1897, belonged to a Gabriel Habib Sakakini, a Christian Syrian who immigrated to Egypt in the 1850s. Like the Al-Khouri family's rags-to-riches story, Mr. Sakakini, a Levant, was a business genius who gained enormous wealth and fame in Egypt. His career started when he worked in the construction of the Suez Canal, impressing the Turks and British with the quality of his work. Many believe that he got his big break with the British authorities in Egypt when he found simple solution to a vexing rats problem. The British asked him to fix the problem and he did that by bringing hundreds of extremely hungry cats to the British grain storages where the rats lived. The rats were quickly eliminated and his reputation as a problem solver propelled him to new heights of fame and fortune. He died in 1923 leaving behind a city square that bears his name and the lavish El-Sakakini Pasha Palace with its unique architecture and multiple marble statues including one of himself adorning its entrance.[55, 56]

I wonder sometimes about what went through my grandmother's, Dad's, and his siblings' minds when they gazed at that magnificent palace a short distance from their apartment in Hayy El-Sakakini. The riches and wealth that they once enjoyed had vanished. The Khouris' luxurious family home and huge fortunes were all gone. They were blessed to have an apartment that they could call home. The Khouri family's immigrant story in Egypt did not end up financially as well as El-Sakakini's. But when it came to accumulation of wealth and possessions, there were no winners in the end. All the accumulated wealth, fortunes, and palaces of that era, including the Khouris' Al-Zagazig home and business and El-Sakakini Palace, were all left behind. They were either demolished or left in disarray, collecting dust as their owners and their immediate heirs eventually all died. The family's apartment in Hayy El-Sakakini became the final hub for my dad's immediate family including his mom and siblings Mousa and Ibrahim, who squandered the family wealth.

Fading Memories, Lasting Legacies

The apartment at Hayy El-Sakakini was the final earthly and temporary home of the original immigrant Khouri family that started with Grandpa's immigration to Egypt in 1862. They lived there, a few left to other countries, while others stayed there until their dying days. The Khouri family, with nine living siblings by the time of Grandpa Hanna's death in 1932, eventually all died and transitioned into their permanent home in eternity. In their story, I can see the cycle of life, with its trials, tribulations, failures, and victories. The last chapter of their lives ended, just as it will end for each one of us one day.

All that remains of the family's Al-Zagazig home, the Hayy El-Sakakini apartment, and all their life stories are the legacies that each had left behind. Dad left me with a good legacy of how to really care, to love selflessly, and to seek others' needs and interests and not just mine. That was how he loved his siblings. Not only that, but he left a footprint of his Christian faith and Christ's teaching for me and my siblings to follow. And that was his enduring legacy.

CHAPTER 9

EGYPT'S BLACK-WHITE COLOR DIVIDE

DAD'S SUDDEN DECISION in the later part of the 1940s to go to the country of Sudan, known to early Arab geographers as "Al-Sudan," or "land of the Blacks" in Arabic, was quite a shock to those in his circle.

"What! Al-Sudan . . . Al-Sudan!" was the usual shock response he got when he broke the news to his family and friends. Sudan, a nation of Black and all-shades-of-brown people, was at the time under the Anglo-Egyptian colonization but primarily under Britain's control. It was a vast, underdeveloped land where the slave trade thrived until the British officially abolished it in 1924.[57]

As a white man, going to Sudan, Dad would be a small minority among a nation of predominantly darker-skinned people. That was a new experience for him. Family and friends were worried about his decision to go to Sudan for that reason. But on the other hand, he was thrilled. Growing up in Egypt, Dad mainly interacted with other white people within his circle. Apart from the casual encounters with Black Nubians, Sudanese, and Ethiopians doing manual work, or former slaves and their dependents in the streets of Cairo, he did not have an opportunity for close relationships with anyone outside his circle. Society's norms at the time would not have allowed it.

But then, enters Giuseppe Verdi's opera "Aida." The opera told of a forbidden love story of an imprisoned, enslaved Ethiopian princess called "Aida" and an Egyptian Army commander named "Radames." The Khedive Ismail Pasha of Egypt originally commissioned the famous Italian composer to compose the opera to inaugurate the newly built Cairo Opera House.[58]

The dazzling and spectacular performance of "Aida" eventually premiered in Cairo on December 24, 1871, when Grandpa Hanna was nine years old.

The opera "Aida" played for decades in Cairo after its premiere, a short distance away from where Dad lived his youth years. It introduced Dad and other opera lovers in Egypt to a novel concept: a romantic love story between an African Ethiopian princess, Aida, and a light-skinned Egyptian military commander, Radames. In an era where Black and dark-skinned people were either slaves, manual workers, servants, or domestic help, the opera "Aida" was an intriguing anomaly.

"Aida," set in Ancient Egypt, is about the Ethiopian Princess, Aida, who was held as a slave by Amneris, the daughter of Egypt's king. Radames, an Egyptian general, chosen by the king as the top war commander against Ethiopia, falls secretly in love with Aida. After a major battle victory against the Ethiopian army, Radames returns triumphantly to Egypt hoping to free the woman he loves, Aida. But the King of Egypt has something else in mind. He decided instead to honor Radames by appointing him as his successor and offered his daughter Amneris as a wife. Radames rejects Amneris's love and chooses instead to set his Aida and her imprisoned father, the Ethiopian king, free. As a punishment, the high priest sentences him to death by sealing him in a dark tomb under the temple. To Radames's surprise he finds his beloved Aida hiding in the tomb to be with him to the very end.[59]

Dad loved classical music and operas. "Aida," with its captivating love story between the dark-skinned Ethiopian and a light-skinned Egyptian, fascinated him as it did other Egyptians. A love story that crossed the color line was a revolutionary concept in Egypt at the time. A few decades after Aida's premiere in Cairo, Dad decided to move to Al-Sudan, where he met and fell in love with Mom, a black-skinned Ethiopian. He decided to cross the cultural and color divide of his time just as in Verdi's "Aida." Unlike Aida and Radames, their earthly love story in Sudan continued for nearly four decades until Dad's passing, with Mom by his bedside. The opera continues to be played in Egypt and throughout the world since its 1871 premiere.

Dad's Journey to Al-Sudan, "Land of the Blacks"

As the top student at his architecture school in Cairo, Dad was eager to advance his career after graduation. He was particularly interested in creative designs including Arabic architectural building designs. Consequently, he entered a competition held in Cairo to choose the best of Egypt's architects to go to Khartoum, the capital city of Sudan. In the late 1940s, King Farouk of Egypt wanted to send few of the country's brightest and most talented architects to design and build his gift to the Sudanese people in Khartoum: The King Farouk Mosque. Dad handily won the competition demonstrating his skills in the Al-Andalus and Fatimid architectural designs needed to construct the famous mosque in Sudan. It still stands in Khartoum and considered as a rare architectural gem and a masterpiece of Islamic design.

Dad's decision to compete and eventually win the architectural competition and to go to Sudan was a major surprise to his family. But to him, it was a well thought-out decision. Following the end of WWII, the political climate in Egypt began to gradually heat up. He felt an increase in anti-Christian sentiment with the gradual rise of the Muslim Brotherhood's influence, anti-British and anti-Western riots, and demonstrations. As a Christian architect chosen by King Farouk's team to build a mosque in

Khartoum, he was very appreciative of the opportunity. He took comfort in the king's religious tolerance of Christians even as he worried about the winds of religious intolerance that he noticed in other segments of society.

Dad was not initially planning to immigrate to Sudan when he became one of King Farouk's elite team of Egyptian architects to build the mosque. That decision came later after the building of the King Farouk Mosque and returning to Egypt. By that time, the king had already abdicated his throne, and uncertainties mired Cairo's political and religious climate.

King Farouk's Architectural Marvel Completed and Dad's New Life in Sudan

As a leading member of an "A" team made up of Egypt's finest Egyptian architects, Dad's name and fame became well-known among Sudan's elite, foreign diplomats, and high government officials. The designing and building of the mosque in Sudan propelled Dad's career and reputation as an architect to new astronomical levels. Since its official opening in 1953, the mosque became an architectural treasure revered by Muslims in Sudan and throughout the Middle East.

Sometime between 1948 to 1949 during the building of the King Farouk Mosque, Dad met and fell in love with Mom, his "Ethiopian Princess: Aida," in Khartoum. The idea of permanently immigrating to Sudan to be with Mom and start his own family began to captivate him. New doors of opportunity to build a family with Mom, advance his career, and make a good living opened for him, and that was like a dream come true. But on the other hand, he loved Egypt. It was home to him, and where his family lived. Dad was at the crossroads of his life, and what he was about to decide on would forever change the course of his life.

Shortly after the end of his assignment in Sudan, Dad returned with his team of architects to Cairo. He had important life decisions to ponder about and needed time to pray and reflect. The violence on Cairo's streets, and the general threat he foresaw to be coming from the Muslim Brotherhood who wanted to end Egypt's secular status troubled him.

The violence and demonstrations on the streets of Cairo reached a boiling point culminating with "The Fire of Cairo" in January 1952 when anti-British and anti-Western rioters burnt hundreds of buildings in downtown Cairo. Jews, Greeks, and other westerners sold their possessions and left after the fire.[60] In July 1952, the Egyptian military dealt the monarchy a final blow forcing King Farouk to abdicate his throne and to permanently leave Egypt. Europeans and other foreigners began to leave the country.[61]

"1951–52 saw several violent uprisings take place in the Opera Neighborhood. Shops and agencies owned by the affluent Jewish and European communities were burned and the merchandise destroyed."[62]

Equally troubling to Dad was leaving his family behind in Egypt's unstable conditions and immigrating to Sudan. But finally, he came to the decision that it was best for him to immigrate to Sudan. Years later, he explained to Mom how he arrived at his final decision.

"Because of my name (Christian family name), they would only give me jobs below my qualifications. All my Muslim colleagues received their bonuses after we finished building King Farouk Mosque. They did not want to give me my bonus."

Three decades after the religiously biased denial of his bonus in Egypt, Dad worried that the same might happen to me. As I was in the process of applying to colleges as my high school education in Sudan was ending, he said, *"I worry because of your Christian name, you might not be accepted in a university."* Education to Dad was as important as it was to his own dad. They both wanted their children to be college educated.

Much like his own father and grandfather who moved to Egypt in search of a better life, it was Dad's turn to follow his inner calling. He was taking a major step of faith to the unknown in Sudan. He needed more of God's encouraging "Fear not," reminders, and less of *"But Gobran!*

Why Sudan? There is nothing there. It is an empty space . . . a wilderness" discouraging and fear-provoking words.

Al-Sudan: Dad's New Home

Sudan, located in the northeastern part of Africa, has always been a country of sharp contrasts and cultural diversity. Up until the fifteenth century, it was the site of the most powerful Christian kingdoms in the world. The North with its hot, dry weather and Muslims of partial Arab lineage stood in cultural, religious, and racial contrast to the South. The southern part of Sudan up until 2011 was the African part of Sudan. Blessed with the water of the Nile, rich soil, heavy rains, jungles, and diverse wildlife, Southern Sudan also suffered from military invasions, wars, and the dreaded slave trade. Sudan was the largest country in Africa until its southern part became the independent nation of South Sudan after two civil wars lasting over two decades. The bloody civil wars between the Muslim Northern Sudan, and predominantly Christian Southern Sudan claimed roughly two million people, mostly civilians dying of starvation and drought. Islamization and imposing of the Sharia law by the Muslim North on the Southern Sudanese were the historically cited causes of the two civil wars (1955–1972 and 1983–2005). The Sharia law became the law in Sudan in 1983.[63]

Sadly, the seeds of division and ethnic fighting continued in the newly formed nation of South Sudan after its independence in 2011. Hundreds of thousands died with many displaced after a new civil war erupted in the new nation of South Sudan.[64]

The Kingdom of Kush

Sudan's history is rich with ancient civilizations including the Kingdom of Kush that once ruled Egypt. It was part of ancient Nubia, a region inhabited by Black people, and included current northern Sudan. The Old Testament has many references to the Kush region and their kingdom. The ruins of its ancient city Napata located in the present-day city of Karima is about 250 miles from Khartoum where Dad and Mom met. The capital city of the powerful Nubian Kingdom of Kush that reigned for over a thousand years was the ancient city of Meroe. The Kushite monarchs invaded Egypt in the eighth century BC, and its monarchs became the pharaohs of Egypt's Twenty-fifth Dynasty. Their rule of Egypt including the enormous influence and contributions of the Kushite Pharaoh Taharqa lasted for a century. Eventually, the Assyrians defeated the Nubians and drove them out of Egypt.[65]

After their defeat in Egypt, the Nubians continued their kingdom in Meroe. They eventually established three Christian kingdoms in northern Sudan: Nobatia, Makuria and Alodia (Alwa) with their capital cities of Kerma, Dongola, and Soba, respectively. Those Christian Nubian kingdoms were able to prevent the Islamic military invasion of Egypt in AD 639 from extending to their kingdoms in Northern Sudan and parts of Southern Egypt. Christianity in Southern Egypt and Northern Sudan continued until the final defeat of the last-standing Nubian kingdom of Alwa by Arab Muslims in AD 1504. The defeat of the last Nubian kingdom, and the fall of Soba, marked the end of nearly a millennium of Christianity in the region. Following the fall of the last Kushite Christian kingdom in present-day Sudan, various Muslim forces ruled the region: the kingdom of Sennar, the Turkish ottomans, and the Sudanese religious leader Al-Mahdi and his loyal followers. Gradually, Christianity disappeared in Sudan among the local population and Islam became the official religion.[66, 67]

Sudan, Dad's New Home

When Dad arrived in Sudan, the only remnants of the ancient Christian Nubian kingdoms he saw were the ruins they left behind. He settled in

Khartoum, just half an hour away from the ruins of Soba, the capital city of the ancient Nubian Kingdom of Alwa. I remember growing up as a child hearing about the old ruins of Soba not far from my childhood home. I never asked my dad to take me there after someone told me: *"No one lives there. It's full of ghosts."* The only remnants of Christianity in Sudan from those ancient empires were churches built by the British for their citizens and other Christians from other countries: Europeans, Americans, Levantines (Syrians, Italians, Armenians, Greeks), and Southern Sudanese.

Fortunately, the building of the King Farouk Mosque and a few other projects established Dad's reputation as a skilled architect. Many officials, foreigners, and well-to-do Sudanese were earnestly hoping for his return. They all wanted him to design their homes, embassies, and churches. In many ways, Sudan was a God-sent new beginning for Dad. The Sudanese, known for their generosity and welcoming of strangers, rolled out the red carpet for Dad.

No one in Khartoum used his Christian family name against him compared to how he was starting to feel in Cairo with the rise in Islamism and the Muslim Brotherhood. It would take another three to four decades for religious fanaticism and the influence of Muslim Brotherhood to spread to Sudan, gain massive political power, and institute the Sharia law. But when Dad emigrated to Sudan in the first half of the 1950s, Sudan was under British and Egyptian colonization, and the relationship between Muslims and Christians was at its best.

Soon after establishing his private architecture office in Khartoum, his fame began to spread, and he became a highly sought-after architect. Multiple jobs to design and build the homes of ambassadors, rich Sudanese, and high government officials, and even a king from Africa began to pour in. And to top it all, he was honored when the country's prime minister personally asked him to permanently stay in Sudan and offered him Sudanese citizenship.

"He urged me to stay in Sudan to help build the country," Dad said to Mom.

Beginning of construction of the King Farouk Mosque in 1949 with Sudanese workers.

Early King Farouk Mosque construction, with Dad somewhere in the photo.

King Farouk Mosque in the early stages of Dad's architectural work.

King Farouk Mosque construction ongoing progress.

Egypt's Black-White Color Divide \ 67

King Farouk Mosque.

King Farouk Mosque near completion.

King Farouk Mosque
Dad's and the Egyptian team of architects' work is all done.

Egypt's Black-White Color Divide \ 69

Dad's architectural designs in Khartoum.

Demonstrators for independence from Britain in the late 1940s in front of the mosque.

PART TWO

MOM'S STORY

★ ★ ★

CHAPTER 10

MIRACULOUS BIRTH AND EARLY CHILDHOOD SEPARATION IN AFRICA'S HIGHLANDS

AFRICA, A CONTINENT OF AMAZING DIVERSITY of landscapes, colors, races, and cultures with about three thousand ethnic groups and one thousand different languages, was where my parents' story began. Dad was born near the River Nile Delta, the last leg of the Nile's journey before it spills its water into the Mediterranean Sea. Mom, on the other hand, was born near the origin of the Blue Nile. From there the Nile continues its long journey to Khartoum where it merges with the White Nile to form the River Nile, just as my parents with their different colors and ethnicities eventually met and merged in Khartoum, becoming one. Their relationship was a match made in heaven, lived, and enjoyed along the ancient Nile where I was born a short distance away from where the Blue and White Niles join.

Mom was born in 1932 in the village of Geldeba, near Adwa, the site of the famous 1896 Battle of Adwa. The region in the Highlands of Tigray, Ethiopia, witnessed the 1896 battle where Ethiopians of different ethnicities united by their Christian faith and nationalism decisively defeated the Italians. Shortly after Mom's birth, her dad, a very devout

Christian, took his wife, his mom, and her younger siblings and moved to a town called Adi Garfa in Eritrea. He wanted to live close to a Christian Orthodox monastery called Enda Abune Brukh and be of service to the monastery priests. A couple of years after doing God's work and serving the priests, he returned to his home village in Tigray, Ethiopia,

"He was a strong believer who prayed all the time. The priests wanted him to move close to the monastery and he did," recalled Mom years later.

Mom's exact month and date of birth are not known as small villages at the time did not keep records of birthdays. She spent her early childhood years not far away from the source of the Blue Nile in the Tigray region of Northern Ethiopia, and Eritrea's highlands. She learned to speak Tigrinya, Amharic, Italian, and grew up in Christian unity and harmony with her Amharic, Eritrean, and Tigrayan neighbors. Her family's temporary home in the village of Adi Garfa was a short distance away from the city of Mendefera, which is about forty miles away from the capital city of Eritrea, Asmara. Both cities were part of Mom's childhood story, especially Asmara where Mom worked the bulk of her early childhood years with Italian families to support her parents and siblings.

Mom's Birthplace

Mom's parents lived close to Axum (Aksum), a city considered holy in the Tigray highlands in Northern Ethiopia. Orthodox Christians of the region regard the city, which was the site of the ancient kingdom of Axum, as sacred and where the Ark of the Covenant is believed to be located. The Aksumite ruler King Ezana embraced Christianity and it became the official state religion in the fourth century.[68, 69, 70]

My grandparents devoted their lives in the vicinity of the holy city to fasting, praying, and serving in the local Christian Orthodox Church.

Mom grew up listening to Bible stories her parents told her, including the story of the Queen of Sheba who is known to Ethiopians as Makeda.

According to long historical Ethiopian traditions, the queen, mentioned in the Bible as the Queen of the South, journeyed from her kingdom in Axum to visit King Solomon in Jerusalem. Scholars disputed the origin and the site of Queen Sheba's kingdom. Some of them believe that she was from Yemen and had led a caravan that followed ancient trade routes to Jerusalem where she met King Solomon. Nevertheless, for generations of Ethiopians throughout the centuries, the Queen of Sheba was Makeda, an Ethiopian royalty from the Kingdom of Axum. They believe that she bore King Solomon's child and gave birth upon her return to a son who became King Menelik I. The king, according to the long-held Ethiopian traditions, continued the Solomonic lineage of royal ancestry that ended in 1974 with King Haile Selassie I, who was known as the "Lion of Judah," and "the chosen of God." [71, 72]

I still remember as a child catching a glimpse of King Haile Selassie I when he visited Al-Kanisa Al-Habashia ("the church of the Ethiopian, Tigrayan, and Eritrean Christians," as it was called) in Khartoum. I and other children from the church sang to the visiting king the Ethiopian national anthem that the church priest spent a long time teaching us how to correctly recite. The Negus (king), who ruled Ethiopia from 1930 to 1974 and died in 1975, remains as a revered figure by the Rastafarians in Jamaica. To Mom, me, and the children singing on that day in Khartoum, he was a Christian king whose ancient ancestor could have been the biblical King Solomon.[73]

Mom's Christian Ancestors

Following King Ezana's embrace of Christianity and declaration of Christianity as the official state religion in the fourth century, many wars followed. But Christianity in Ethiopia still managed to survive for generations even as Islamic control and influence spread in the nations surrounding it. Eventually, Christians in Egypt and the kingdoms of

Nubia (present day Sudan) became a minority. But, nevertheless, as my parents often told us, the ties between the Egyptian Copts and the Christians in Ethiopia remained strong for centuries. I grew up hearing the story of how Ethiopia threatened to block the flow of the River Nile if the remaining Coptic Christians in Egypt were killed, thus saving the Coptic church.

Sir Francis B. Head, the biographer of the renowned traveler James Bruce, who searched for the source of the Blue Nile in Ethiopia in the late 1700s, wrote:

> Never did the seed of the Christian religion find more genial soil than when it first fell among the rugged mountains of Abyssinia . . . no war to introduce it, no fanatic priesthood to oppose it, no bloodshed to disgrace it; its only argument was its truth; its only ornament was its simplicity; and around our religion, thus shining in its native luster, men flocked in peaceful humility, and hand in hand, joined cheerfully in doctrines which gave glory to God in the Highest, and announced on earth peace, goodwill toward men.[74]

The roots of Christianity there seemed to be very deep. Emperor Yohannes IV of Ethiopia fought many wars to preserve Christianity in his kingdom and died defending his faith. According to the book *Historical Dictionary of Ethiopia*:

> ". . . Yohannes IV defeated Egyptian forces that advanced on Ethiopia from Eritrea. In 1888, a large Islamic army of Mahdists attacked Ethiopia from Sudan, sacking Gondar and burning many of its churches, the following year, Yohannes defeated the Mahdist forces at Metemma on the Sudanese border but died in the battle."[75]

The Italian Invasion of Ethiopia & WWII in Mom's Neck of the Woods

Italy invaded Ethiopia in both the nineteenth and twentieth centuries. But its plan to conquer Ethiopia in 1896 ended with their defeat in the Battle of Adwa. The Ethiopian forces led by Emperor Menelik II defeated the Colonizing Italian army in March 1,1896, in the First Italo-Ethiopian War. The war raged in the mountainous terrains of Adwa in the Tigray highlands of Northern Ethiopia, a short distance away from my ancestral home, and Mom's future birthplace.

According to some scholars, the 1896 defeat of the Italians in The Battle of Adwa became a source of national humiliation in Italy. It led to anger and agitation in Italy that eventually contributed to the eventual rise of Italy's Benito Mussolini. In October 1935, thirty-five years after that major battle, Italy's dictator Benito Mussolini avenged that defeat by invading Ethiopia. Mom was four years old when the Second Italo-Ethiopian war started. Mussolini's troops occupied Ethiopia's capital Addis Ababa on May 5,1936, and then the country in 1937. The war claimed many lives including one of Mom's relatives whose husband went to the war front but never returned.

Emperor Haile Selassie I who led Ethiopia in the war against Mussolini's army went to exile after the fall of Addis Ababa. He continued his efforts to seek help from other European countries to free Ethiopia. WWII (1939–1945) ushered many drastic changes to Ethiopia and Haile Selassie's efforts to liberate his country. Benito Mussolini's decision to declare war on Great Britain and join Hitler's Germany led to Britain's support of King Haile Selassie I in his fight against the Italians in Ethiopia. In 1941, the British began the East African Campaign and attacked the Italians in Ethiopia. The king who was in Khartoum at the time in anticipation of returning to Ethiopia to liberate his country joined them. On May 5, 1941, Emperor Haile Selassie I had a triumphant return to Addis Ababa, the capital city of Ethiopia after the defeat of the Italian army. In September 1943, remnants of the Italian troops who engaged in guerilla warfare surrendered. The Italians under Benito Mussolini were only able to occupy Ethiopia for a brief time before their final defeat.[76,77]

In those turbulent days of the war, and the guerilla warfare that followed, Mom, her parents, and her siblings were miraculously able to stay safe. Mom, who was a young child at the time, worked as a domestic help for Italian families in the city of Asmara. After the Italians left following their defeat, she worked with British families who came to the region. Her parents' and siblings' survival during that time depended on staying away from the war zones, a good harvest, and Mom's income that helped them avert starvation. The end of the war and the departure of the Italians, and then the British brought a new beginning, but uncertainty in Mom's heart. *"How can I work to help Mom, Dad, and my siblings if all the Italians, and the British leave?"* she worried and wondered.

Mom's Parents Sweet Love Story

Mom's parents, Grandpa Tesfi and Grandma Mislal, started their life together in the beautiful highlands of Tigray in northern Ethiopia. Their love story under the splendid African sky began in the first decade of the 1900s. Tesfi, a tall, good-looking man with a black complexion, like Mom's, fell in love the moment he laid eyes on his Ethiopian beauty with long hair, Mislal, who was very light-skinned just like her family. In a culture affected by European colonization where a lighter skin color was viewed more favorably, she was highly desirable for that and for her beautiful hair and looks. A family relative recalled years later how their love story began.

"Tesfi was walking on the village dirt road when he first saw Mislal weaving baskets through a window in her family house. He was awestruck. It was love at first sight."

Desperate to meet her, he went directly to the house and knocked on the door hoping to see her. But to his dismay, a young girl who was visiting her opened the door instead. Determined to see Mislal, he asked the girl for a cup of water hoping that his dream woman would bring it to him.

"She sent the young girl instead with the cup of water. He refused to take the cup and told her that he wouldn't drink unless Mislal brought it personally to him. But after the going back and forth of the girl with Mislal refusing to bring him the cup of water, he got upset. He pushed away the cup of water which ended up falling on the ground and told her, 'I only want Mislal to bring me the cup of water.'"

That was enough to bring Mislal to the house door to lecture him about his rudeness and for pushing away the cup of water the young girl brought him.

They finally met and the rest is history. Grandpa Tesfi did not waste any precious time. True to tradition in an age of no dating allowed, phone calls, texting, or emailing he expediently sent his family to ask Mislal's family for her hand in marriage. Love and marriage in early 1900s Ethiopia were not as complicated as they are today. Just one single look through a house window is all that it took!

Tesfi and Mislal's marriage, officiated by a Christian Orthodox priest, was a match made in heaven. She was a blessing to him and a true lifetime partner. Mom recalled how her mom loved her dad and worked hard to help him.

"She would regularly walk a long distance to the village well to bring water to the family. She refused to let the young children carry the heavy water from the well. She did it herself."

Grandpa Tesfi was a man of prayers who prayed with his children, fasted, and regularly went to church with his wife, Mislal. He was a man known for his superb knowledge and gained a reputation of being the wise man of his village, and its storyteller.

"Abouy (my dad) used to sit under a 'Neem tree' where many people from the village gathered to listen to his stories. He knew about everything," Mom recalled.

Mom and the community viewed Tesfi as someone akin to an encyclopedia or a modern-day Google. He repeatedly told his adoring listeners stories shared by one generation to another about Tigray's highlands, Ethiopia's history, the Italian invasion of Ethiopia, the Battle of Adwa, Christianity, and world history. Many assembled faithfully and regularly around him surrounded by centuries-old, rock-hewn churches as sheep and cattle meandered on the green grass of northern Ethiopia's highlands.

Mom's Miraculous Birth and Childhood

Mom was one of six siblings: three sisters and two brothers, plus a younger brother who died in childbirth. When Mom was about two years old and her mom was nursing her two-month-old sister, the family moved from Mom's birthplace near the historical city of Adwa into the Eritrean town of Adi Garfa. Her dad, at the request of a high-ranking Ethiopia church bishop, obeyed what he believed was God's higher call. He decided to leave his land, possessions, and home of his ancestors to live in close vicinity to Enda Abune Brukh monastery. His journey of moving away from his home mimicked that of immigrants throughout Africa, Dad and his ancestors, and many figures in the Bible such as Abraham and others. My heritage, much like many in such regions of the world, is full of such stories of those who take steps of faith and move to what they believe is God's higher call for them and their families.

The Holy Man

Mom's birth was regarded by her parents as a "miracle." At the third trimester of Grandma Mislal's pregnancy with my mom, things started to deteriorate, and Mislal started to lose weight. Mom's parents started to despair when there was no movement in her womb and the delivery was past due. But just as they started to lose hope, a miracle happened.

Miraculous Birth and Early Childhood Separation \ 81

"*Dad was walking on the road when he met a priest who was looking for a monastery in the area. My dad asked him where he was from and invited him to come to our home to eat and drink since he had a long way to go,*" Mom recalled her dad's words.

The man of God accepted the invitation and surprised Grandpa Tesfi when he told him:

"*Well done by inviting me. I know your wife is pregnant, and the baby is not doing well. But don't worry because the newborn will be a daughter, and she will be blessed and a gift.*"

There was no doubt in Tesfi's mind that he just met a "holy man" because he knew about his wife's pregnancy and its complication without ever being told.

The man of God asked for a large container, filled it with water, and began to pray. He then began to write on a piece of paper biblical scriptures from the book of Psalms, put it in the water-filled container, and continued to pray.

"*He told Dad to use the water in the container to wash his body with, to drink from it, and to make sure to fill the container whenever the water goes down. He also told him to feed her good food like eggs, meat, soup, and to take good care of her. The priest then told my parents about future events in my life that came to be true. It was like he was looking into the future,*" Mom said.

In a culture that was so rooted in faith, being literally soaked in the words of the Holy Scriptures was not questioned by my grandparents. They believed God can do what seemed impossible for them. They felt helpless and needed a miracle. The mystery priest was right. Grandma's condition miraculously improved, and Mom was born a healthy baby, just as promised. She was named Tikabo which means "gift" or "blessed one." Judging by how she grew up to be a true blessing to her parents, siblings, and eventually to Dad and their children, the holy man's prophecy did come true.

Early Childhood in Tigray's Highlands of Ethiopia

Mom's miraculous birth in her parent's modest village home in Gelebeda—close to Adwa, site of the 1896 Battle of Adwa—led *to* a life of faith and Christian devotion. Growing up a short distance away from the ancient holy city of Axum—the capital of the ancient kingdom of Axum and the sacred church of Lalibela—kept the family close to their Christian heritage. During Mom's early childhood years, she grew up hearing the rhythmic sounds of the orthodox priests chanting the "*Mizmor*" (a Psalm) in Axum. The city with its old ruins, scattered obelisks, and churches with distinct Byzantine and Coptic architecture, has been for generations a site of religious pilgrimages. Worshippers flocked on Sundays to Axum's churches where the paintings of the Virgin Mary holding the baby Jesus, the apostles, and St. George slaying the dragon had been displayed there for centuries.

Mom lived in a politically and militarily uncertain time in Tigray's Northern Ethiopia where most of the Christians in Ethiopia called home for many centuries. Southern Ethiopia where Muslims, animists, and Ethiopian Jews known as the Falasha, or Beta Israel[78] lived were half a world away from Mom's tiny village. Multiple wars and invasions of Christian Ethiopia including from neighboring Islamic forces[79] had failed to erase Christianity from the region.

Mom's ancestors held on to their Christian faith for centuries passing the baton from one generation to another.

My grandparents Tesfi and Mislal passed the Christian faith they received from their ancestors to Mom. She, in turn, passed the baton of her faith, so did Dad, a generation later, to me and my siblings in the Muslim majority country of Sudan. My parents and others did exactly what their own parents and ancestors did for many generations. They faithfully passed their faith in Jesus Christ to the generation that followed them thus guaranteeing Christianity's survival.

Unconventional Childhood: "Who Is Mom? Who Is Dad?"

What followed Mom's miraculous birth story was a series of curious turns of events. She described those peculiar events many years later with tears welling up in her eyes.

"Mom gave birth to a baby every two to three years, but my aunt Sahitea was barren. She asked Mom when she was pregnant with me to let her have the baby if it was a girl. Mom, who was having a difficult pregnancy, was very worried that I would not be born alive. She made a vow to my aunt that if I was born a healthy girl then she will let my aunt take me to live with her."

In a deeply religious culture where vows made are vows kept, Mom's birth brought a lot of joy but worries about the vow that my grandparents made and felt obligated to fulfill. That solemn promise made by grandma at a time when she deeply feared losing her baby proved to be the hardest decision in her life. Allowing Mom's aunt Sahitea to take the baby soon after birth was hard for my grandmother.

"My aunt agreed to not take me until Mom gave birth to a new child. Eventually, she took me to live with her when I was about three years old after Mom had a baby," Mom recalled.

Eventually, her aunt came to Adwa to take her from her godmother Alasow and her grandparents where she stayed during her mother's last pregnancy. Her aunt, determined to hold my grandparents to their vow, took her to the village of Maragous on the outskirts of the town of Mendefara.

"It was like a dream. I've no idea how I remember that, but I do," she said holding back the tears.

Mom vividly recalled decades later riding a mule as her aunt took her back and forth between her home and the village where her parents lived. She stayed with her aunt until the age of ten and only saw her parents when they visited her.

"Initially, I did not know they were my parents, but I started to get attached to them. As I grew older, I used to cry . . . cry . . . cry if they missed coming for a week. Then I would hear the people say, 'Why didn't her parents come? Did they come?' That was when I started to know that they are Mom and Dad."

Her aunt Sahitea was upset when Mom found out about her parents. She worried that Mom was becoming overly attached to her parents after knowing that the two nice strangers she often saw and grew to love were Mom and Dad. Regrettably for Mom, Sahitea decided to stop her from seeing her parents altogether. Thankfully, Sahitea's decision did not stop Mom and her parents from secretly meeting.

It is hard for me to imagine how seriously Grandma Mislal and Grandpa Tesfi viewed the vow made to leave Mom with her aunt. To them, making a vow before God was sacred and they did not want to break it. In our age of broken and discarded vows, their decision seems so unreal. Despite my grandparents' decision not to break the vow taken, they decided to see Mom in secret in the *Souk* (open market) of Adwa. The city of Adwa, in addition to its religious and historical significance, was a big marketplace and a trading center for the region. It drew people from the surrounding towns and villages to buy and sell food and products. The busy *Souk* became the once-a-week meeting place for Mom and her parents away from the watchful eyes of Sahitea. The time of bonding between Mom and her dad and mom was always special and memorable to them, but always ended with Mom crying when it was time to say goodbye.

"*My aunt told me not to see them, but I used to see them at the* Souk. *But whenever I returned to my aunt's home, I would start crying . . . crying. My aunt used to ask me 'why are you crying?' She began to follow me to the* Souk *and that was when she found out why I was crying. She told my parents to stop seeing me,*" said Mom recalling that sad chapter of her childhood.

CHAPTER 11

THE TEARFUL YEARS OF YOUNG CHILDHOOD

Mom's childhood was most definitely not a typical one. The vow made by her mom to let her live with her aunt Sahitea in a city far away created a deep yearning and longing for her parents' love that never left her. The years of raging wars in Ethiopia against the Italians, the ever-present threat of starvation, and many sleepless nights of hard labor marred her precious childhood years. As a young child, she started a long-term career of working with Italian families as a domestic help. She cooked, cleaned, and took care of their babies and young children.

She did not enroll in any school. She had no school bus to take her anywhere, no warm meal waiting for her after a long school day, or childhood activities to enjoy. She had none of that. She had a full day of uninterrupted work, a child taking care of other children. All what she remembers of her young childhood are those occasions of feeling hungry and close to starvation. Tears always flowed from her eyes every time she talked about those days of yearning for her parents, and how hard she labored to send them all the money she made. With her dad Tesfi gradually losing his eyesight and no longer able to fully support his large family, hunger and famine were like vultures always awaiting them.

Before her dad's visual impairment and eventual vision loss, there were joyful days where the land produced plenty of harvest. On those days, you could see the family's cattle feeding on the surrounding pastures with wheat, barley, teff, and sorghum grown and harvested. On those days of plenty, she shared with her family delicious meals; chickpeas, lentils, *zigni*, and *injera*. Her mom and aunt taught her how to cook, and decades later in Sudan she cooked those very same delicious meals that reminded her of those precious childhood moments. For her dad Tesfi, it was essential that the children were all well-fed before going to sleep. He often asked his wife, Mislal, when the children lay asleep next to them, if any of them went to bed hungry.

"*I do not hear them passing gas. Did they eat enough?*"

Mom's childhood memories often brought her laughter and smiles but mostly tears. She easily cried whenever she talked about those days when she constantly "walked . . . walked . . . walked." She walked and walked barefooted to and from work or in search of a job. Occasionally, she stepped on dry grass, thorn bushes, and hot sand, and rested under an acacia or eucalyptus tree. Mom never got over her fears of hyenas, and large pythons that "*can even swallow cattle*" and who lived in the rugged highlands. But mostly, she never forgot her intense yearning for her mom and dad's warm love, and the unfulfilled dream of spending all her childhood with them.

On the Brink of Starvation

Mom was about ten years old when the British Empire began their military campaign against the Italians in colonized Ethiopia and Eritrea. The East Africa campaign, June 1940 to November 1941, started after Italy's dictator Benito Mussolini allied himself with Adolf Hitler and fought with Germany against the Allies in WWII.[80]

The repercussions of the war between Italy and Britain affected the region including her aunt Sahitea's household where she lived. Sahitea's husband became a soldier and left home for the battlefields of the raging war. She never heard from him again. The fierce Second World War against the Italian army in Ethiopia and Eritrea took a toll on every home in the region, including Sahitea's home. In desperation, Mom's aunt left home to look for her husband and left Mom behind. Feeling hopeless and in despair, Sahitea decided to leave Mom with a preteen relative girl, *"a helper,"* alone at her home as she embarked on the dangerous journey in search of her husband. She promised to return soon and left them with enough food to last for a couple of weeks. Mercifully, there was food stored in the house for a potential future marriage that Sahitea was arranging for the young *"helper"* girl who had been left with Mom in the house. And with the temporary absence lasting for months, the stored wheat, barley, and teff flour saved them from certain starvation.

"*My aunt had flour and food stored for the wedding, but after we finished eating the food, we started to get hungry. We did not know what to do,*" Mom recalled.

Shockingly, Sahitea left the two children alone at a time of war with dwindling food supply! Fortunately, Nietzsche's statement, *"What doesn't kill you makes you stronger,"* was true in Mom's life, starting with a painful early separation from her parents. Her resilience and faith in God, shaped and formed by those very perilous days of childhood work, separation, and uncertainties, made her into a strong woman of admirable character. Decades later, Dad was swept away by her good character and beauty.

Mom's Child Labor Years

Mom's journey into the hazard of childhood labor started with the near starvation stretch at her aunt's home. *"Necessity is the mother of invention"* became true in Mom's life as she and her young housemate consumed all the food left in her aunt's house. They started to get hungry and feared starvation after they finished the remaining food.

"I joined other children in the neighborhood who went house to house dancing during Christian Orthodox religious ceremonies. There were three festivals in that year where we danced with other children to the beat of the kabero (Ethiopian/Eritrean traditional drum) and bought food with the money that the people gave us."

Mom bought *himbasha* (an Ethiopian-Eritrean decorated flat bread also known as *ambasha*) with her portion of the money and brought it home to share with her young housemate. But soon enough, they were back again at the brink of starvation when the religious festivals ended. Mom could no longer dance with the other children to make money to buy *teff* flour and wheat. Mercifully, a moment of divine intervention saved their lives. Mom would have many of those miraculous moments throughout her life that strengthened her own faith in God.

"A next-door neighbor saw me and noticed my big belly. She suspected something was wrong and that I was starving. She invited me to her home. "Come Tikkabo. Are you OK?" She realized I was very hungry and fed me Injera (a soft and spongy Ethiopia-Eritrean flatbread made from teff flour) and shiro (an Ethiopian-Eritrean curry or stew made from chickpea). I ate it so fast and almost devoured all of it but then I stopped. I refused to finish the food she offered me because I wanted to take some of the food to feed my friend who was also hungry."

Thankfully, the kind neighbor, whom Mom saw as God-sent, figured it out and loaded Mom with a plate full of half *kisra* (a Sudanese name for *injera*) and half *shiro* and told her to take it with her.

The Long Dusty Road to Home

The next day Mom's kind neighbor came to check on her and offered to take her back to her parents' home before she starved to death.

"She told me to go home. I asked her 'but how do I go?' Then, she asked me if I knew the way back to Dad and Mom's village. I used to go there every two to three weeks, but I had no idea how to get there because they always took me on a mule. She told me to get ready early in the morning and came to take me," she recalled.

The neighbor was true to her word. She woke Mom up early in the morning and walked with her on a long dusty road that led to her parents' village. She could not go with her all the way to the village but told her to walk close to the people on that road. Many people regularly took that route to villages close to where Mom's parents lived.

Mom did exactly what the neighbor told her. She walked in the middle of a crowd of people, some walking on foot, others riding their donkeys and mules heading toward their villages. Her youthful age, hungry looks, and smallish figure must have elicited compassion and pity among many of the travelers who shared their meals with her.

The long journey on the road back home that they all started at sunrise often became perilous and hazardous at sunset. Experienced travelers knew well the grave risk of being on the long road when it got dark. They would usually pick up the pace late afternoon to make it to their homes before sunset. As the sun began to disappear below the western horizon, Mom realized that fellow travelers and mules on the road disappeared except for a lone woman speeding frantically. The woman who was hoping to make it back to her village before it got dark, saw Mom, a child, frightened and walking all alone. Mom knew why everyone wanted to desperately make it home before nighttime. The howling sounds of the vicious, hungry hyenas roaming the vast African savannah looking for a prey filled her heart with panic.

"I saw the woman running fast. It was a miracle from God that she noticed me walking alone. She asked me: 'Where are you going to?' I told her: 'Adi Girfa.' But then she told me 'You can't go now!' I was so afraid of Al-maraphean (hyenas)."

For the next hour, the woman sped swiftly down the dusty road as Mom tried to keep pace. Mom's biggest fear as darkness descended was an attack by a hungry *Zybee* (*hyena*) or one of the other highland predators. But what she saw scared her more than her fearful hyena encounter.

"*As I followed her, we both noticed a very tall man with big Afro hair. He was lying down on a branch of a giant tree. When he saw us, he suddenly stood up and we panicked. She told me 'He is not human! He is too tall,' and we ran and ran and didn't stop until we reached her village.*"

In an age of no TV, Google images, Instagram, or Facebook, living in a small village in the highland plateau of Tigray meant isolation from other humans who look different. They doubted that a person that tall with a big Afro haircut could be human, got scared, and ran. The poor man who was most probably a member of the *Hadandoua* tribe as Mom figured out decades later was just as startled. Seeing a woman and a child walking in near darkness on a road where most humans avoid at sunset was a strange sight to see. They finally made it to the woman's hut where Mom was fed and offered a warm bed for the night.

"*In the morning, she walked with me for an hour until we arrived at Adi Hease. From there, we walked alongside a creek. She then stopped and pointed me to the direction that I needed to take to my parents' home. Then she watched me from far away as I walked, walked, and walked.*"

As she approached the home with great anticipation, she could see her mom from far away. She was pregnant with her last child, Mom's youngest brother, Tawaldi, but was still managing to work hard to help her visually impaired husband and to feed her young children.

"*She was planting potatoes and tomatoes and removing weeds. I was wearing my Damouria dress (traditional fabric) and as soon as she saw me, she ran toward me. She picked me up and cried . . . cried . . . cried 'WY, WY, WY!' (words used to describe shock and surprise) 'It is Tikkabo! Oh, my daughter, I sold you! I didn't know all this happened to you.*'"

Finally, Mom made it home! Her happiness and excitement were indescribable. As a child deprived for years from her parents, coming back home to their love and warm embrace was a cherished moment. It brought her tears of joy, back then, just as it continued to do throughout her life.

Finding and Then Losing the Joy of Childhood

After coming back home, Mom enjoyed for a year an uninterrupted childhood in the comfort and love of her mom and dad. That was to her a dream come true. One of her memories of those precious days included the joy of enjoying warm meals with the whole family. Each night her dad would ask her mom a variation of the same routine question when the children were sound asleep or pretending to be asleep.

"*He used to ask Mom when the room was too quiet at night. 'The children are not passing gas. Did they eat well last night?*'" Mom recalled.

But out of all the stories of her one year of childhood bliss with her parents, this unforgettable childhood story of Shashou stood out the most.

"*I had a chicken that I called 'Shashou.' I loved Shashou and enjoyed playing with her. Then one day after eating the zigne (spicy chicken stew) and injera that Mom cooked, I went out to play with my chicken, but I couldn't find her. I started to cry out 'Shashou Shashou, Shashou' where are you? I screamed and wept when Mom told me that Shashou was in the zigni and injera lunch that we just ate,*" said Mom recalling the short life of her beloved pet chicken.

Sadly, Mom's childhood joy of finally being home with Mom and Dad was short-lived. Her aunt suddenly appeared out of nowhere following her return from the war front after failing to find her husband. She demanded that Mom be returned to her home to work, given her previous arrangement and grandmother Mislal's previous vow. But soon after Mom returned to her aunt Sahitea's home, disaster struck. Her aunt succumbed to a severe illness and decided to defy her Christian Orthodox church's teaching and seek healing from a witch doctor. Many years later, Mom vividly recalled the scary day when the witch doctor performed a bizarre ritual at her aunt's request.

"For hours, the witch doctor was chanting, dancing, and shaking ceaselessly around her bed. Then suddenly, he ran out of the house screaming in panic at the top of his voice, 'SAHITEA WILL DIE . . . SAHITEA WILL DIE. SHE WILL DIE.'"

Oddly enough, Sahitea died shortly after that weird ceremony and Mom found herself without a source of income to support herself and her family. Soon after her aunt's death, Mom returned home to her parents hoping and praying to never leave again.

Sadly, her childhood joy with her mom and dad after her aunt's death ended quickly. Soon after Sahitea's death, another female relative showed up at her family's home asking to take Mom to live with her. She promised to take care of her and to send my grandparents desperately needed money in return for Mom doing domestic help at her far away home. Sadly, the woman turned out to be an out-of-control psychopath who whipped and slapped Mom for every trivial thing. Those were the days of no phones or text messaging to let her parents know what was happening to her. Mom, still a child, had no hope of escaping her abusive relative without a miracle.

Curiously, the miracle she prayed for came after a terrible, incessant beating Mom got after she refused to lie to cover up for one of her female relative's big lies. The slapping and pummeling Mom received in public, after the woman ran after her and stopped her on the street, eventually led to Mom's final escape from the vicious woman. Many decades later, Mom's recollection of the incident was vivid.

"She asked me to lie to a man she had a relationship with about where she was, but I didn't. She got mad and wanted to beat me. I ran, but she stopped me on the street, pulled my dress exposing my back, and began to whip me so hard. Then suddenly a policeman who saw her beating me and the man that she wanted me to lie to, came running to us. They stopped her from beating me, and then one of them began to whip her hard. They helped me to go back home to my parents."

Returning Home Again

Mom was finally home . . . again! There she was back to her sweet home with its four *Agdos* (round huts) built close to each other. The four spacious *Agdos* were huts constructed with round walls made up of mud and dry cow manure. They had thatched roofs made up of straw and branches, among other materials. The kitchen and bathroom were outside the main round hut, with a clean *Agodo* for guests built next to them. Mom slept in a bed made up of well-constructed circular mud walls that fit two to three people. Multiple layers of cow and sheep hide covered by a *Zouria* (cotton cloth) served as a comfortable mattress.

Her dad's two favorite oxen that he often called *"Ata B'arai"* (You cow!) and *"Ata Finjan"* (You handless coffee cup!) when they plowed his corn and grain fields frequently mooed as Mom slept soundly in her mud bed. One mule, goats, sheep, and chicken—including her favorite one, *Shashou*, that her mom cooked for a tasty *zigni* dinner—gave Mom the nostalgic feeling of being home. Mom cherished every moment there and yearned to never leave her parents, siblings, and the safety and security of her home ever again.

In the peace and comfort of their home, her parents showered her with love and diligently taught her about the foundation of their Christian faith. Her mom showed her how to cook the delicious *zigni*, *injera*, and other meals that delighted many for many years to come. Interestingly, her learned cooking skills helped her to find and keep jobs with Italian and British families that she desperately needed. Even more important, she used her acquired cooking talents decades later to make mouthwatering meals for her own family in Sudan that no local restaurant could match.

It amazes me every time I reflect on how Mom showed her devotion and love to Dad, me, and my siblings through the art of cooking. Cooking to her was much like a talented ballerina expressing her love and passion in a "Swan Lake" ballet performance. Mom cooked with a deep passion and excelled in it. Those brief but formative years of her childhood transformed her into a warm and loving mom. She taught us the foundation of her Christian faith that her parents had taught her and created a peaceful home environment. Ours was a warm home that reminded Mom of the brief but joyful time she spent with her mom and dad in a simple hut in the highlands of Tigray.

Sadly, Mom's joyful reunion with her parents and siblings was short lived. Mom stayed for about a year after leaving her abusive relative's home but then things quickly changed. Grandpa Tesfi began to experience severe eyesight loss that prevented him from working in the fields. Glaucoma, known as the "silent thief of sight," stole his vision, rendering him unable to take care of his farm and cattle. In an era of colonization and in a war-torn part of the world where government assistance did not exist, working in the farm meant putting food on the table. Sensing the real risk of hunger that the family would face because of Grandpa Tesfi's visual impairment, his sister Azieb pleaded with him to let Mom go back to work.

"I heard her say, 'you don't see, and your children are still small. She is now older and familiar with everything. You must let her work to help you.' When I heard that, I started to cry and cry in bed while trying to go to sleep. I didn't want to leave them. Mom and Dad didn't want me to leave. Mom said 'NO.' Dad said 'NO.' Let us be hungry together. What we eat she eats and whatever God wills for us.'"

After Azieb's repeated persistence and pleading to Mom and her parents to find a job in the "city," Mom agreed to go. Her mom and dad finally relented.

"I finally said 'Hiray . . . Taiib' (OK in Tigrinya and in Sudanese Arabic). On the day I left home, I began walking on the road and was frequently looking back to wave goodbye to Mom. She was standing on a rock and waving back at me. I remember how she was rushing to find a spot where she could see me as I walked along the road. 'Bakait . . . bakait . . . bakait' (I cried, cried, and cried) as I kept walking and looking back to see if she was still there."

A few years after saying goodbye, her mom, Mislal, died. Her dad had a total loss of his vision following her death.

"*Dad cried till he lost his eyesight,*" Mom surmised.

Child Labor in Little Rome: Asmara

Mom's lengthy career of childhood labor to feed her family started after that tearful goodbye to her parents. Her journey of working with many Italian families who called Asmara home began soon after that farewell. Italy first colonized Asmara, a beautiful Eritrean city 7,628 feet above sea level in 1889. It became a home to thousands of Italians who moved from Rome and Milan.[81]

They transformed the city that became known as Piccola Roma (Little Italy) into futuristic and modern architectural designs. They built railways, opened fancy cafes and pizzerias, and created fancy boulevards that resembled those found in their Italian cities.[82]

In an era where the natives of Asmara stayed away from where the Italians lived, dined, and entertained themselves, Mom, a small child, began working as a domestic helper with Italian families in Asmara. Mom's domestic help jobs were a lifeline. It provided her parents and siblings with enough money to ward off starvation. Even as she advanced in age, she never forgot those difficult days of childhood labor. She carefully and gently fed, and put the little Italian babies entrusted to her to sleep. Her extensive list of home chores included cleaning the whole house, cooking, and washing dishes and piles of dirty cloths and bed sheets. The jobs assigned to her were hard. But she survived those years energized by faith and the knowledge that she must work hard to meet her family's basic needs.

"*One of the Italian families I worked for made me take care of two brothers who lived in adjacent homes with their wives and children. I worked so hard from early morning to late at night taking care of their baby children, washing their cloth and bed sheets. I cooked and cleaned the floor with soap* and water. One of the children was sick and soiled the bedsheets badly. I had to remove all the sheets and put them in a tin container filled with boiling water and ashes. After washing the cloth, I would then hang them outside. I used to feel cold. It was cold in Asmara. That was how we used to wash the cloth back then. When I washed the dishes, I had to place a big rock to stand on it so that I can reach the sink. I was too small."

Working day and night as a child left a physical and emotional toll on Mom.

"I cried whenever I saw the children play. I worked like a donkey. I would tell myself 'Why do I have to work and not play like the other children?' I felt tired, hungry, and cold. I didn't buy any new clothes. I walked barefooted and didn't want to spend any money.

I never had a childhood."

Some of Mom's Italian employers were kind and caring, while a few others were demanding and unreasonable. Her greatest challenge, much like any employed adult in the workforce, was what to do when an employer was terrible. God only knows how as a child she managed to deal with such employers, but she miraculously always managed.

"I remember, one of the Italian women I worked for accused me of eating the food that I prepared for her baby. The food I cooked shrank in size when it got colder. Her husband who was on a ladder changing a light bulb in the kitchen knew that I didn't eat it. He defended me and told her that I didn't eat any of the food. But she told him 'No, she ate it . . . she ate it.' He told her 'NO! she didn't', but she yelled and argued with him. Then she yelled at me and fired me. She told me 'USCIRE DI CASA' (get out of the house in Italian)," recalled Mom many years later.

Mom was shocked and frightened.

"I ran out of the house as soon as she screamed 'uscire di casa.' I cried . . . cried . . . cried. She told me to leave without paying me for the work that I've already done. I started walking on the street not knowing what to do next. But then I saw her husband who was so kind, running toward me. He gave me money and told me to take it. I did."

That traumatic, unjustifiable act of firing reminded Mom of her childhood away from her parents. Unkindness such as this revived the old memories of missing her parents and abandonment.

"As I grew older, I began to suspect that Dad and Mom were actually my parents. When they told me that they were, my aunt was not happy. They began to meet me in secret under an acacia tree without her knowledge. I often thought 'Why did Dad and Mom give me away? Did they love me? Why were they not taking me back?' All I wanted is to be with them. I missed them so terribly after our meetings under the tree."

It's hard for me to fathom how Mom survived her childhood. Working instead of playing with children her age was not fair. But with wars raging, and her dad's loss of vison, she was her family's main source of income. No work meant hunger and starvation. Working as a child exposed her to many risks and potential dangers. Yet, her only worry was not any of the above but whether she would be able to work to support her family. Hard as those childhood labor years were, they helped to grow Mom's faith and character.

A marketplace in Mom's place of birth. She spent a long time secretly seeing her parents in a marketplace like this.

A mountain in Tigray near Mom's birthplace.

Oxen plowing the field in the highlands of Tigray.

The Obelisks of Axum. Erected by Ezana, the king of Axum, in the 4th century.

CHAPTER 12

MOM'S FAREWELL TO ASMARA: THE SEARCH FOR ITALIANS AND BRITONS

AFTER THE ITALIANS' DEFEAT IN ETHIOPIA and Eritrea during World War II, the Italian families that Mom worked for began to leave Asmara. She could no longer find an Italian family to work for. Mom's only hope then was finding one of the British families who came to Asmara after Great Britain's victory over Italy. Mom, who was just a child during that era, did not grasp the full meaning of colonization or the Europeans' "Scramble for Africa" adventures. All what she wanted was to find a job that would keep her family alive. The Italian families provided her with that opportunity, and she appreciated them for that.

But as the Italian families packed up their life belongings and left Asmara, gloom and worries filled her young heart.

"I cried because all the Italians were leaving. The two Italian brothers that I worked for told me that they were going back to Italy. All what I could think about was to find another Italian family to work for."

In Asmara, Mom stayed with her kind aunt Azieb during her days off work. There, she enjoyed rare, precious moments of playing with Azieb's young daughter who was close to her age. After the exodus of the Italians,

Azieb wanted her to look for jobs with Eritrean or Ethiopian families in the area. But Mom, and a young friend who only worked with Italian families, had a different plan. They wanted to work with the Italians or the British because they could afford to pay them well.

"*My friend was two years older than I was. She told me 'Let us take the Babour (train) and go to the city of Keren. I hear there are still Italian and British people there.' I was determined to find an Italian or a British family and so I agreed. We went to visit my aunt and her daughter. I left her home without telling her of my plan to go to Keren.*"

The Train Ride: From Keren to Teseney in Search of Italians: The Journey to Keren

Mom was barely fourteen years old when she began her courageous step of faith through the vast wilderness of Eritrea's highlands. Her journey by train with another young child, two years her senior, through the mountainous terrain of East Africa had one objective. They were both determined to find a job with any of the Italian or British families that might still be left in the country. As the train rolled along the tracks, further and further away from her familiar surroundings, she began to reflect. The significance of stepping out of her comfort zone and leaving everything behind began to dawn on her. Many decades later as a teenager, I had my own worries and hope when I left my family home behind and ventured into the unknown future awaiting me in America. Mom repeatedly experienced throughout her life of pursuing a better life for her family, a mix of fear and hope.

Leaving her childhood home was not a totally new experience to Mom; after all, she lived through multiple temporary separations from her parents from a very young age. But taking a train through the mountains and valleys into foreign terrains, with unfamiliar people, and far away towns was. The further the train ride took her away from home, the more

Mom's Farewell to Asmara: The Search for Italians and Britons \ 103

intense were her emotions. Her awareness that she might never be able to go back home finally hit her.

"We bought tickets for the Babour (train) to go to Keren. I cried a lot because I missed my parents and didn't know if I would ever see them again. I cried at every station when the train stopped. My friend and the passengers who were with us on the train tried to console me, but I couldn't stop crying. I wanted to be home with Mom and Dad. I never stopped crying even after the train stopped at the last station and we were told to leave."

The scenic view of the splendid Barca River in its 640 miles journey from Eritrea's Highland offered her little solace.

"I couldn't stop crying."

Mom's train left "Little Rome," Asmara, once home to many Italian inhabitants, for the smaller city of Keren. She was hoping against hope that some Italian or British families might still be in Keren or nearby cities. She heard that a sizable Italian community once lived in the cities of Keren, Agordat, and Teseney. Mom and her young friend were heading there to look for those who chose to stay. According to Berhane, a family relative, and his family who lived for many generations in the area, the Italians employed for years many locals in their textile and button factories, cotton fields, gardens, and farms. But at the time of Mom's job search adventure much fewer Italians remained in the area. Yet, she was determined to find a job in one of those cities. To Mom, whose family relied on her financial help, failure was not an option.

The sixty-mile train trip between Asmara and Keren lasted a few hours, and it felt like days to Mom and her friend. But they finally arrived.

"When the train got closer to Keren, I started sobbing. Keren looked to me like Aldahara . . . Hagarasab (a faraway underdeveloped village) with Goutia . . . Agodo (circular straw huts). I started to cry, "No Italians can be here. No Italians or British live in a Goutia!" Mom recalled.

Keren, a city with a large Italian population before WWII, had its fair share of Italian- built infrastructure. Mom must have missed seeing the more developed side of the city as the train passed by circular straw huts surrounding Keren. But Mom and her friend could not see any Italian or British people there. They were on a mission to find a job and the disappointment of not finding any in Keren did not discourage them. They just continued their train journey to the next city of Agordat.

Agordat: Mom's Last Train Stop

In an era of no internet or smartphones, Mom's job search was quite different. She rode trains and buses to cities with names she could not read. Post-WWII, jobs were scarce in Agordat just as they were in Keren. Unbeknown to Mom at the time, both cities lost their Italian inhabitants following the defeat of the Italian Army by the British. The Britons and their allies scored a victory in the Battle of Agordat in January 1941, followed by the Battle of Keren a couple of months later.[83]

The scenic train ride took them across a terrain of 1,500-feet elevation. A savannah of shrubs, *doum* trees, and scattered grass surrounded them. Through the train windows Mom could see the Barka River on its flowing journey from the highlands of Eritrea. The view fascinated her. She had never swum in the waters of a river before or played on a river's sand. But the Barka River was not a safe place for a child's water play and splashing.

The river, which passes through the city of Agordat, dries up during the rainless seasons. During that time, people would cross it on foot. But locals knew how treacherous and unpredictable the river could be. At the onset of the rainy season when the water level unexpectedly rises, many drown as they try to cross the river. The rainfall that would bring blessings and life to the region often brought flooding and drowning at its tail end.[84, 85]

Mom's reaction to the city of Agordat of the mid-1940s as the train was approaching the city late in the evening was a mixture of shock and dismay.

"I cried nonstop during the last part of the train ride from Keren. When we approached Agordat, all that I could see was a small village that looked like a vast grassland area. There were scattered doum trees, banana plants, and goutias made up of mud and straw. I could count the mud huts with my fingers! I began to cry again 'There can't be any Italians or British families who live here. Where do I find any work here? I was crying hysterically, 'It's even worse than Keren.'"

The train arrived at night at its final station at Agardat. From there Mom and her friend had to wait for a bus arriving the next day to take them to the city of Teseney. Having given up quickly on finding a job in Agordat, their last hope of finding *Ta'laina* (Italians) or *In'glease* (British) to work for was Teseney.

"When we arrived at night, I started to ask, 'Where can we sleep?' There was no place to sleep until the next morning when the bus to Teseney would arrive. The only place we could sleep was outside the train station. I was terrified of the hyenas and couldn't go to sleep. I just kept on crying and couldn't stop my tears. People would stop by and ask me: 'You girl, your tears never stop, why don't you stop crying?' But I couldn't."

The Bus Trip to Barentu: Mom's Cultural Shock

Mom and her friend survived their outdoors sleeping in the vicinity of the area's barking and laughing hyenas. They made it in one piece! The next morning, they rode the bus to Barentu, a small town on the way to Teseney. That large city was their final hope of finding a well-paying domestic help job with Italian or British families. Mom spent the nearly forty-mile bus trip from Agordat to Barentu crying.

"What if there are no jobs in Teseney. What will I do next?" she wondered between her tears.

In the 1940s, Barentu was a small agricultural town made up of mud and straw huts. The *Kunama* tribe, a dark-skinned Nilotic ethnic group, inhabited the area during Mom's job search adventure. They were mostly cattle farmers at that time.[86, 87]

Except for the Italians she encountered, Mom grew up, much like most people, sheltered and surrounded by her own people and tribe. As the bus arrived at the Barentu station, she was able to see for the first time the *Kunama* and other dark-skinned tribes. They had different looks, culture, and cloth that she had never seen before. That was a new experience that was permanently engraved in Mom's childhood memory.

"Men were walking naked, and women had a tiny belt. Their breasts were showing. 'They are the type that will eat us,' I cried. But others in the bus told me not to cry and explained to me that this was their habit."

Colonization in Black and White: Biases and Prejudices

Slavery in Africa, where Arabs, Turks, and later European slave traders bought and sold slaves, was a widespread practice for centuries. The institution of slavery followed by decades of western colonization reinforced the false notion that black color is inferior to white. Many generations in Africa and around the world grew up believing that being white or light-skinned signifies superiority. Unfortunately, this prejudicial and false belief still predominates the psyche of many. It still negatively affects the self-esteem and sense of value of the young and old.

Ethiopia and Italian-colonized Eritrea of the 1940s were much like other colonized countries in Africa. They were a mixture of many races, ethnicities, and colors. At the time of Mom's journey in search of a job, whites, Italians, and British were there but dwindling in number. Mom had no contact with the dark and Black tribes—*Surma, Shanqella, Kunama, Nara*—who lived far away from her family village. *Tigrayans, Amhara, Oromos, Somalis* and mixed-race groups, among others added to the region's diversity.

In colonized Africa of the 1940s, someone's skin color determined his or her "beauty," level of success, and value. Generally, natives did not frequent areas where Europeans lived and played. That is unless they worked or served as domestic helpers, as Mom did. As a child, Mom's paramount interest was to get a good-paying job with a good Italian family. Not only did she work diligently and wholeheartedly, but she loved the Italian children and families for whom she worked.

Mom did not believe that the white skin of the Italians she worked for made them superior to her with her dark skin. Nor did she harbor any ill feelings toward them because they were white. Mom appreciated the work opportunity they offered her and cared deeply for them and their children. And for that, the Italian families liked her and treated her well. Albeit for those occasions when some overworked her or when an Italian mother falsely accused her of eating her baby's hot meal! But even then, she never forgot her Italian husband's act of kindness. He could not convince his hotheaded wife of Mom's innocence. He decided to do the next right thing. He ran after Mom and paid for her work.

Even as a child, Mom was aware of the prevailing biases regarding her skin color. Mom had the darkest skin color in her family and striking blue eyes, a rarity in Africa. Sadly, as a child, she grew up hearing disparaging and mocking remarks about her dark skin color—not from her employers but from family, friends, and acquaintances.

"My mother was light-skinned with long, soft hair. I was the darkest one of my siblings and my hair was coarse. I was called names like 'the unattractive, ugly dark one' and was treated like I was less because of my dark skin. I struggled for a long time with a feeling of being inferior because of how people viewed me, and what they said about my skin color," she reflected many years later.

Mom, with her attractive dark skin and uniquely blue eyes, was not just beautiful outwardly. But more important, she was a well-mannered child with a pleasing personality inwardly. A few years after her train journey, her job search led her to the country of Sudan where she met Dad. He was smitten by her skin color, beauty, and most important her character, inner beauty, and heart of gold.

Teseney: Mom's Last Chance for Finding Italians

Teseney was Mom's last hope of finding a job with an Italian family. She could not wait to get there. The scenic seventy-five-mile trip from Barentu to the city of Teseney kept her distracted from the job search worries. From the bus window, she could see the Gash (*Naren*) River flowing in its three hundred miles journey. It starts near the city of Asmara, and travels through Teseney, Mom's destination. The Gash River continues its course to the Sudanese city of Kassala, and the lower plains of Sudan. It eventually vanishes in the hot sands of the desert.

As the bus approached Teseney, Mom could see the green wildlife region of the Gash-Setit, home of the Kunama people. Mom's spontaneous decision to travel as far as Teseney to look for a job turned to be a consequential one. The proximity of Teseney to Kassala in Sudan, a country she had never heard of, changed the course of her life. Unexpectedly and in a miraculous turn of events, Mom would soon find herself smuggled across the borders to Kassala.

As she and her young friend got off the bus, she began to cry again. Teseney was not what she expected it to be. Her fears of never finding a well-paying job to support her family intensified.

"I saw houses made of straw . . . huts! I cried . . . cried . . . cried. Bystanders stopped to check on me. I told them 'I'm here to look for a job but there are no Italians!'"

After nearly 225 miles and an exhausting long journey across the Eritrean highlands to Teseney, Mom felt emotionally drained.

Divine Intervention in Teseney

For a moment, all hope seemed lost. Mom felt stuck. But miraculously, her seemingly impossible circumstance changed, and she began to feel hopeful again. A good Samaritan who saw her crying at the bus station approached her.

"*Do you have any family in Teseney?*" he asked. All what she could utter between her tears was "*Tadalish . . . Tadalish,*" her relative's name who once lived in the city.

The kind stranger stopped what he was doing and promised to help Mom and her friend. He took them to the home of a woman named Tadalish hoping that she was the relative Mom was looking for.

"*You have guests,*" he announced as he entered Tadalish's home.

Influenced by the centuries-old tradition of hospitality to strangers, Tadalish brought coffee and food to perfect strangers she had never met before.

"*She made us coffee, but I was too hungry. I ate the food that she brought with the coffee. Then she asked, 'Who knows me?' I said, 'Me. I'm Tikkabo.' She was shocked to see me. She dropped the coffee and cried, 'You are Tikkabo!! Oh, my girl, it's you. What are you doing so far away from home?' She hugged me,*" Mom recalled.

After the warm welcome, Mom and her friend told Tadalish *the reason for coming to* Teseney. But Mom's initial joy and hope of finding a job, with Tadalish's help, turned to gloom. It soon became clear to Mom that the prospect of finding a job in Teseney was close to zero.

"*There are no more Italians or English families here. They've all left,*" said Tadalish.

The only option left for Mom and her young companion was to return to Asmara. There at least there was some hope of finding a British family that hadn't left the city yet.

"*Tadalish offered to take us with her to Asmara in two months. She planned to visit her sick mother there and wanted us to stay with her in Teseney until* then. But two months without work meant no money to support my parents and siblings, and no food. I told her 'I must go now.' She took us to the bus station when she saw how insistent I was."

Miracle at the Last Second

As Mom and her friend waited at the bus station with Tadalish, another unexpected event happened.

"We arrived at the bus station with Tadalish and waited for our bus. I was telling her my reason for leaving, 'I don't want to work in the Dahara (small villages) but only with Italians . . . and if not Italians, then with the British,' when a man that Tadalish recognized suddenly approached us. He greeted us and then asked, 'Why are you leaving?'"

The man who had just arrived by bus listened attentively to Tadalish's story about Mom's disappointing job hunt. Then to their surprise, he told them of a work opportunity in Teseney that he knew about. That job opportunity turned out to be a God-sent open door for Mom. Little did she know, the decision to stay in the city for that job would change her life forever. It would lead her into a new path, purpose, and the center of God's plan for her life in Sudan.

"I just came from Barentu; there is a job for one or maybe for two girls with a British man and his family. The man is in the British military, the only British left there. He will be leaving with the rest of the British Army in about two months. You can look for a job with Habasha (native Eritreans, Tigrayans, or Ethiopians) after he leaves," he said.

That was welcoming news to Mom. Her blue eyes lit up as she heard the potential of a well-paying job with an English family. But she did not like at all the idea of looking for a job with a *Habasha* family in two months.

"No! I don't want to work with Habasha. Only with Italians or British," she tearfully told the man.

Mom's Farewell to Asmara: The Search for Italians and Britons

Mom's reason for wanting to only work for Italian or English families was a purely practical one. They had money to pay her good wages while her native Habasha people could not afford to pay her. Her fellow Habasha were struggling just like her own family, and barely surviving the post-Second World War economic disasters. The money Mom made was immediately sent to her parents. It was their only dependable income at the time. Even as a child, she took her task as the provider of her family very seriously. That was a role she was committed to play even after she met and married Dad in Sudan.

In every way, Mom lived up to the name "Tikkabo" that her parents gave her at birth. That was the name they gave her when she was born healthy after almost giving up hope. Her name signified their faith that God had blessed them with her and that she would live to be a blessing to them and to many others. Mom, who left the security of her home as a child to put food on her family's empty table, was, indeed, a blessing. Not only to them but also to countless others.

Sensing Mom's uneasiness, Tadalish encouraged her to take a step of faith and work with the British family. Mom took her advice to heart and agreed to take the job. She prayed for God's help and guidance for after that short assignment was over.

New Opportunity and a Hard Decision

As the two months job ended, another divine intervention redirected the course of Mom's life. Mom's prayers for a new job after her assignment ended were answered in an extraordinary way.

The British officer had a Sudanese *Ghafir* (a guard) called Hassan who made horseshoes for the British military cavalry. Hassan was married to an *Amharic* (Ethiopian from the Amhara group) wife named Teru.

"He spoke fluent Amharic and Tigrinya and was a kind and caring man."

Although she was a perfect stranger to him, Hassan was determined to help Mom find a job to support her family.

"After the British family leaves, I'll go back to Sudan with the British Army, and my wife Teru will follow us. There are many English people in Sudan, and they pay good money, about 400 to 500 a month. Do you want to go to Sudan?" he asked Mom.

"Sudan? Where is that?"

Mom had no idea where Sudan was! Soon after the short assignment ended, Hassan left Mom with a major decision to make: to join his wife Teru and cross the borders to Sudan or go back home to her parents.

"Teru asked me if I want to secretly cross the borders with her to Sudan. I didn't know where Sudan was. But my dad couldn't see. I had to work. Hassan told me of a big city called Khartoum (the capital of Sudan) filled with English families where I could find a lot of work. There weren't any more English or Italians left here. Teru told me that going to Khartoum was my best option to find a job. I said 'OK.'"

Even as a child and a young adolescent, Mom always chose the well-being and interest of others over her own comfort and safety. She continued to do that throughout her adult life as a wife and a mother. Her 1946–1947 decision in Teseney to say "OK" to be smuggled to a country she never knew existed was risky. But it was a selfless decision, one that sought the well-being and interest of her family more than her own.

In Search of Peace and a Better Life

Mom's decision to go to Sudan and look for a job in Al-Khartoum (the Khartoum) was a bold one. Dad made a similar bold decision around the same time. He left his home and comfort zone in Cairo and moved to Sudan. But the difference was he was a professional architect in Egypt sent by the king of Egypt to Khartoum. But not Mom! She left her comfort zone and was about to cross the borders of a country she had never heard of. There was no job guaranteed for her, and Arabic, the officially spoken language in Sudan, was foreign to her. But all of that did not matter to Mom. The survival of her family was at stake, and that was what mattered.

In reflection, my paternal and maternal families' stories were a series of exoduses and immigration from their homes to elsewhere. Like many in America and other countries in the world, they fled wars, violence, religious intolerance, or dire economic hardships. That included my dad's family journey that ended in Al-Zagazig, Egypt, and his eventual immigration to Sudan in search of a better life. Mom's family did something similar. They moved from the city of Adwa in Tigray in the Ethiopian Highlands into Eritrea led by a spiritual passion to serve God in an isolated monastery. And then there was Mom in Teseney! She was about to start her own immigrant journey as a teenager into the unknown awaiting her in Sudan.

After a quiet time of prayers, pondering, and reflection, Mom felt peace about her decision. She decided to cross the borders into a country that was unknown to her. The benefit of sparing her family the risk of starvation by supporting them outweighed the real risks she would face. Many decades later, I followed the old heritage and tradition of my maternal and paternal families. I took a comfortable plane from Sudan to America, a much easier journey than Mom's illegal border crossing.

In a region plagued by the aftermath of WWII—poverty and instability—Sudan was peaceful and economically stable in comparison. Sudan in the mid-1940s was a land of opportunity and a haven for many job seekers and refugees. Many people like Mom came to Sudan's capital, Khartoum, at the time in search of peace, tolerance, and prosperity. Sadly, decades later, civil war, religious intolerance, and economic problems drove people of all races and religions out of the country.

Mom's final decision to take a risk and go to Sudan was not an easy one. But once she made the decision, she never looked back. Most of all, she became appreciative. Mom was deeply thankful to God, Teru, Hassan, and Sudan and its generous people once she made it there. Years later, after I personally experienced the peace, freedom, and amazing opportunities America offered me, I, too, became thankful. I finally began to understand Mom's heart of appreciation. And how can any immigrant in America or elsewhere fleeing a past of persecution, adversities, or economic hardships not be appreciative?

Mom grew up surrounded by the beauty of mountains and forests in Ethiopia's highlands of Tigray.

CHAPTER 13

THE JOURNEY: CROSSING THE BORDERS: TESENEY TO KASSALA

Soon after Mom agreed to go to Sudan, Hassan took Mom and his wife, Teru, to meet a trusted "coyote." The skilled border smuggler (a.k.a. guide) knew how to cross the borders from Teseney, Eritrea to Kassala, Sudan, without being caught.

"*The British would never allow you and Teru to enter Kassala. If they catch you, they will put you in jail,*" said Hassan as he prepared to depart with the British cavalry to Khartoum. "*I'll meet you in Khartoum.*"

The man who would take them to Sudan belonged to a Sudanese tribe from the region. He was a family man and perfect for the job with his vast knowledge of the Teseney-Kassala borders. After the meeting, Mom began to worry. She began to ponder her future and her family that she was about to leave behind.

"*I started to think, 'If I go, how will they eat? Who will help them when I leave?' But then, I knew that I needed to go anywhere where I could find a job. I had to leave so that I can help them.*"

Nelson Mandela once said, "*I learned that courage was not the absence of fear, but the triumph over it. The brave man is not he who does not feel afraid, but he who conquers that fear."* To me, Mom, as a young girl, showed that example of courage, and so did my dad. He had an easier life as a child than Mom. Nevertheless, he possessed enough courage to overcome his fear, leave the comfort of Egypt behind, and go to Sudan. Albeit, in a plane and with a valid Egyptian passport. Both eventually became immigrants in Sudan who supported one day my own immigrant dream of a new life in America. At heart, we are all immigrants who dream of conquering our fears in pursuit of a better life.

Following Mom's sobering meeting with the guide, she felt determined to leave the Highlands of Ethiopia and Eritrea behind. She believed that she would find a new and financially better life in Sudan and agreed to go. As the time grew closer for Hassan to leave with the British military to Sudan, he met with Mom's relative. He and Teru took Mom to Tadalish for the final goodbyes. Tadalish, who felt personally responsible for the well-being of Mom, held Teru's neck in a traditional fashion and said,

"I'm entrusting this girl to you. I'm entrusting her to your hands."

"Don't worry. Don't be afraid. She is like our daughter," Teru responded.

Early Morning Journey from Teseney to Kassala

Mom and Teru arrived in the early dawn at the home of their border smuggler. The friendly family man kindly agreed with Hassan to be their guide in the journey across the Sudanese border to Kassala. As a member of the *Beni-Amer* tribe who inhabited Kassala and the border region between Eritrea and Sudan, he knew the area well. As soon as they arrived at his family's hut, he offered them food and prepared them for the long walk ahead. Soon others began to join them. They were men, women, and children escaping economic hardships in their hometowns in search of a new beginning in Sudan. Once the group assembled, they helped to load a donkey with food and heavy belongings in preparation for the long walk. Mom and Teru were finally ready for their journey on foot from Teseney to Kassala.

The Journey: Crossing the Borders: Teseney to Kassala

Teseney, considered a market town, is located southeast of Kassala on the Gash (*Mareb*) River in a region called Gash-Barka. The area is rich in vegetation and fertile and was once a common habitat for wild animals. Lions, elephants, leopards, baboons, monkeys, and what Mom described as "pythons that can swallow a cow" once lived there. That was before the gradual deforestation that has befallen the area. Teseney, where Mom's walking journey started, was also a region where the flooding of the Gash River regularly occurred during the rainy months of the year.[88, 89]

With wild animals in the forests and a challenging landscape, the journey was perilous and unsafe. Luckily for them, the *Beni-Amer* guide was experienced and was familiar with the surrounding terrain.

The nearly thirty-mile journey between Teseney and the borders of Kassala would take them up to nine hours on foot. They needed to finish it during the daylight. The risk of wild animals and hyenas hunting for prey after the sunset was too high to take. There were other risks besides the devouring hyenas. Mom and Teru were taking other major risks. *Haras al hodud* (border guards) could apprehend them at the borders and throw them in jail, and criminals could rape them, or even worse. Mom with her youth and small stature risked being kidnapped and forced to marry someone against her wishes. She was taking a huge risk for a mission she felt was God's plan for her life. From Teseney with its high altitude, Mom could see Kassala in neighboring Sudan from a distance. That kept her motivated as fatigue and sore feet overwhelmed her young body.

Sudan was governed by the Anglo-Egyptian condominium (1899–1955) at the time of Mom's border crossing. Without a passport, identification card, or valid entry papers, Mom had no chance of entering Sudan through an official port of entry. The Anglo-Egyptian government and the Italians built robust modes of transportation in the region to support their military operations. Unfortunately for Mom, her only mode of transportation to Sudan was quietly, discreetly, and on foot.

But Mom decided not to dwell on the dangers and risks of being caught on the Sudanese borders. The perils of the journey and the dangers of being snatched by a wild animal kept her focused on the long road. She walked under the tall *doum* trees and brushed her small body across thorny bushes. Keeping pace with the guide, Teru, and the rest of the group was not easy. With the midday sun shining brightly, Mom could now see farmers selling their produce in Teseney's busy *Souq* (open-air market). She could see more piles of sorghum, millet, teff, and chickpeas than she had ever seen before. Herdsmen could be seen from a distance standing with their cattle as cows and sheep grazed on the hillsides.

"*When it got dark, I could hear the howling of the* marapheen *(hyenas) not far away from us! I used to hear that they ate people who walked on the road, and I cried because I was so afraid,*" recalled Mom as daylight gradually gave way to darkness.

The experienced guide placed Mom in the middle of the group hoping to calm her fears. That plan worked well for a short time as Mom felt safer and stopped crying.

Mom, a confident and beautiful married African woman, years after crossing the borders of Sudan as a frightened teenager.

"*But then, I started to cry again when I heard someone say that the hyenas can still snatch people from the middle and eat them. The guide tried again to stop me from crying. He said, 'Khalas!' (enough) 'You can walk behind the donkey.' I was quiet after that until we finally stopped.*"

The Journey: Crossing the Borders: Teseney to Kassala \ 119

This was Mom's surrounding before crossing the borders to Sudan.

CHAPTER 14

CROSSING THE BORDERS TO SUDAN: WALKING TO KASSALA

As darkness began to fall, Mom's small caravan slowed down as it got closer to the Sudanese border. The *Beni-Amer* guide signaled to the group to follow him as he led them through the forest. Then he stopped where they would camp for the night, gathering the group in a circle around a small fire.

"*We sleep here tonight and cross the border early in the morning,*" he said.

His vast knowledge of the territory where to stop, and when to cross the borders made him a skillful guide. He was a caring man who wanted Mom and the group to cross safely and to succeed in Sudan.

"He cooked asida *(a soft corn or wheat flour dough eaten in Sudan and various African countries), placed it on hot rocks, and then made* shy bil'laban *(tea with milk) for us to drink. He was from the Beni-Amer tribe. A very, very, very good man,*" recalled Mom.

After enjoying the traditional *asida* meal and the *shy bil'laban*, the good guide explained the exact plan for the would-be border crossers.

"*Pay attention. Tomorrow morning you will cross the borders with the shepherds who graze their cattle very early in the morning.*"

Mom, who was too frightened of the hyenas, began to cry. She thought about the possibility of being snatched in the middle of the night by one of them.

"I was afraid of a *Marfaeen* (a hyena) coming to eat me at night and I started to cry. The *Beni-Amer* guide made sure that I slept in the center surrounded by everyone. There was a fire surrounding us. He told me 'Don't be afraid,' but I was because we were in *Al-khala* (wilderness)."

Mom could barely hear or comprehend the guide's instructions because of her crying. As a young teenager about to cross the borders of a country she never heard of, Mom relied on Teru. She became like a parent to her.

"I asked Teru because I was confused about what the guide just said, 'Are we going to be shepherds?' But she told me, 'No, we have our donkey to walk with. But we just need to mix with the shepherds as if we're part of their group,'" Mom recalled.

In the early morning hours after Mom and the small caravan woke up, they followed the guide's instructions. Mom, Teru, the donkey, and everyone in the group mingled with the *Beni-Amer* shepherds and their cattle. They safely and miraculously entered Kassala, Sudan, without being caught! The combined forces of the British and Sudanese armies, who guarded the borders at the time, failed to see them. If you would ask Mom, she would tell you that God was guarding her at that time. The guards failed to see her because God protected her during those frightening moments of her life.

In 1980, I entered America legally after finishing high school in Sudan. My passport was thoroughly reviewed by an immigration officer at JFK International Airport before I set foot in my future home, America. Mom was about five years younger than I was at this point when she entered Sudan after evading the border guards. She was disguised as one of *Beni-Amer's* shepherds, and without any passport or documents. Both of us needed courage to leave our comfort zones and the warmth of our childhood homes. We were both young, innocent, and possessed with a childlike faith that shielded us from the fear of the unknown. But in comparison, I had it much easier when it came to the pursuit of our hopes and dreams in new countries.

My challenges and hurdles as a teenager entering America were mental, emotional, and spiritual. Hers were all of the above plus the physical hurdles and dangers of hungry packs of hyenas and wild predators. She faced the risk of malaria, typhoid, meningitis, yellow fever, and a host of other tropical diseases. Not only that, but as a young female border crosser, Mom was in danger of being caught or kidnapped. She could have been sold to human traffickers or even been killed. But with the innocence of a child, she saw none of the above perils and potential dangers. She only saw herself in Khartoum working for an English family and sending the money she made to her family.

Her dream of providing for her folks was not buried or obscured by the mountain of difficulties in her path. It was real, in vivid colors, and felt within her reach. Years later after Mom's border crossing, my own dream in America to be a doctor was similarly real and crystal clear. No mountains of impossibilities, failures, defeats, or hardships could bury her dream or mine. I learned from her and my dad what their Christian faith inspired them to do. They never let any of their life problems, falls, and failures stop them from pursuing and achieving their God-given dreams. Their individual decision to lean on their faith in God to overcome the fear of the unknown inspired me. Ultimately, it became my own battle cry as I faced my own setbacks in America, Land of My Dreams.

Making It to Kassala

Early in the morning, Mom and Teru, surrounded by grazing cattle and *Beni-Amer* shepherds, crossed the borders to Kassala. Kassala was the beginning of Mom's long and hard adventure in Sudan. She approached the city quietly after successfully crossing the open borders without being caught! As she entered the city in the early morning hours, she could see the majestic Taka mountains. The mountains' massive rocks and boulders scattered at their bases fascinated her. In the open city market, *Al Souk;*

she saw Sudanese men and women sipping their *ja'bena* with *ginzabil* and *girfa* (coffee with ginger and cinnamon). Some were preparing *fuul* with *falafel and gibna baida* (fava beans with falafel and feta cheese) for breakfast. She walked quietly past restaurants preparing *bamya* (okra) with *kisra* ("paper bread" or *Injera*) for the upcoming lunch hour.[90]

Mom began to miss her family and her mom's delicious cooking. The sights and sounds of the Rashaida tribe nomads trading goods with their veiled women in colorful robes intrigued her. She was comforted by Kassala's hospitable people who delightfully greeted her and each other.

"*Al-salamo Alikom. Hababkom Ashra*" (a traditional Sudanese greeting).

The city of Kassala located in eastern Sudan was founded in 1834 as an Egyptian garrison. In 1885–1894 it was occupied by the Sudanese religious leader Al-Mahdi who wanted to spread what he considered a purer form of Islam. He believed that he was the chosen one to do that and to rid Sudan of the British. Al-Mahdi's forces were eventually defeated in 1898 by the British near the Khartoum in the Battle of Omdurman. During WWII, the Italians invaded Kassala in 1940 but were defeated by British-led forces in 1941. When Mom crossed the borders to Kassala in the late 1940s, Britain and Egypt ruled the country of Sudan. Thankfully, Kassala was no longer a battle zone for colonizing forces when she entered the city with Teru.

Kassala's history dates to the Kingdom of Kush who ruled it centuries ago. It was a Christian city inhabited by the *Kushites* and known for its trading and large market. Years later, the Ethiopian Christian Orthodox Kingdom of Axum took control of the city after defeating the kingdom of Kush. The city was eventually invaded and converted to Islam in the sixteenth century by Muslim conquerors.[91,92]

Mom briskly walked past the crowds of *Hadendawa, Rashaida* nomads, and *Beni-Amer* tribes and wondered, "*What's next? What's in store for me?*"

She was secretly led to a home of an elderly Sudanese couple in the city and told to wait there.

"They were good people. It was a family, husband, wife, and their married daughter. They made kisra (flat paper bread) and injera and had a place that looked like a restaurant. People used to come, eat, drink, and buy njera from there. After we ate, they offered me one of the rooms adjacent to their home that was used for rental. They asked me: 'Are you going to be afraid to stay in that room by yourself? Would you rather spend the night with us in the hut?' I told them: 'It is not Aldahara (wilderness). I can stay by myself in the room.'"

Mom stayed her first night in Kassala in that room adjacent to the elderly couple's home. The man's wife brought her food, water, and tea, and instructed her not to leave the room.

"Stay in your room and use the outdoors bathroom only when it's dusk, or early in the morning. If someone sees you, he might think that you are not Sudanese. No one should see you."

Mom gratefully obliged. She waited patiently for Teru and the guide to come and take her to Khartoum. But then, a week passed without any news. Mom was starting to feel worried and very frustrated.

"I started to cry and told the man: 'Please take me to a train station. I want to go back to Teseney. I want to go home.' But he told me: 'The authorities will catch you because you don't have any papers.' Back then the authorities would catch you and put you in jail. They 'played' with people there."

To calm her down, the elderly couple asked her to be patient and wait.

"OK, someone will come to take you back across the borders to Teseney and then to your parents in Adwa," they promised Mom.

But Unbeknown to her, they had a secret plan to transport her subtly by bus from Kassala to Khartoum. With their original plan delayed and Mom's restlessness for a job, they were at a loss what to do next.

Mom's fears intensified with every passing day. She did not know how long she was going to wait in hiding. She began to greatly miss her mom and dad.

"I cried a lot and told them: 'I just want to leave and go back home. I don't care even if I go to jail. You can send me back home now.' But they *pleaded with me: 'You can't go now. You will be happy when you go there (to Khartoum) and begin to help your family. It's true! You will start working with the English.' I said, 'OK.'"*

Mom was comforted by their words and decided to trust them and wait. She was young, naïve, and trusting. Confined in a tiny room in Kassala, she had no clue how to go to Khartoum or where to stay. She had faith in God, and trusted Teru and her husband Hassan, but the couple were not there. But suddenly things became clearer to her. She overheard a conversation in her language between the elderly couple in their small restaurant.

"I heard them say, 'This girl will now be able to go and work legally in Khartoum. One of our men prepared papers that say she is married and will bring them with him.'"

Mom was clueless about the meaning of what she had just heard. Yet again, with one of those strategic divine interventions, a stranger eating in the restaurant overheard the conversation too. The man who was from her homeland heard the couple talking about waiting for someone with fake marriage papers to arrive. He signaled for Mom to come to his table and told her about the marriage trap she could fall into.

"He warned me, 'Don't follow what they tell you to do. Don't go' (meaning don't let someone deceive you to go to his home as his wife). He told me, 'Awey Tamshe (don't go).' I put this man's words in my heart. And when a man came with the fake marriage papers and I was told that he will take me to Khartoum, all that I could think of were the man's words. I remembered his words 'Awey Tamshe,' and I began to cry, 'I want to go home. Nowhere else. No thank you. I don't want to go with him. I don't want to.'"

Mom grew up in a strong Christian home. In her faith, marriage is sacred where she would marry a parents-approved man in a Christian church ceremony. Her parents married after a brief love at first sight. They were officially married by the priest of their local Tigrayan-Ethiopian Orthodox Church after their parents' approval. Their life as a couple was that of devotion to God and to each other. A sham paper marriage was a concept she had never heard of. That is, until the stranger in the restaurant told her about it and warned her not to go there.

In a region in the world where female child marriage is traditionally and culturally prevalent, the risk to Mom was real. She could have been forced by an older man into an actual marriage that started as a sham one. For generations, many families in Mom's homeland lost their young girls to foreign invading tribal and religious forces. Those girls were never heard from again. Many of them were forced into marrying men of a different religion and alienated forever from their families and Christian religion. The sobering words of the man at the restaurant were a red flag. What had happened to those unsuspecting young girls for centuries could very well happen to her.

Mom, with her trusting and unsuspecting heart, had no clue that Teru and her husband had set that arrangement up. They never told her about the fake marriage arrangement! In their genuine desire to help her get a job, they decided not to tell her about the scheme. They knew that she would never accept a sham marriage even if it helped her find a job with a British family. Teru felt that she was doing the right thing to help Mom. The man who finally showed up with his fake marriage papers assured the elderly couple of his "good" intentions. He convinced them that it was a fake marriage that was meant to help Mom get a job in Sudan.

The perfect stranger at the restaurant was like an angel placed on Mom's path to warn her about the risks of a sham marriage. His advice helped her think about something that her innocent mind could not have conceived of. I still think about what could have happened (and the legacy of children she and Dad brought together) without his warning. Years later, I pause and think. I would not be a doctor in America writing about Mom, Dad, and my own immigration journey but for that supernatural intervention.

Mom's objection to the paper marriage and her tearful plea to return home became a problem. The whole plan of helping her find a job in Khartoum was falling apart. Meanwhile, returning her back across the perilous borders to Teseney was unthinkable for Teru, who had finally arrived to see Mom, and the elderly couple. They all wanted her to find a job to help her family who depended on her financial support. Mom's insistence to return to her family in Adwa bewildered them.

"The elderly married couple tried to convince me not to go back home. The old man fell on his knees. His wife put a stone on her back and begged me: 'You only have one day left for you to decide to go with him and Teru to Khartoum!' Then Teru told me: 'How can you go back home now? You're 'Amana fi ragabtee' ('you're entrusted to me' in the Arabic language, Mom's new learned language after immigrating to Sudan). 'When you go to Khartoum, you'll be able to help your family!'"

I still don't know the significance of putting a stone on someone's back. But to my mom who understood the cultural traditions of the time, it signified humility and honesty. It was a way to assure Mom with a solemn promise that the man would never be her real husband. It was a vow that she was not the man's wife, and the arrangement was just to have legal documents. Mom was left with two difficult options: crossing the borders back home or going to Khartoum with fake documents! She thought about her family's dire financial needs and decided to trust God and hope that Teru was right.

"Teru and the couple told me that the man who came with the false marriage papers was only doing me a favor. They told me, 'You should thank him.'"

Mom had no other option but to believe them and pray that they were sure and right. But the advice of the man at the restaurant made her vigilant and prepared to run if anything went wrong. His words proved to be prophetic. They moved her to action when the supposed fake husband decided to renege on his agreement and almost kidnapped her.

"*I said* Hiraie . . . Hiraie (or Tayeb . . . Tayeb *in Arabic which means* OK . . . OK) *from my lips but my heart didn't want that. I didn't ask the man any question or thank him,*" said Mom as she vowed to never be snared into a real marriage with him.

CHAPTER 15

THE BUS TRIP TO KHARTOUM: MOM AND A FAKE HUSBAND

AFTER MANY ASSURANCES, including the elderly woman placing a stone on her back and Teru's promises, Mom began to reconsider. She finally relented after being reassured that the marriage was not real. Seeing the elderly man's humble act of kneeling at her feet ended her resistance. Mom began her long bus ride to Khartoum, frightened but full of hope. The bus was crowded with people going to the capital city of Sudan to visit their families and for work. Mom was told to sit quietly in the seat next to the man who pretended to be her husband. She held tightly to her fake marriage papers.

"During the time of the English, it was very strict. They wanted all paperwork and documents to be accurate and ready when asked."

It was almost impossible to convince Mom to take the bus to Khartoum with a fake husband. She had no idea that this marriage plot was part of the plan. In her young girl's mind, crossing the borders was all that was needed before working with an English family. Mom's one condition to agree to take the bus to Khartoum was for Teru to be with her on the bus. Teru and Hassan were the only people she knew and trusted in her new unfolding chapter of life in Sudan.

The bus ride between Kassala and Khartoum, a 258-mile distance, lasted nearly 9 to 10 hours because of the frequent stops along the way. Mom was exhausted and fell asleep, unfazed by the loud noises in the bus and the many stops. As the bus continued its long journey, Mom suddenly woke up and looked around her expecting to see Teru. She was not there!

"Teru, Teru, Teru," she cried. She got out of her seat and tried to get out of the bus when she could not find her. *"Teru, Teru, Teru!"* she screamed in panic. She was a foreigner in a foreign country with a language she did not understand or speak. She was gripped by the fear of being alone with a man holding documents that say she was his wife.

As Mom's crying intensified, the man scolded her.

"Don't leave your seat. Don't cry, Teru is riding in the bus that's behind us."

She stopped crying. As the bus slowed down and approached the busy and chaotic main bus terminal in Khartoum, she could hardly wait to find Teru. Mom was out of the bus the moment the conductor announced *"Khartoum station. Y'ala (Let's go), all out, all out."*

The noises of buyers, sellers, and the crowds shouting in various languages were deafening. Mom's voice and Teru were both lost in the sea of people surrounding the bus. She was finally in the heart of the capital where her dream of finding a job would come true. But she was lost, confused, and all alone.

Mom's heart was racing. Teru was not in the bus as the man with the fake marriage documents told her. He quickly assured her that she must have taken the bus that just arrived at the station. She ran to that bus to find her as the passengers started to disembark. As she anxiously waited, the bus drivers in the busy open terminal began to shout 'Omdurman... Sangaat' Mom did not know what those words meant but figured out that they must be city names.

"I had no idea what 'Sangaat' or 'Omdurman' were. I ran and waited near the bus that the man told me Teru was riding in. I didn't read Arabic, but I could tell the words written on that bus were different than the ones written on the bus I just came from. I figured out that the buses must have come from different cities. Teru couldn't be here. I started to shout 'Teru, Teru, Teru,' but she wasn't there."

Mom's suspicion of the man's true intentions was right. He deceived her about her trusted friend's whereabouts. His assurance that she was in the bus behind theirs was a lie. Mom realized when he led her to another bus heading to his home in Omdurman that she was in trouble. It became clear to her that he intentionally misled her and lost track of Teru.

"I cried so loud, 'Ouwooy . . . Ouwooy (*a traditional expression of shock and disbelief*) Teru, Teru, Teru.' I started to scream and cry, 'This man told me that she is in the bus behind us. Teru, Teru, Teru.' People started to gather around me. Men and women wanted to know what was wrong with me but all I could shout was 'Teru, Teru, Teru.' They wanted to know who Teru was, but I couldn't explain anything to them."

Nearly seventy-five years later, after crossing the borders, that memory at the bus terminal in Khartoum never went away. It was clear that the con man lied to her. Apparently, he was planning all along to take Mom to his home in Omdurman as a wife. But Mom refused to enter a real marriage against her Christian beliefs and parents' teachings. And despite her fervent desire to find a job in Khartoum, going against her faith was not an option. Mom was ready to suffer any consequences for her beliefs. That included being jailed for not having legal papers to stay in Sudan.

Rescued at Khartoum's Bus Terminal

Shortly after the crowd gathered around Mom, the man rushed to Mom with his fake marriage papers in his hand. He raised his fraudulent documents with one hand to assert his authority as a husband. Then he reached out to pull Mom from the crowd that surrounded her. But Mom's resistance and determination to never allow him to take her was fierce. She refused to leave with him and began to scream loudly in her *Tigrinya* language hoping someone would understand her, "NO. NO. NO. HE IS NOT MY HUSBAND. WE ARE NOT MARRIED."

The crowd seemed perplexed. It was hard for the people who surrounded her to know what was happening. It appeared to them as if Mom was a young wife refusing to obey her husband. But just as the con man began to pull her away from the crowd, Mom experienced yet another miraculous intervention. Out of nowhere, a man in the crowd quickly stepped forward to stop him from taking Mom away.

"He looked like he was mixed . . . half Egyptian and half Sudanese. He stopped the man from taking me. Someone later translated to me what he told him. He told him: 'If what you say that she is your wife is right, and you're married to her, she wouldn't be crying and screaming like that. She has a problem; she has a problem that we don't understand. Once we know what the problem is, you can then come back and bring the marriage papers with you to show us.'"

Following the unexpected turn of events, Mom felt very safe with the stranger who came to her rescue. She believed God saved her at the right time through a brave and caring "half Egyptian . . . half Sudanese" man. She gladly left with him just like a child who trustingly follows her father. The "Good Samaritan" took her to the safety of his home to stay with him, his wife, and children.

"He took me to his home *fee amanti Allah* ("*with God's protection and security*" in Sudanese Arabic, her newly learned language), and my heart felt peaceful. His wife was nice and so were his children. *Galbee irtah* (*my heart felt comforted and rested*). The man who had the marriage papers didn't show up and I felt at peace. They fed me and gave me water. But I couldn't understand them. I couldn't do anything."

Sadly, Mom's respite did not last long. The crook suddenly showed up at the home that she was staying in and wanted to go in. He demanded to talk to the man who saved her at the bus station. The Good Samaritan's wife refused to let him in.

"The man of the house is not here now. You need to return when he is back from work," she said.

Sure enough, the man returned with his fake marriage papers. He told the man, who rescued her, and his wife to give him back Mom and demanded to take her. Thankfully, his attempt failed as the compassionate "Half Sudanese . . . half Egyptian man," a total stranger, refused to let him. Mom never forgot that day.

"*He came back again insisting to take me with him. But the man of the house told him 'You can't take her from here. She doesn't want to. If your papers are right, you can show it to the court.'*"

Finally! Freedom from a Fake Marriage

Mom felt safe with the man and his family as they tried to figure out what to do. They were all trying to keep Mom away from the man who claimed to be her husband. To them, he was a predator trying to take advantage of a young, innocent girl. Her plan to immediately start working with "the English" after arriving to Khartoum was on hold. Without Teru and her Sudanese husband, Hassan, she was at a loss, and did not know what to do next. They secretly arranged for Mom's border crossing, and a fake paper marriage that they never intended to be real. She fully trusted them and wondered if she would see them soon. Their original plan to get her legal papers to help her stay in Sudan stalled. The crafty man wanted to force Mom into an actual marriage and thus far she was protected by the kind gentleman and his wife. "*But where are Teru and Hassan?*" she wondered.

Then suddenly, there was a bit of good news! The host family told her that they got hold of Abeba, an Ethiopian woman in Khartoum, who spoke Tigrinya. They invited her to come and interpret for them.

"*I understood what they meant to say. I thanked God there was finally a Habasha woman that I could talk to. Abeba's husband was from Kassala, from the Beni-Amer tribe. He also spoke Tigrinya.*"

Abeba's highly anticipated visit finally happened, and Mom was ecstatic. After a time of socializing, extensive talking, and drinking coffee, it was time for her to leave.

"She said her goodbyes and was getting ready to leave. But I got up quickly, followed her, and held tightly to her Toub (a colorful Sudanese thin cloth women wrap on top of their dresses covering the body and the head). I begged her, 'Please take me with you. I can't stay here.' But she gently told me, 'What would the people say . . . that I took you away. Maybe I can come another time. Stay for now.'"

Mom feared that the man would return with his fake papers. She held tightly to Abeba.

The sight of Mom holding tightly to Abeba's *Toub* refusing to let go deeply touched the kind man and his family.

"Bil Lahi (By God), please take her. Please take her with you. She really misses her people," he said.

To Mom's delight and joy, the host family genuinely wanted what was best for her. It was best for Mom to be able to communicate with Abeba and they understood that. They were like angels who saved her from danger at the most vulnerable time of her life. Abeba decided to continue their good work and to take Mom with her.

"She took me to her home where I met her husband. He spoke clean habasha *and I told him everything . . . everything that happened. I was so happy,*" Mom recalled.

Mom stayed with her new host family for over a month. She felt safe with them until the man showed up again with the fake marriage papers demanding to take her. Abeba's husband welcomed him in a typical Sudanese generosity. He invited him in, offered *shai* (hot tea), and then confronted him.

"*This girl is married,*" *said the man.*

"*Married!! Then why is she afraid of you?*"

"*I don't know, but I want to take her now.*"

The Bus Trip to Khartoum: Mom and a Fake Husband \ 137

"No, you won't take her."

To Mom, it was nothing but God's intervention that brought perfect strangers in her life who became her fiercest advocates. Abeba and her husband began looking for clues from Mom's story when she first arrived in the bus terminal. They wondered if the city of Sangaat, which Mom had heard a bus driver announcing, might be where Teru went to. Apparently, the con man planned to take her to his home before Teru could find her at the terminal. Did Teru wait for Mom at the bus terminal and then leave for Sangaat when she didn't find her? Finding the whereabouts of Teru and her husband, Hassan, became of paramount importance to them. They were determined not to let him take Mom.

"If you're married to her and claim to have papers to prove it, then here is the plan. She told me everything about Teru and her husband, Hassan, and all that happened. I will go to the town of Sangaat. If you want to come, then come," said Abeba's husband.

He refused to go! Abeba and her husband's instincts were right. They were able to locate Teru and Hassan in Sangaat and confirm Mom's story. The reunion of Mom with Teru was heartening and nothing short of a miracle. Mom's dream was becoming a reality. All what she could dream of now was finding a job with an English family. She was now back to Teru's care! She and her husband Hassan were about to fulfill their promise of finding her a job in Khartoum.

But before that, the problem of the man demanding to take Mom as his wife had to be solved. Now that his scheme was discovered, he decided to go directly to Teru's home in Sangaat. He knew all along where she lived.

"Where is she?" he said with forged papers in hand.

"What do you want from her?" asked Teru.

"Of course, I want her. She is my wife."

"YOUR WIFE! Give me the papers that you faked and now are using to tell lies. If you don't give them to me, we will go to court," said Teru.

He complied and gave her the papers. Thankfully, that chapter of trickery was soon cut short when he handed over the documents to Teru.

"*She cut it . . . cut it . . . and kept on cutting it to many small pieces. Then she threw it away and told him 'Go away . . . you're a deceiving liar. Get out of here. You said that you're doing this as a favor to help us and now you decide to do that and scare the girl. Now get out and leave.' She kicked him out of the house,*" said Mom.

How perfect strangers suddenly appeared out of nowhere and stepped in to help Mom will forever intrigue me. They guarded, fed, and sheltered Mom, an innocent and helpless child, who was a total stranger to them. To me it was like a God-orchestrated conspiracy of kindness that saved her repeatedly using different players. God watched over her and saved her again and again. She came to Sudan with the sole mission of saving her family from starvation in Tigray and Ethiopia's Highlands. Through a series of miraculous interventions, her good mission was about to start in Khartoum.

CHAPTER 16

KHARTOUM: MOM'S NEW HOME THE "HOLY WAR" AGAINST BRITAIN AND ETHIOPIA

Nearly six decades before mom's arrival in Khartoum, Al-Mahdi, a Sudanese Muslim military leader, besieged the city. Al-Mahdi believed that he was chosen by God to spread his religious movement throughout Sudan. The siege lasted nearly a year and ended with Mahdi's forces breaking into Khartoum and taking the city. His forces massacred the Anglo-Egyptian garrison protecting Khartoum, including the British governor-general Lord Charles Gordon. He was killed on January 26, 1885, in the governor's palace near the confluence of the White Nile and the Blue Nile in Khartoum.

The British Army reinforcement that was to help Gordon and break the siege of Khartoum arrived two days late! And eventually, it withdrew back to Egypt once they realized that Khartoum had fallen. Five months after the capture of Khartoum and the death of Gordon, Al-Mahdi died. His loyal followers, the Mahdists, continued his movement and extended their control over most of Sudan after his death.

The Mahdists' control of Sudan stretched beyond Khartoum. They occupied Kassala in 1885. The city became a launching ground for many future wars given its proximity to neighboring Eritrea and Ethiopia. Khalifa Abdallahi, the Mahdi's heir, continued the campaign of *jihad* (holy war) to spread Islam in Christian Abyssinia (Ethiopia).

In the years 1885 to 1889, the Mahdists attacked Ethiopia's Christian kings and their military forces. A renowned military general from the Highlands of Tigray-Ethiopia, Mom's birthplace, came to great fame and prominence at that time. Ras Alula, also known as Alula Aba Nega, served as the general of Ethiopia's King Yohannes IV. He was viewed by his contemporaries as the bravest and greatest military general in Africa. Ras Alula led his forces against the Mahdists' "Holy War" including the Battle of Gallabat in 1889 (known as the Battle of Metemma). The emperor of Ethiopia, Yohannes IV, was killed in that battle, and was replaced by Emperor Menilek II. Ras Atula joined the new king and continued his military victories including defeating the Italians in the Battle of Adwa in 1896.[93, 94, 95, 96]

Mom's knowledge of the legacy of Ras Atula and Ethiopia's religious wars against the Mahdists made her pause and reflect. She was now in Khartoum where the Mahdi once ruled after defeating the Egyptians and killing the British General Gordon. But Khartoum in the late 1940s, when she arrived, was no longer a religious battleground. She felt safe.

Khartoum

The name "Khartoum," or *Al-Khartoum* as it is known in Arabic means "the Elephant Trunk." For many years, the city was used by slave traders as a slave market and was shattered by wars. Khartoum was occupied by Egypt in 1821 until the Mahdists defeated the Egyptians in 1885 and killed British General Gordon. Subsequently, the city was reoccupied in 1899 by the Anglo-Egyptian forces under the British Major General Kitchener. Young lieutenant Winston Churchill, who fought in the *Battle of Omdurman* against the Mahdists, recounted the battle in his 1898 book *The River War: An Account of the Reconquest of the Soudan*.[97, 98]

Mom arrived in Khartoum during the Anglo-Egyptian colonization of Sudan. The British were at that time actively discussing with popular Sudanese political figures the future of Sudan after the colonization. Some of the politicians wanted Sudan to be fully independent, contrary to Egypt's wishes at the time. While others, such as the Al-Azhari, a prominent Sudanese political figure, wanted Sudan to form a unity with Egypt. Mom's arrival to Sudan coincided with the British allowing parliamentary election leading to Sudan's self-determination.[99]

That decision was against the wishes of Egypt and King Farouk who viewed himself as "King of Egypt and Sudan." The country was eventually granted its independence from Great Britain in 1956.[100]

But none of Khartoum's bloody war history, days of slavery, or its uncertain future after the British left troubled Mom. Nor did Khartoum's hot and dry weather with the frequent summer *Haboobs* (large sandstorms) sway her from staying. Finding a job with an English family who would pay her good wages was all that mattered at the time. That was her sole focus. The Blue Nile that originates from Ethiopia's Highlands and merges with the White Nile in Khartoum reminded Mom of her home. It brought her fond memories of her family and early childhood. She was a teenager who came to Khartoum to make money for a mission. Her mission was to save her family from starvation.

Finding a Job: A New Beginning in Khartoum

Now that the swindler with the fake marriage papers faded away for good, things looked brighter for Mom. Khartoum's hot temperatures reaching up to 102° Fahrenheit in the Summer, and its *Haboobs* were but minor distractions to her. Getting a job was her main pressing goal. Mom's appreciation to Teru and her husband Hassan for what they had done to help her was heartfelt. They stood by her just as they promised. And now that getting a job was her next most pressing goal, she still needed their help and generosity.

Soon after Mom's arrival at Khartoum, one of Hassan's elderly relatives brought her good news. He worked with a German family who decided to stay in Khartoum after Germany's defeat in WWII.

"*Young girl, I'll take you with me to work tomorrow. The German family I work for needs help.*"

To Mom's great relief, she got the job! Her dream of finding an immediate job with a British family came true albeit with a German family in Khartoum.

"*The next day he took me with him to work. They gave me four hundred (Sudanese pounds) and they were so, so, so kind. Because I worked with the Italians and knew how to take care of children, I knew everything. The German woman in the house was happy with me because I was able to work hard. She trusted me to take care of her daughter's sleeping time and feeding time.*"

Thankfully for Mom, the German woman spoke Italian, and Mom was able to easily communicate with her. The family was kind and generous. They cared about Mom a lot and made sure to secure her a job with another family when they left for a vacation.

"*They once got me a job that paid six hundred pounds when they were gone for a three months' vacation! They were very nice.*"

With time, Mom worked with other Europeans in Sudan. Working with them exposed her to new and more liberal cultures, and a few family secrets that she did not like. One of those secrets that greatly distressed her involved a European wife who decided to cheat on her husband.

"*The wife used to see a man who took her at night from home when her husband wasn't there. I didn't like it at all. It made me so angry. He was such a good man who took care of me when I was feeling sick. He used to check my temperature and bring me food. But she didn't care.*"

Most of all, Mom's fondest memory was that of a German woman and her family who genuinely cared for her. Miraculously, they inadvertently helped to change the course of Mom's life by introducing her to my future godmother: Habouba Zanabesh.

Mom and Dad's Unlikely Meeting in Khartoum

My parents' unexpected meeting in Khartoum was indirectly facilitated by one of the German families Mom worked for. They introduced Mom to Habouba Zanabesh who was at that time the main go-to person in the *Habasha* community in Khartoum. Zanabesh played a major part in introducing my parents to each other, convincing Mom to speak to Dad, and to eventually marry him. She became an integral part of our small family in Khartoum, in addition to being my godmother.

Dad saw Mom for the first time at the home of a British family where she worked as a nanny and domestic helper. He came to discuss an architectural remodeling design for their home when his eyes fell on Mom for the first time. Mom must have reminded him of Opera Aida's Ethiopian princess as she was cleaning up the house and doing her domestic chores!

"*I met your dad for the first time when I was walking after work to the Metro Station. He was waiting for me with his car outside the home where I worked. He offered me a ride and said, 'come ride,' but I didn't want to. When I was a child, I used to hear that the Egyptians viewed the human being's spirit as valuable as that of a chicken,*" said Mom explaining her reason to avoid Dad.

Mom's grandfather lived at the time of Ottoman-controlled Egypt's invasion of Ethiopia and the ensuing Ethiopian-Egyptian War (1874–1876).[101] The Ethiopian Empire won the war and remained independent until the "Scramble for Africa "and the ensuing Italian invasion of the country. The tales of victory and how Egypt was stopped from occupying Ethiopia, and potentially other countries in Africa, was told by Mom's grandfather to her dad. It was a frequently shared story of pride and victory that was told and retold in her village community.

The old village stories of Egyptian invading forces who killed her people and 'viewed the human being's spirit like that of a chicken' came back to memory as Dad, an Egyptian citizen, offered her a ride. But Dad was one of the many gentle and kind men born in Egypt who would not hurt a fly—or a chicken for that matter. Nor was he an Egyptian man who would give up easily or concede defeat.

"He used to wait for me at the end of my workday at the main house gate to offer me a ride to my place in Bahri. (Al-Khartoum Bahri is a city close to Khartoum.) When I said no, he would follow me slowly with his car and say, 'The distance to your home is too far from here and the sun is hot, come on ride the car. I'll take you there.' But I used to say 'NO' and would walk on foot to the Metro station. There were two trains at the time, but they were crowded with people dangling from the doors. I couldn't do that, and I used to wait until I find one with a place to sit."

There was a definite language barrier. Dad never got a clear-cut message of "NO" that he could understand from Mom as he continued his persistent pursuit. He felt a deep sense of caring for her as she walked in Khartoum's boiling hot weather. He even unsuccessfully attempted to give her a ride at the station where she disembarked.

Dad's fascination with Mom's beauty, dark skin, down-to-earth appearance, and character was unabated. He decided to visit my future godmother Zanabesh given her leadership position in the *Habasha* community and to tell her of his desire to marry Mom! Zanabesh, in turn, told her Greek husband about Dad's proposal, and they both decided to tell Mom about it.

"Zanabesh told me that a man with a car is coming to her and her husband asking to marry me. But I used to tell them every time they asked me that I just wanted to work to help my family. At that time, I wasn't yet able to send any money and felt very upset. I was saving my salary to send it to them, but I didn't know how to."

Not being able to send money to her family weighed heavily on her and made Dad's marriage proposal low on her priority list. Sending money to her family in the late 1940s to a remote village in Ethiopia's Highlands was a logistical nightmare. But once again, through a set of circumstances that could only be attributed to divine intervention, Mom was able to send the money that her family desperately needed.

"I overheard a conversation about a professional soccer team from Asmara coming to play in Khartoum that would be visiting a local Ethiopian restaurant. I had a relative named Berhane who was a good soccer player and I hoped that he would be one of the soccer players in the visiting team. I found the location of the restaurant and went there by taxi hoping to find Berhane."

Fortunately, Mom's childlike faith was rewarded. She found her relative Berhane in the restaurant. She gave him all the money that she had been saving since coming to Sudan and urged him to find her family and give it all to them. Mom never forgot the special moment in her life when she heard that the first installment of her hard-earned money was safely delivered. Her objective of crossing the perilous borders from Teseney to Kassala to provide for her family was at last accomplished when the money was finally received. She prayed and rejoiced.

"I prayed, 'May God give him (Berhane) more of His blessings.' He delivered the money and sent me a letter to let me know. He told me that 'Twalde (one of her brothers) came, and I gave it to him. They are blessing you and praying for you.'"

Mom, barely a sixteen-year-old teenager at the time, was driven by a consuming passion to keep her family alive. She was thankful to God that her family could now survive. The price she paid was to travel to Sudan and risk never seeing them again. But to her, the price she paid was all worth it! Her family back home could buy food and would be able to live.

Mom finally began to relax. There were plenty of available jobs for her in Khartoum, and fewer worries about being able to send her hard-earned money back to her family. It was finally a good time to listen carefully and reflect on Zanabesh and her Greek husband's advice regarding Dad's marriage proposal. And so, the gentle nudging, genuine appeals, and encouragement by the couple returned in full force. They knew Dad would make a great husband to Mom. But first, Mom had to let go of her long-held learned childhood bias that Egyptians "view other human spirits like chicken." That was the result of the brutal legacy of the old Egyptian invasions of Ethiopia where people were killed "like chicken." That was the past and Zanabesh did not want that old bias to affect Mom's potential future with Dad, a good Egyptian who was determined to marry her.

"Ajee (a Sudanese word that indicates being surprised), but you're now working. Do you think you can make the same amount of money that he makes? He will help your family more than you can," said Zanabesh, hoping to lay the Egyptians and human-chicken comparisons to rest.

"She repeated these same words to me over and over again. And when I refused to listen to them, she would get upset and tell me, 'When you get older no one will be there to see you or help you.'"

Zanabesh, an elderly wise woman, noticed Dad's kindness, and love for Mom. She saw that he shared Mom's Christian faith and was a man of solid character who would take good care of her. Her own marriage to a white Greek man convinced her that it was not color nor race that mattered, but a man's heart and character. Zanabesh was determined to convince Mom to marry Dad. She did not want to see her growing old alone in Sudan without someone like Dad by her side.

My Godmother Zanabesh

Zanabesh, or Adey Zanabesh as Mom called her, was a sweet and mysterious figure. I recall *Habouba Zanabesh* ("grandmother" in Arabic), as I called her, was short in stature with more wrinkles than I had ever seen before. She was commanding, sharp, and energetic. I was told as a child that she was my godmother. That meant to me at the time that she would bring me candy and treat me more special than other children. In a culture that revered the role of a godmother, she genuinely cared for me beyond gifts and candy. She continued her mission of being my godmother until her health deteriorated and she died in Khartoum's main hospital. It was only many years later when Mom shared with me the secret past of Habouba Zanabesh.

Many decades before she was my godmother, she was a military fighter. Zanabesh worked as a soldier in the Royal court of Empress Zawditu (1876–1930) the daughter of Emperor Menelik II.[102] She served the empress who ruled Ethiopia between 1916 to 1930 until she was captured either by the Italians or the enemies of the empress. She was subsequently sentenced to death by hanging. But miraculously, Zanabesh was helped to escape prison disguised in a dark dress and smuggled to Kassala, Sudan, just before her execution date. The exact details of her capture and escape from prison died with her when she passed away in that Khartoum hospital.

In Kassala, Zanabesh hid in the home of a Greek widower and eventually got married to him. The couple moved to Khartoum where Habouba Zanabesh met Mom, became her mentor, and introduced her to Dad years later. I was too young to comprehend any of her past wars' stories. But an old and trusted family member recalled one of those tragic stories that Zanabesh never forgot.

"*She hated the Mahdist fighters. She talked about a night when many of her people died. 'Many of Al-Mahdi men came to one of the small villages in Ethiopia and said they were on their way elsewhere and needed a place to rest. The elders of the village decided to accommodate all the men by placing each one of them at the homes of the welcoming families in the village. But at about 3:00 a.m. all the Mahdist fighters woke up and killed all the men in the homes in which they were staying. They took the young boys and girls, and all the women with them. The women were forced into marriages.'*"

Her stories of those years were collaborated by a very old woman, Mariam Al-habashia, that the same family member met in one of his trips to Western Sudan. The woman was abducted by the Mahdist fighting men when she was a child.

"She told me how glad she was to meet someone who reminded her of her own childhood heritage. She cooked for me a traditional zigne and injera meal and began to tell me about how she was abducted as a child by Al-Mahdi soldiers from her Ethiopian village. She was forced to marry one of the fighters and to become a Muslim. She ended up having two children who were grown up when I saw her. She was so excited and crying when she saw me."

As Habouba Zanabesh became old and frail, she was seen at times placing rocks on the sand depicting soldiers in various battlefield formations. She would then begin to move the rocks showing how the soldiers in their battlefield positions would strategically attack each other. I will always wonder if she was relieving childhood memories of the 1896 Battle of Adwa against the Italians. Or perhaps she was describing one of her military battles as one of Empress Zawditu's loyal soldiers.

Mom in her early twenties in Khartoum.

Taking good care of Italian and British babies.

CHAPTER 17

MY PARENTS: A BLACK & WHITE LOVE STORY IN KHARTOUM

M OM AND DAD CAME TO SUDAN not just with big dreams but with their rich cultures and deep Christian faith. They wasted no time in searching individually for other Christians from their homelands: Mom within the Ethiopian/Eritrean communities and the Ethiopian church and Dad in the Coptic, Syrian, and Lebanese circles. There were multiple denominational churches in late 1940s Muslim Sudan: Catholic, Coptic, Armenian, Greek, Anglican, and American Evangelical congregations to choose from.

But Dad soon realized that he was more at ease with mingling and furthering his community to include Ethiopians, Eritreans, and Sudanese in Khartoum. Unlike some of his Levantine and Egyptian contemporaries in Sudan who preferred to stay within their own groups, Dad formed solid relationships and friendships with many *Habasha* and Sudanese. He saw beauty in every skin color but particularly loved black and all the shades of brown skin color. Consequently, reaching to the brown, and dark-skinned *Habasha* community, including Zanabesh, in his pursuit of Mom came naturally to him. His rejection of prejudice in words and actions at a time where racial and ethnic prejudice was the norm impressed Zanabesh. To her, that was another good reason to passionately encourage and plead with Mom to accept Dad's marriage proposal.

Mom and Dad could not have been more different. Apart from their Christian faith, Mom an Ethiopian Orthodox, and Dad a member of the Egyptian Coptic orthodox church, they were in almost every aspect polar opposite of each other. He was a white, thirty-six-year-old Arabic speaker, college educated, and a well-off architect who was sent to Sudan by King Farouk of Egypt with a team of highly skilled architects. Mom, a Black, barely sixteen-year-old *Habasha*, spoke no Arabic. She was an unschooled teenager smuggled on foot across the Sudanese borders in search of a domestic help job to feed her family. Despite their differences, the subtle criticism of his white peers, and his personal belief that his family would reject his marriage, Dad never wavered in his decision.

Mom and Dad: Different and Unequal in Colonized Sudan

Mom and Dad's experience and treatment in Anglo-Egyptian colonized Sudan, and for a few decades after the country's independence were quite different. Her dark skin color and ethnicity subjected her to a few derogatory terms, a product of the long years of slavery that bedeviled Sudan.

"*Habashia*" (a word that can be used as a derogatory term to describe an Ethiopian or Eritrean female), "*Abda*"(a female slave), and "*Khadama* (servant) were a few of the choice words that she heard in Khartoum. She was confused for a Southern Sudanese, a Nubian, or a Western Sudanese, recipients of some of those derogatory words. She had no idea what those words meant until many years later.

In contrast, Dad was revered with the term *Khawaja* (a term reserved for white Europeans). His white skin color guaranteed him the highest status and first-class treatment in Anglo-Egyptian colonized Sudan. Mom's dark skin color on the other hand placed her at the bottom of society's social status scale and guaranteed her a second-class treatment. That mindset was prevalent in the late 1940s not only in Sudan but also throughout the world, including my dad's birthplace of Egypt. Egyptians

My Parents: A Black & White Love Story in Khartoum \ 153

at the time lived in a culture that poked fun at dark-skinned Sudanese in theatrical shows and in the media. Sudan was viewed as a vast land where hot deserts, jungles with wild animals, and Black Nubians populated the land. To Dad, all the above added to the mystique and sense of adventure. He embraced all of the above and fell in love with a dark Tigrayan woman that some of his peers assumed to be a Black Nubian.

Not only was he viewed with professional reverence as a renowned architect, but also his white skin color gave him status, privilege, and the name *Khawaja*. To Dad, a deeply Christian man, the label of *Khawaja* did not make him feel better or superior to others. To him, Mom, with her beautiful black skin color, was his Ethiopian-Tigrayan princess, and his equal. Ultimately, she was the main reason he decided to make Sudan his new permanent home.

Mom, a proud Tigrayan, did not care a bit about Dad's presumed higher status in society. Dad's white skin color, car (a rarity at the time), well-designed suits, and money were not good reasons to be married to him. She did not care about the things that many privileged women at the time in Khartoum were captivated by, including a white man with money. Mom recalled how Dad used to say that he loved her dark skin color. Essentially, he was a color-blind man who saw Mom's beautiful heart just like he saw the beauty of her skin color. To Dad, who once shared that he almost married a famous white Lebanese singer named "Sabah" when she was in Egypt, instead choosing Mom, a simple, dark-skinned young woman surprised everyone. Dad, who often said that some of the white Levantine people he knew "do things (with women) at night that they don't do in the morning," found in Mom what he could not find in any other woman. Choosing to not marry one of the white women, including a rich and famous one, who were interested in him, and choosing instead to marry Mom surprised many. But to Dad who saw the beauty in Mom that others blinded by color biases might have failed to see, all that he hoped for was for Mom to say "Yes" to his marriage proposal.

Experiencing a Taste of Colorism and Ethnic Discrimination

Growing up, Mom had her own experiences of being viewed inferiorly because of her dark skin color. She was the darkest of her siblings in a societal culture that esteemed lighter skin colors. In Sudan, she faced something similar but with the added bias that people immigrating from Eritrea and Ethiopia occasionally experienced. Some natives used terms like "*Ya Habashia*" (for females) and "*Ya Habashe*" (for males) in a derogatory fashion to describe them. Thankfully, the kindness of many of the Sudanese she knew made up for the offenses of those who uttered those ethnic insults.

Compared to Mom's harsh racial experience, Dad had it good. Under the Anglo-Egyptian rule, white skin was the right color. It was a time when one's position in society was mostly influenced by how close to white was his or her skin color. The system was openly discriminating at that time with white British, Europeans, Syrians, Lebanese, and Egyptians receiving preferential treatment and privileges. They were always welcomed to dine and entertain at the "Grand Hotel Khartoum," Sudan's first hotel built a short distance from the Nile between 1902 to 1906. Non-whites, Black, and dark-skinned people like Mom were not usually welcome. They were mostly not seen there unless they worked as waitresses, gardeners, and janitors.

For many of the Ethiopians and Eritreans who flocked into Sudan fleeing conflicts and poverty life wasn't easy. Many endured scorn and contempt because of their ethnicities. A few unfortunate women chose to meet their daily bread needs with prostitution as they hoped for a better future. That, in turn, added another layer of scorn and ill repute to the community of *habasha* women of good character who took their Christian faith seriously. Fortunately for Mom, an innocent sixteen-year-old teenager, Zanabesh became her mentor. She helped her understand the complexities of a racially and ethnically charged society.

In many ways, she was a God-sent woman of courage and character who helped Mom rise above the cruel stereotyping insults she heard. Mostly, she showed her by example how not to judge a person by his skin color. Her marriage to her white Greek husband was going well. Zanabesh wanted most of all to help Mom focus on Dad's character and not his ethnicity. Mom, who grew up hearing that white Egyptian men did not value human lives, but 'viewed the human being's spirit like that of a chicken' needed a major step of faith to trust Dad. To entertain Zanabesh's advice of accepting Dad's marriage proposition, she had to confront her own stereotypes about him.

"He told me that I'm beautiful and he loved my skin color. I wasn't sure why a famous white architect would want to marry me but Adey (mother) Zanabesh convinced me that he was a caring man and will help me take care of my family back home. So, I agreed to marry him."

Dad's firm determination and reason to marry mom were based on Mom's innocence and character. He often shared with Mom the reason for marrying her with his favorite Arabic proverb: *"Khoud alasyla walou hata ala alhasira."* (Choose for a wife an authentic compassionate, and honorable woman of character even if all that you end up with is a straw mat for a bed). Dad believed that a good and compassionate woman with a noble character will bring him happiness and peace of mind. He believed Mom was that woman.

Mom and Dad Denied Marriage in Khartoum

Finally, Mom agreed! All what she wanted was a Christian church wedding. But that did not come easy in Sudan at the time. The hurdle of Mom's initial reluctance to marry Dad was replaced with a bigger hurdle. Regrettably, they faced hindrances and were discouraged from getting married by the priests they talked to.

"We visited different churches in Khartoum, but they refused to marry us. Maybe they didn't feel it was right for a white man to marry a Black woman.

Or maybe because they wanted Gobran (my dad's name) to request lots of papers about his life in Egypt and he just got tired of it and didn't want to. One of the priests told us: 'If you are still together in six months apply again if you want.' There was no official Ethiopian, or Eritrean church in Khartoum at the time to marry us," recalled Mom.

After experiencing rejection and frustration, Dad and Mom decided to have a courthouse wedding in Anglo-Egyptian colonized Sudan. Their official church wedding in the Christian Orthodox church of Enda Mariam in Asmara had to wait for a few more years. Meanwhile, they had to be content to being legally married albeit not in a church, much to Mom's disappointment.

Mom and Dad's racially related challenges did not end with their courthouse marriage. Fortunately, their marriage was rooted in love and respect, which helped them survive the difficult challenges they had to face. One of those challenges was taking Mom with him to places where she was not welcome. Dad, who valued Mom's wisdom and sought her opinion about the high-rise buildings, mansion, and lavish villas he designed, couldn't take Mom to certain places with him. He often worried about someone making her feel unwelcome or treating her inferiorly.

Dad's protection of Mom did not end there. He shielded me and my siblings from any gatherings or places where he felt we were treated (or potentially treated) inferiorly because of our skin color. And because he worried that his own family would not accept us, he kept us away from them. When he had enough assurance that Mom, my siblings, and I would be welcome and treated well by them, he finally agreed for us to meet! What a challenge he had to face! He worked and prospered in Khartoum among his white peers where he was revered as a *"Khawaja"* in a culture that viewed Mom, the love of his life, as less. How he managed, in such unsettling racial tension, to be a renowned architect, a devoted husband, and a loving father is nothing short of miraculous.

My Parents: A Black & White Love Story in Khartoum \ 157

Return to Childhood Home and the Death of Her Mom

Following my parents' civil wedding, Mom's life changed for the better just like "Adey" Zanabesh assured her. She became a stay-at-home mom and took care of Dad and their growing children. The initially impossible dream of going to Sudan, finding a job, and taking care of her family became a reality. She was now happily married to a generous man who took care of her and helped to take care of her own family. But she still missed her family. And the longer she lived in Sudan, the more intense was the yearning for her parents and siblings.

Four years after Mom's border crossing to Sudan she was able to return alone to her childhood home and visit her family in Adwa. She left them as a young teenager looking for a job with an Italian or a British family in Khartoum. But she was returning to see them as a married young woman and a mother. She missed them terribly and could not wait to see them. Soon after her arrival at her childhood home near Adwa, she began to look with high anticipation for her parents. Her mom was not there.

"My mom Mislal died from a severe asthma attack a short time before I arrived. My family decided to keep her death a secret until I came in person to visit them. I remember as a child how, despite her asthma and difficulty breathing, she would walk uphill with a big container to bring water home. She regularly planted and watered vegetables near our home," said Mom.

Mislal dedicated her life to her husband and children. Her husband cherished her and did all that he could do to help her as she suffered from her asthma exacerbations. But, despite his efforts, he was unable to do much because of his visual impairment.

"There was one more child born by Mom after me. Once she gave birth, she told Dad to please take her back to her childhood home because her asthma symptoms were getting worse. Dad decided to move to her childhood home because he loved her," recalled Mom's youngest sister.

Grandma Mislal died from an asthmatic attack two weeks after attending her son's wedding. Grandpa never remarried. After her death, he lived thirty more years with one of his sons, Mom's brother, Tawalde.

Mom grieved the loss of her mother for many months after that visit and never forgot her sacrificial love, caring, and kindness. She remained fully committed to taking care of her dad, and all her siblings after Mislal's passing. Supporting her remaining family, including her youngest sister, who came to live in our home in Sudan, became a life mission. She and Dad shared that caring mission of helping their siblings and families for life.

Finally, Holy Matrimony in Church

It was not until the year 1954 when Mom and Dad finally had the chance to travel together to Asmara, Eritrea, to have the Christian church wedding they both longed for. Mom and Dad got married by the welcoming Christian Eritrean orthodox priests of Enda Mariam (the Place of Mary in Tigrinya) Cathedral in Asmara. Mom's earnest desire to have a Christian wedding that Dad promised her was finally a reality. Their church marriage in Enda Mariam brought them joy and vindication after the rejection they endured in colonized Sudan.

Their wedding in Asmara, a city with an elevation of over 7,500 feet in Eritrea's Highlands, brought Mom a lot of childhood memories. She remembered the Italian families she once worked for as a young child. The memory of her long and tearful journey from Asmara to Teseney, and then to Kassala where she crossed Sudan's borders came alive. To Dad, it was an enchanting experience. He marveled at the sight of monasteries, the many ancient underground churches, and those built high on the mountains.

A Very Traditional Wedding Reception in Adwa

After the church wedding in Asmara, they went to Mom's birthplace of Adwa where a lavish traditional reception awaited them. It was Dad's first time meeting her dad and siblings. Mom left her childhood home as a child to support her family but in 1954 she returned with Dad by her side! It was a joyful occasion and the marriage festivities started as soon as they arrived. Traditional songs filled the air, sheep and chicken were butchered and made into delicious spicy (made less spicy for Dad) dishes eaten with injera. Dad never noticed, or cared, that he was the only white person in the crowd as he delighted in the food. He enjoyed listening to the Tigrinya drumbeats and singing as he watched their unique traditional dancing. Dancers shuffled as they followed each other in a circle. Their heads and shoulders moved with the rhythm of the drumbeats. That, in turn, culminated with increasing movements of their shoulders as the dancers faced each other as the music intensified. Dad was lost in the crowd of dancers and for a moment they all became one. There he was not viewed, nor did he think of himself, as a *Khouaja* because of his white skin color. He was one of them and color did not matter.

My Parents' Biracial Marriage Challenges

After the wedding festivities and reconnecting with Mom's family, my parents returned home to Sudan. The two major milestones in Mom's life—supporting her family and seeing them again—had been accomplished. And so was the dream of having a Christian church wedding. Dad, on the other hand, found a new family in Mom and her people. But the decision to introduce Mom and his growing family to his own family in Egypt was a difficult one for him. Out of genuine worry that Mom and the children would be rejected, he decided not to tell his family in

Egypt about his marriage. He feared that Mom and we children might be viewed inferiorly and not treated well.

"Your dad worried about our family being rejected and treated disrespectfully by his family in Egypt because of our skin color," said Mom.

The arrogant and condescending looks Dad noticed from some of his white circle of acquaintances and clients when they knew he was married to Mom frustrated and angered him. Mom was always able to notice Dad's frustration and anger when some people treated him poorly because of her skin color.

"That used to annoy him, and he would tell me, 'You know I get treated badly because of your skin color. They wouldn't do that if you were white.' I used to get upset when I heard him saying that. But I knew he was right! The bad treatment he received at times was because of my skin color. That was upsetting to him."

In Sudan, Dad was, at the time of marrying Mom, the top architect in the country. His work included buildings considered "the first skyscrapers in the Middle East"! Many people stopped in front of his buildings in admiration and would then contact his office requesting him to build a similar design for them. He was considered the first architect in the region to build high-rise buildings that were viewed as "skyscrapers" to many at the time. One of those high-rise buildings included the American Embassy building in Khartoum. Many pedestrians at the time avoided walking under its shade in fear that it might fall on them!

Dad's fame rocketed with his European- and modern-style homes and international embassies in Khartoum. Shortly after immigrating to Sudan, he became that renowned architect whose good reputation spread beyond Sudan into other countries. As an avid and talented photographer, Dad chronicled his astounding success with numerous rare photos of his designs. Those included detailed stages of the construction of the historical King Farouk Mosque, and many other impressive projects. Those photos and numerous others spanned his long professional career. They showed his breathtaking architectural designs that had fascinated the public for years. Yet, all those accomplishments could not spare him the prejudices of those who disliked his choice to marry Mom.

The Abyss of Prejudice: "Whites Only"

Many beautiful places in colonized Sudan were "whites only" where Mom was overtly or covertly not welcome. For years, she heard from Dad about the beauty and the splendor of the historic Grand Hotel in Khartoum and the British Officers Club. Native Sudanese and non-whites were generally not welcome during the years of colonization in such places.

"Dark-skinned and Black women seen with white men in places like that were considered prostitutes. Gobran (Dad's name) wouldn't take me there," said Mom.

Another place that Dad avoided taking Mom and our family to was Al-Nadee Al-souri (the Syrian club) in Khartoum. The lavish club with its Olympic-style swimming pool was designed by Dad! The dark-skinned people and people who worked in the club at the time were mostly servants and not members. Dad shared with Mom that he did not want anyone to view her or treat her as a servant. He was concerned that she and their children would not be welcome there.

As my siblings and I grew up, he finally decided to take us to the Syrian club after he felt assured that we would be fully welcome. Thankfully, the biases there gradually changed. By the 1970s we were treated as full members of the club and had great memories swimming in the magnificent pool that Dad had designed!

Mom's biggest challenge of living in Khartoum in the 1950s centered on the evil of racial prejudice. What she encountered as a dark-skinned woman married to a white man affected her marriage, family, and even her car rides with Dad. She had to deal with demeaning nuisances such as stooping down to avoid being seen by a white person while riding in the car with Dad!

"Your dad felt bad that I had to do that. He wasn't happy that some of those men 'do with Black women things at night that they wouldn't do in the daytime.' Some lived with Black Southern Sudanese women but ended up leaving them. They would leave them and their children behind choosing to return to their countries to marry women of their own race," Mom recalled.

A woman, a family friend, whose white Levantine dad was married to her Black Southern Sudanese mother, once shared with me her sad childhood story.

"After Dad died in Southern Sudan, his brother and his wife didn't want to have a relationship with us. They treated Mom's culture with disgust. My uncle managed to take the inheritance Dad left for us through the court system. We were left with nothing," she said, nearly in tears.

Another similarly tragic story was that of a woman my family knew well. Her white Levantine dad left her and her siblings behind when they were young. He went back to Lebanon without leaving them with any address or a goodbye note. She eventually began a desperate search for him when she was older. That eventually took her to Lebanon where she found his home address. She knocked on his door only to find out that he was married to a Lebanese woman and already had a few children with her! And such was the dark abyss of prejudice at the time. It drove fathers to abandon their children, family members to reject their own, emotional injury, and Mom to duck down so as not to be seen with Dad!

Dark Skinned, Black, and Beautiful in 1950s Khartoum

Given the color-biased mindset of 1950s Khartoum, many single white women were jealous of Mom. They considered Dad as one of Khartoum's most eligible white bachelors. To them, it did not make any sense that Dad chose to marry Mom instead of one of them.

"Many young white women wanted to see me in person. They were curious to know why a famous man like Gobran would choose to marry me," Mom said.

One specific Levantine woman who pursued Dad's attention for years was shocked to know that he chose to marry Mom.

"She climbed the wall of the house and then asked me, 'Could you please remove your Toub?' (a traditional veil-like silk fabric that women in Sudan wrap around their dresses). When I did, she started to walk around me and then asked me to turn around as she looked at my dress and figure. I didn't know why she wanted me to do that, but I did what she asked me to do wondering what was in her mind."

To Mom's surprise, the woman stopped walking around her and said as if she had a "eureka" moment: "Now I know why he married you. It's because of your body!"

Fortunately for Mom, Dad, who took his Christian faith seriously and craved the books of the American preacher Billy Graham, saw in Mom more than her body. The attractive white woman who decided to inspect Mom's features and body as if that was all that mattered missed seeing what Dad saw in Mom. He saw her gentle, compassionate, loyal, and down-to-earth character. He saw the loving, kind, and caring heart that the white woman who climbed the wall failed to see.

The tiring complexities and toxicity of the racial prejudices my parents encountered was at times quite overwhelming. But thankfully, their marriage was blessed with close-knit friends who became the family they both did not have in Sudan. They felt loved and accepted as a couple by Habasha and a few Sudanese families. Thankfully, racial and religious differences did not divide or break those caring relationships. My childhood home was a place to rest, grow, and prosper. It was the safe sanctuary that kept us away from the racial and religious biases that often awaited us outside its safe walls.

Mom in Khartoum.

My Parents: A Black & White Love Story in Khartoum

Dad and mom in Asmara.

Dad, Mom, and my older brother Joe.

Dad, a friend, and probably the same car that he offered Mom rides in when he first met her.

Mom holding my brother Anwar, and my oldest brother, Joe, standing by.

Dad and Mom at an evening party in Khartoum in the 1970s.

My parents growing old together in early 1980s.

PART THREE

SUDAN 1960–1980: MY CHILDHOOD YEARS

★ ★ ★

CHAPTER 18

LIFE AND PERSONAL TRAGEDY IN SUDAN

Sudan of my childhood, once the largest country in Africa, is a country of many contrasts. Mansions and Mercedes-Benz cars in the rich suburbs of Al-Amtidad, Al-Manshia, and Al-Riyadh stood in sharp contrast to other neighborhoods. Donkeys and packed buses were more common than cars in the poorer neighborhoods. There were childhood fun and activities even as a never-ending civil war raged between the predominantly Christian South and the Muslim Arab North. The Southern Sudanese were fighting for autonomy and against the Islamic Sharia law that became the law of the land in 1983. After decades of war with millions of dead and wounded, the South finally won its independence in 2011. Over a decade later on April 15, 2023, a violent war erupted in Khartoum between the Sudanese Armed Forces and a large paramilitary group that was formerly part of the army. Khartoum, where I abundantly enjoyed my childhood, became a battleground!

Sudan, the one country that I grew up in, became two divided countries. Thousands of Southern Sudanese who once called Sudan home had to leave their jobs and schools in the North. They moved to the new country of Southern Sudan leaving their childhood homes behind and starting their lives over again. Decades before, my parents did something like the Southern Sudanese who had to abandon their homes in Sudan. They moved away from their close-knit families and support systems, trying to start their lives in a new place all over again.

After my parents' church marriage, they settled down in their home near Khartoum and began to quickly grow their family. Sadly, a tragedy befell their new family soon after their wedding in Asmara. Their second born, my brother George, died unexpectedly from severe diarrhea when he was only two years old. Mom vividly recalled his death many years later.

"*I was alone with him when he died. I cried hysterically. None of the doctors could help him. He died when your dad was out of Khartoum working in a project in a remote area of Sudan. Because he was not given a bonus like his Muslim colleagues after finishing the King Farouk Mosque, he needed these projects. I couldn't get hold of him, and the only option was to bury George before his body began to smell. Your dad didn't know that he died or that he was buried until he came back from his work trip,*" Mom recalled.

Dad took George's death very hard. He cried a lot and Mom heard him asking himself in frustration: "*Why would they deny me my bonus just because I'm a Christian?*"

Dad felt that he would not have been far away from his home for so long to make money if he got his expected bonus. My parents kept George's name and the memory of those two brief years of his life alive throughout my childhood. He was always the seventh sibling missing from our gatherings; but always loved and present in our hearts. Shortly after George's death, Dad left for a long trip to Egypt and Europe. He was grieving and needed time alone and to visit his family in Egypt. Concurrently, that was the time when he faced some of his fiercest spiritual and emotional battles.

Marital Challenges After George's Death

Dad left Khartoum to visit his family in Egypt with a broken heart. That was a difficult and trying time for my parents. Mom was aware of the stories of some Levantine men who permanently left Sudan leaving behind their women and children. The loss of social status, and the rejection of their families and friends of their Black wives and dark children was too much of a burden for them.

"*Would he ever return? Is he going to be influenced by those around him in Egypt to leave me and our children?*" she pondered. She worried that what happened to some of her abandoned friends might also be her fate.

But somehow, she trusted that he would return and waited patiently for him. Dad, who experienced society's biases because of his marriage to Mom, was at that time in a vulnerable emotional state. He was grieving the loss of his son George who died and was buried while he was far away. The mental and spiritual battles within and without briefly took a toll on him. But thankfully his faith in God and unfailing love of Mom and their children prevailed. Dad returned to Mom and to his children as a devoted husband and committed loving father.

What helped Dad to fight the surrounding society's color distinction and obsession that rendered him superior because of his white skin color and Mom inferior because of her dark skin color was his faith. He believed what the Bible said about all people being created equal regardless of their race, sex, or ethnicity.

To Dad, Mom's good, kind, loving character, and her dark skin color were truly beautiful. Even in his deep grief, he decided to defy the norms and racial prejudices of his surroundings. In that regard, Dad was much wiser than many of his white friends and acquaintances who abandoned their devoted Black wives. They left them to marry white women back in their home countries only to suffer miserable marriages. In essence, they married what society considered the "right" color wives who turned out to be with unloving hearts and wrong characters.

Dad always attributed his phenomenal success as an architect to Mom's encouragement and support. He often asked her about what she thought about his new architectural ideas. And oftentimes, he incorporated many of her good design ideas and suggestions to his projects and designs.

"He was always under a lot of pressure to finish important projects. He worried and was at times anxious if he started a new foundation of a big building and then a strong storm with heavy rain began pouring. I used to comfort him when worries about the rain ruining the new building's foundation prevented him from going to sleep. I used to tell him 'Gobran, don't worry. You are the best architect. The foundations of your buildings are always done so well, and no rain will affect it.' He always told me 'wara koul rajoul azeem emra'a (an Arabic proverb that means behind every great man there is a supportive and caring woman/wife),'" she recalled many years later. Dad saw Mom as God's blessing to him. He often told her that he would not have succeeded in his stellar career as an architect without her.

My Childhood Home by the Blue Nile

I was born one of seven children in *Al-Manshia*, an affluent suburb of Khartoum. Dad, being the consummate architect, designed and redesigned our large, two-floor home and finally settled on a Spanish-European design. He added an exotic, large tropical and Japanese style garden creating an international flavor to our home. Just a short walking distance from the house, the waters of the Blue Nile (*Al-Neal Alazrag*) streaming from the Highlands of Ethiopia could be seen. The river continues its flow and joins a few miles away from our home the White Nile (*Al-Neal Al-Abiad*) at Sudan's capital Khartoum. Their waters merge forming the River Nile in front of the Presidential Palace where the British general Charles Gordon was killed in 1885. From there, the majestic River Nile travels north through Egypt's dry land on its way to the Mediterranean Sea, its final destination.

As a child, I remember how content and proud I was of my heritage. My parents created a home environment where I felt loved and valued.

I was born in Sudan, yet not fully Sudanese in culture or religion. My parents were from Egypt, Ethiopia's-Tigray's Highlands, but I was not fully Egyptian, Tigrayan, or Ethiopian either. In many ways, I felt like a tree rooted in every culture where the River Nile flows through and that felt good. As I grew older and my parents began to teach me about their Christian faith, I began to see that my roots go beyond the River Nile and the cultures that surrounded it. Home was warm and peaceful. It was also like a training ground where I learned about faith, right and wrong, value, and, most of all, humility. We enjoyed a high standard of living, traveled to Europe, had a personal gardener, and hired domestic help. But my parents would not allow us to ever use the word "rich" to describe ourselves. They wanted to make sure that we never saw ourselves less valuable or more valuable than others because of our money or wealth. Others saw my family as rich, but that was a word that we never used in our home.

My childhood home in Al-Manshia was a warm and welcoming place. Dad and Mom offered refugees from Ethiopia and Eritrea sanctuary and shelter as they prepared to immigrate to Europe and America. It was a place where Christian missionaries from America visited, and where Dad shared with us tons of Egyptian colloquial proverbs that influenced his life:

"*Doukhul al-hamam mish zay khuruguh*" means "entering the Turkish bath is not like getting out" (used to advise someone that it is much easier to get into a new direction, choice, and situation than to get out of it).

"*Ya pharoun, ya pharoun mean al-pharanak*" means "pharaoh, pharaoh who made you a pharaoh (a tyrant)" and the pharaoh answers, "*Min gilat had ma yoroudani*" (I am pharaoh because there is no one to stop me).

"*Albab albigy mino al rih sido wastarih*" means "the door that brings you the wind, close it and rest."

And of course, his favorite one: "*Khoud al-asila wa'law hata ala al-hasira.*"

My Childhood 101 Introduction to Colorism and Prejudice

I do not exactly recall at what age the culture's obsession with skin color began to affect me. My childhood home was a safe place for my siblings and me where the black, brown, and white skin colors of my family were the norm. But when I started school, I was exposed for the first time to my classmates' and friends' views about race and skin color. I heard for the first time statements about race and color that I could not grasp or understand. A lot of what I heard made me think about my own skin tone and that of each member of my family.

"You mean your dad is this white Khouaja (a term used for white Europeans)?"

"You mean the Black woman that was with you is your mother?"

"Is she your sister? She is so much whiter than you!"

Shortly after I was exposed to the world's and society's biased view about race and color, I began to wonder. It did not take long for me to feel their negative effects. Like a growing cancer, my mind was invaded by new and troubling world and societal views. Those disturbing views seemed to rank Mom inferior because of her skin color, and Dad as superior because of his white skin color. My color-blind world nurtured at my childhood home was now being challenged by something disturbing and unsettling.

I was a child whose mind was now attacked, as if in a battleground, by foreign beliefs coming from around me. The society that surrounded me seemed to view Dad as more valuable than Mom because of his white skin, and my sister more valuable than Mom, me, and my siblings because of her light skin color! And in society's color obsession, my family in general was viewed and treated as more valuable than those darker than us. The message heard and perceived was that the color of someone's skin—white, light, or dark—determined his or her value. That felt as sickening and nauseating to me back then as it still feels today.

The love and encouragement that I received from my parents at home helped me to excel in school and to accomplish a lot as a Boy Scout. I was one of the top students of my school, and as a Boy Scout I reveled in camping by the River Nile, winning badges and rising through the ranks. When I was growing up, Mom and Dad kept me focused on the many blessings that we found in Khartoum and not on our or someone else's skin color. Yet, there was that troubling dichotomy between how I saw Mom and Dad as equally valuable and cherished, and society's view of Dad as more valuable and acceptable than Mom. Growing up in Khartoum as a child and a teenager where such dichotomy never abated was hard. It was emotionally exhausting. After all, how can a child ever fathom and make sense of his mom, whom he deeply loves, being viewed in society as inferior because of her skin color, and his dad, whom he equally loves, being viewed as superior because of his color?

In a world that is so obsessed with skin color rather than character, this is probably the inner battle many biracial and mixed-race children like me go through. Seeing ourselves, regardless of our skin color, as beautiful, valuable, and God's unique creation is the battle that many of us must conquer and win. Many generations in Sudan, other African countries, and throughout the world where white Turks, Arabs, and Europeans invaded and ruled were treated as inferior based on their skin color. Their worth and value were determined by the color of their skin. And even when the outcome of such invasions was not long-term slavery, the ultimate long-term destructive outcome still lingers. Many generations grew up believing that their skin color and racial features determine their significance, worth, and value.

In Sudan of my childhood, like in many other African countries and throughout the world, white skin colors like that of my dad were esteemed the most. The closer someone's skin color was to being white, the more he or she was valued and esteemed. The challenge to many people of mixed races and darker colors was to see themselves as beautiful, equal, and valuable despite society's hellish color-based ranking. At school, my friends treated me as an equal when it came to my skin color. My skin color was similar or lighter than most Sudanese. Hence, I was spared the term *"Abd,"* a term that means "slave" in Arabic. This derogatory term was unfortunately used for generations to describe the Southern Sudanese or other native Sudanese who were black or with dark skin colors. Not all my friends used the word *"Abd"* and probably most of those who used it were just repeating a word that has been ingrained in the culture. Many used this word as part of their vocabulary without thinking of its racist roots, meaning, and how demeaning it was to others.

Indeed, for people growing up in Sudan, racial and ethnic issues and challenges were hard to escape. But equally challenging was growing up as a Christian family in Muslim Sudan.

Staying Christian in Muslim Sudan

I grew up with my siblings in a nurturing home that was color-blind but not religion-blind. Both Mom and Dad came from an extensive line of Christian ancestry and were determined to pass the mantle of Christianity to us. They viewed themselves as Olympians passing the prized Olympian torch of faith from one runner to another until the finish line. Outside the gate of our family home, Islam ruled supreme with the voice of the *Alazaan* (a Muslim cleric calling Muslims to prayers) blasting from hundreds of mosques in the city. Throughout the day, one could see the faithful Muslims praying as the call for prayers came from the public radio and tall minarets. But in our home, Jesus and his teaching ruled supreme as Mom and Dad taught us all about Christianity.

As a child, it was a challenge to remain a Christian in Sudan where my friends, the media, and government officials preached and regularly talked about Islam. Not every Christian parent was able to pass this mantle of Christianity to their children. That task became particularly harder as the children grew into adventurous teenagers and young adults. Some of them developed close relationships and romantic interests with their Muslim friends. That, in turn, led a few of them to change their religion to Islam to get married to their love interests.

Certainly, Dad and Mom had a big job before them as I and my siblings became teenagers. Their job to keep us committed to our Christian faith wasn't easy especially as we formed close friendships with Muslim classmates and neighbors. In addition to the regular teenage peer pressure, I was often encouraged and enticed by my Muslim friends who would have liked me to change my religion to Islam. That was mainly at the beginning of forming our friendship relationships but would usually stop after becoming a close circle of friends.

"Adel, why don't you convert to Islam. You're really very nice."

Mom and Dad decided not to take any chances. They wanted to ensure that their children would be following in the footsteps of their Christian faith. Their ancestors carried the mantle of Christianity for many generations. They remained committed to their faith despite the persecution and extreme hardships that many of them had endured. Christianity in that part of the world was handed from one generation to another, and it was my parents' role to do the same. My parents were both determined and committed to teach me and my siblings about their faith in Jesus Christ. And so, we went regularly to the Coptic Church and eventually every Sunday to the Protestant church in Khartoum. They encouraged us to observe the fifty-five fasting days preceding Easter, sent us to Christian Church camps in the summer, and celebrated Christmas in a grand style.

In a country where Christians in the North were a small minority, Dad and Mom kept close and long-term friendships with our Muslim neighbors. They regularly visited their homes and invited them to ours, especially our Christmas parties. But to keep us grounded in our Christian faith, they also watched me and my siblings closely. They worked diligently to steer us away from being involved in situations that could potentially lead us to doubt or abandon our faith. My parents, just probably like my Muslim friends' parents, were often worried that any of us might fall in love with someone outside of our faith.

They loved their Muslim friends and neighbors but being torchbearers igniting the flame of Christianity in us, just like what their forefathers did for them, was the most important legacy they wanted to leave us with. To accomplish their goal, Dad kept an eye on me as a teenager. He wanted to make sure that I did not spend too much time in front of the mirror trying to look "cute." Like other parents, he worried about his children falling in love and converting from Christianity. Or the repercussions of being immersed in a love relationship forbidden in society and culture.

"Kafaia ba'ah *(It's enough), are you combing your hair to look cute for the girls? Enough standing in front of the mirror,*" Dad often said.

My parents did exactly what generations of Christian families had to do in predominantly Muslim countries. They got along with their Muslim neighbors, held tightly to their beliefs, practiced their Christian faith, and passed it to their children. And that was the way it has been done for two thousand years.

Dad.   Mom.

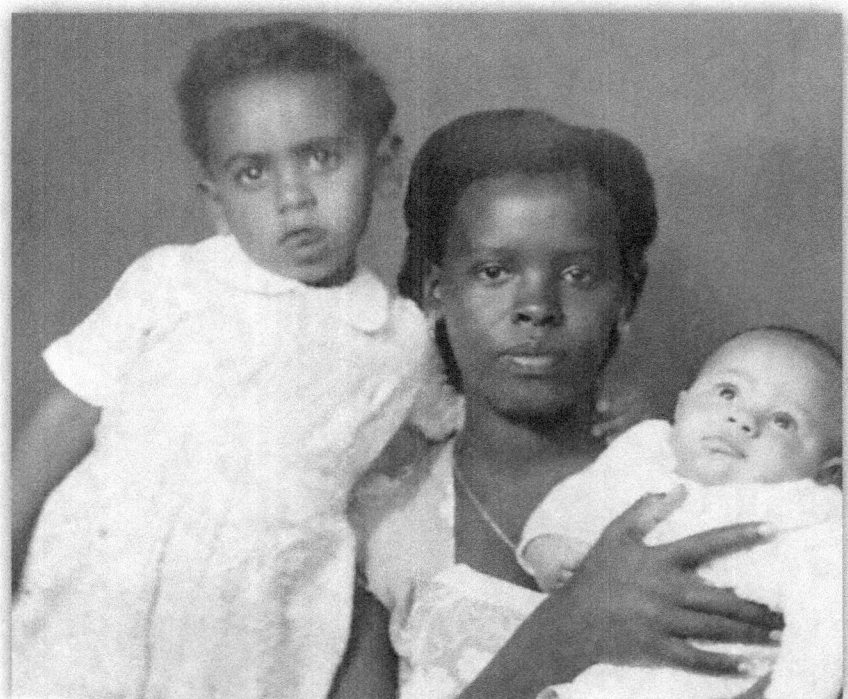

Mom, my older brother Joe on the left, and my brother George who died as a baby, on the right.

CHAPTER 19

MY SCHOOL DAYS AT A CATHOLIC SCHOOL IN MUSLIM SUDAN: COMBONI COLLEGE KHARTOUM AKA CCK

My primary to high school educational journey in Khartoum was in a private Catholic school system run by Italian nuns and priests. My school days were filled with fun, adventures, and close friendships with people of all colors, races, and religions. CCK, also known as "Al-Comboni," was originally named after Bishop Comboni, an Italian missionary priest. Comboni traveled to Africa in the latter half of the 1800s and started several schools for the natives there. Located in the capital city of Khartoum, CCK became known in the early 1900s for its excellent standard of education. Its high standards have been maintained by a cadre of highly educated Italian priests for close to a century.

For nearly a century, CCK with its school motto of "Always More, Always Better," remained a favorite center of education. Sudan's top government officials, and the well-to-do were educated there and routinely sent their sons to the all-boy school. The equivalent all-girl school "Sisters' School Khartoum," run by Catholic nuns, was also attended by the daughters of Khartoum's most elite. But students with fewer financial means to afford the tuition were also able to attend the school.

It was Bishop Comboni's original mission to educate Sudanese of all religions and to offer what Sudan's public schools didn't offer: a dedicated period of Christian religious education to Christian students. The Christian Italian priests and nuns devoted their lives in predominantly Muslim Sudan to do exactly that. That was their way of demonstrating the love of God to Sudanese of all religions and races. And that became their life mission! Their Christian influence of sacrificial love and humility was so impactful that I often thought of becoming a priest just like them. But not all was easy or simple for them. The Italian Catholic priests and nuns often walked the fine line of being foreign Christian priests in a predominantly Muslim country with finesse and kindness. Throughout the decades, they learned to garnish the respect, support, and trust of many of Sudan's political leaders. As a matter of fact, many of the Italian priests were eventually offered Sudanese citizenship and chose to live and die there!

"Al-Comboni," "Sisters' School," and the other Roman Catholic elementary and middle-school systems in Khartoum offered their top-notch education in English. They had state-of-the-art biology and chemistry labs, science education, sports, Boy Scouts, and extracurricular activities that were unmatched in Sudan. Many who attended CCK before me became doctors, engineers, businessmen, and government officials who helped build and run Sudan. The Italian priests and nuns remained committed to their mission even after many Christian and Muslim Sudanese left the country.

After the strict Islamic Sharia Law became the law of the land in 1983, many Christian and Muslim Comboni-educated students left Sudan. But the Italian Roman Catholic priests and nuns stayed. In a country where military powers and politicians had come and gone, CCK and its school affiliates are still standing. They continue today to teach Sudanese and foreigners of all races, classes, and religions their motto of "Always More, Always Better" and unparalleled education—all without breaking any of the changing strict Islamic religious laws that could limit the rights and freedoms of their Christian faith.

Introduction to America 101

It was most probably the CCK priests who first introduced me and other students to America through the movies. Every Saturday evening, a priest would set up his movie projector in the elementary school's large open-door theater, and with the help of Hussain, one of the priest's favorite Sudanese students, the show would begin. They played clean American movies, after a few cartoons, featuring actors and actresses with foreign names such as John Wayne, Jerry Lewis, and Elizabeth Taylor. They all spoke English with a strange foreign accent that I could not understand. But still, I could not wait for the Saturday night movies. Right after the school day and the Saturday Boy Scouts meeting in the school yard, I would rush across the basketball court to the theater. I was supposed to help in selling tickets and refreshments as a Boy Scout. But what I wanted most was to find the best wooden seat in the house before the movies started.

All that I knew about America back then was that it had an embassy in Khartoum located in a "skyscraper" that Dad had built. Dad designed in the 1960s the two tallest buildings in Sudan at the time. The American Embassy was in one of them, and the other one was home of the "Excelsior Hotel." But apart from that, I had no clue as a child where America was, and who lived there. But that all changed when I saw John Wayne and other cowboys riding horses and shooting bad people and outlaws in the Saturday evening movies at my school.

There was yet another side of America in other movies that I saw in the "Blue Nile Cinema," and "Cinema Coliseum" in Khartoum. There were cars driven at insane, manic speeds chasing others in America's city streets. There were so many beautiful women called "baby," which I assumed was the most common name in America. The women seemed to be naughty and often kissed men (with scenes censored but assumed) whenever asked. That was my "Introduction to America 101."

To me and to some of my friends, America was what Hollywood movies displayed, and what the media told us. It was years later after coming to America that I learned that "baby" wasn't a common American woman's name, and American girls do not randomly kiss strangers. Hollywood's version and portrait of America were not real!

Halfway through the movie, the priest and Hussein would stop the projector. It was time for a brief intermission. To many of us that was the best part of our Saturday night experience. It was time for the all-boy CCK students to see the girls from the all-girls "Sisters' School" in the school's playground. There were smiles, quick innocent chats, winks, and short walks within the fenced school. But those were quickly interrupted by a predictable warning that Hussain and the priest were about to start the second part of the Hollywood movie.

The American Embassy in Khartoum, Our Home, and Malik's Grocery Store

Sometime after my introduction to America through the movies, I saw for the first time an image of the USA flag with two hands shaking each other in front of it. The image was displayed on an oil canister and on a sack of flour sold at Malik's (name changed) local grocery store. The items were sold as premium American products from the United States, which made them a big deal. It was many years later that I learned that the food items came from USAID. The U.S. Agency for International Development (USAID), an American government organization, offered millions of dollars in humanitarian aid to Sudan. That oil canister and flour bag I bought from Malik's grocery store were American products all right but most probably not meant for sale. I wonder how many children starved to death during the civil war waiting for the flour and oil that I and others inadvertently bought.

Seeing the oil and flour from America for needy people in Sudan confused me. The country's media portrayal of America and the Westerners as anti-Islamic did not make sense considering those oil canisters and flour sacks with the American flag. Nor did the millions of dollars that America sent through the USAID organization to Muslim-majority Sudan fit that media narrative. It took meeting American Christian missionaries and hearing about their country and Christian faith, including the concept of America's Judeo-Christian tradition, to know more about America.

The fact that many Muslim countries with money and means to help Sudan, a fellow Muslim country, were not helping, but Americans influenced by the teachings of the Bible were the ones helping, intrigued me. As the days and years passed, I became fascinated by America. I saw her as a faraway foreign country that chose to be kind and generous to total strangers in Sudan. Dad's admiration of an American preacher named Billy Graham, whose books translated in Arabic adorned our home library, only helped to grow my interest in this mysterious country where Christians seemed to thrive.

Gradual Wind of Religious Change at High School

My friends at school included Sudanese of all backgrounds: Syrians, Ethiopians, Tigrayans, Eritreans, Armenians, Indians, mixed races, Copts, Jews, Muslim Northern Sudanese, and Christian southern Sudanese. We all got along well. There were plenty of activities to keep us busy and amused: school sports, Boy Scout events, and schoolwork where I managed to be one of the top students in my classes.

None of my Muslim schoolmates was excessively religious or strict when it came to Islam, except for perhaps one of them. The ultrareligious student led the first ever Muslim Friday prayer at the Catholic school. He and a few other students spread their prayer rugs in the schoolyard at the end of the short school day on a Friday. I have seen a few times our long-term Muslim gardener and security guard from western Sudan praying in front of his room at the back side of our garden. But that Friday in the schoolyard was the first time in my life that I have seen Muslims praying together in public. I wondered why they chose not to pray in a nearby mosque, including King Farouq Mosque, which was only a few blocks away.

The Italian priests' mission went beyond quality education. They also offered the students encouragement, support, and wise advice when a clueless student like me would occasionally ask unexpected questions.

"Father Di Nicolo, Father Di Nicolo, marriage is bad, right? That's why you're not married, right?" I once asked the friendly Italian priest.

I was a fifteen-year-old at the time and had a few vexing questions about God and marriage.

At the time, a new religious group in Khartoum called "Jehovah's Witnesses" was visiting people's homes, knocking on doors, and telling the Christian wives and mothers when their husbands were at work about their beliefs. They told the women who opened their doors, including Mom who once invited them in, about their brand of faith and what "Jehovah" expected of them.

She and other women were made to feel guilty, as Mom recalled, if they did not participate in door-to-door proselytizing. The Jehovah's Witnesses who talked to Mom and the women in her neighborhood believed that the earth was ending in 1975. That was just around the corner, and hence the group's great urgency to knock on doors to spread their beliefs. But soon enough, Mom realized that the core of their beliefs differed and was in opposition to mainstream Christianity.

"They told me 'The church is an adulterer' and said wrong things about Jesus. They started to tell me that no one should get married because the end of the world was about to come in 1975. But then they were all married and had children," she recalled.

To Mom, a devout Christian, who believed in Jesus Christ as the Bible and her parents taught her, the Jehovah's Witness teachings differed from the Christian faith she knew. She regularly worshipped God in church and saw marriage as God's superior design. What she heard from them and was told to do seemed wrong and unacceptable. Consequently, she told Dad about what the Jehovah's Witnesses told her, including their beliefs that education and marriage were not good. She shared with him their belief that there was only a brief time remaining on planet Earth and hence no need for marriage. And that was it. Dad was shocked to hear that, and they both decided not to allow them in our home again.

But by the time my parents stopped communicating with Jehovah's Witnesses, I had been partially exposed to their teaching. They preached that Jesus is not God and described a God who was quite different from the gentle and forgiving Jesus my parents told me about. Jehovah's Witnesses' God seemed so different. To me and many in the neighborhood, including Mom, exposed to their teachings, God was suddenly a fearsome force of anger and vengeance. He was a god who expected nothing but perfection. A demanding power who expected us to knock on neighbors' houses and who hated marriage. We'd been told that 1975 was just around the corner and that God seemed to no longer allow marriages on earth. That was a bummer, I thought.

But the notion of an angry God who was constantly in pursuit of sinners to punish them scared me. That god seemed like a hot-tempered, guilt-tripping, maniacal entity who demanded perfection, which I certainly did not have, and always ready to punish me and the rest of the neighborhood. In addition, the dream of marrying a beautiful woman of my dreams was starting to feel like a guilt-provoking nightmare. It took me a few decades to finally realize that God is always pursuing me but for an entirely different reason—not to punish me, but because He loves me.

Meanwhile, the notion that the end of the world would be happening anytime brought me a curious sense of relief! Theoretically, I no longer had to go to school, study, or do any homework. I luxuriated in that concept.

"Mom, why do I have to go to school if the end of the world is coming in 1975?" I told Mom as she looked at me in disbelief.

Years later, she told me that my question about quitting school made her realize how adversely the teachings of Jehovah's Witnesses were affecting the family. The religious group was told by my parents to never come back to our home soon after I asked that question.

Sensing my confusion about marriage, Father Di Nicolo, who knew me as a Christian student, stopped to listen to me. He gave me the final verdict and answered my vexing question in a quiet hallway in front of the classrooms.

"NO . . . NO . . . NO. *Marriage is a holy sacrament. It's good. God blesses the marriage.*"

The year 1975 came and left but I, the world, and the school were still there. There were still early morning alarms blasting to wake up for school, take tests, and do homework assignments. But on a positive note, thanks to Father Di Nicolo, I celebrated the liberating thought that marriage is still allowed. Maybe one day, I would fall in love, get married, and have children without guilt, fear, or punishment by God. And that sounded refreshing and good.

In 1970s Khartoum, my Muslim friends at school and in my neighborhood of Al-Manshia were fun to be with. None of them ill-treated me because of my Christianity or my family's old Christian heritage. In fact, our religious and cultural differences never stopped us from forming strong and caring friendships.

During the Anglo-Egyptian rule of Sudan, and following Sudan's Independence in 1956, Christian, Jews, and other religious minorities enjoyed a life of tolerance and religious freedom. Many Christians from Tigrayan, Eritrean, Ethiopian, Egyptian, Syrian, Lebanese, Italian, Greek, and Armenian heritages, among others, worshipped in one of the many ethnic community churches in Khartoum.

During my teens in the latter half of the 1970s, a tall, decorated Christmas tree adorned a square close to the presidential palace. The Christian Southern Sudanese could be seen on Khartoum's streets walking in large groups carrying banners celebrating the birth of Jesus! Christmas was truly a joyous time when Christian homes were beautifully decorated, and churches were packed with Christmas Eve crowds. It was the time when Mom's delicious cookies *ka'ak*, *biskawheat*, and *kaik* were baked in abundance and shared with our neighbors.

My Muslim friends celebrated Christmas and the New Year just as much at one of the many international clubs in Khartoum. In those years of religious tolerance and excitement, we could hear disco music and live bands playing during the Christmas and New Year holidays. Music blasted from the Catholic, Arabic, German, Armenian, Syrian, and American clubs. Those were the years when Christian, Muslim, Jewish, and Hindu men and women celebrated Christmas and the New Year together.

In 1983, three years after I left Sudan, the Sharia law was imposed. A lot of my Christian and Muslim friends, including women who experienced new restrictions, felt their rights and freedoms were curtailed. Many of them chose to emigrate elsewhere, or not to return to Sudan from their new homes overseas.

My aunt holding me, posing with Dad, Mom, and siblings somewhere not far away from the Nile.

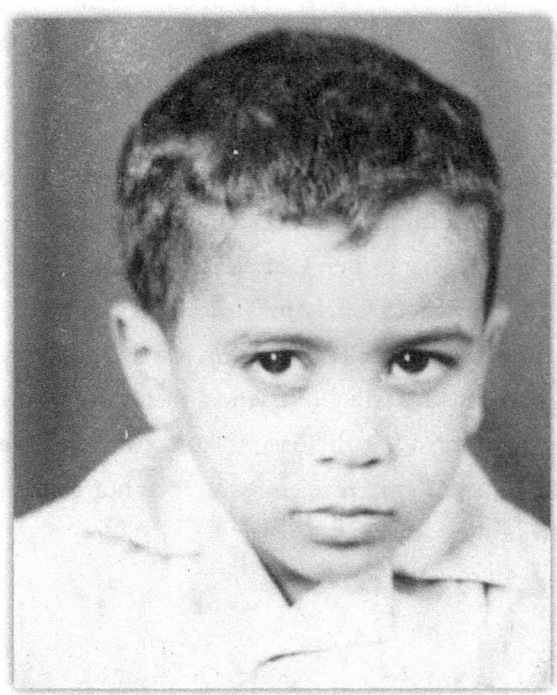

Me as a child. Someone said I look mean but I was just reflecting on my future.

Mom holding me again next to my siblings.

Me as a Boy Scout in front of my room in Al-Manshia.

Mom holding me, posing with my aunt and siblings.

Our second family home in Al-Imtidad. My lifelong friend posing on the right.

Playing my accordion at home with my brothers hoping that I would stop.

Me (posing in front of my older brother on the right), and my siblings.

My School Days at a Catholic School in Muslim Sudan

I always read the newspapers front to back and every article. Someone captured me doing just that.

Our home in Al-Manshia, a short walking distance from the Blue Nile.

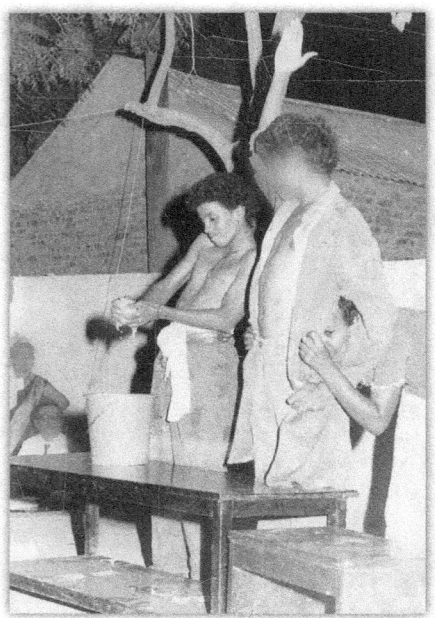 

On stage as potentially an accomplished actor representing my school at the Indian Embassy in Khartoum.

Traveling to Europe as a teenager.

CHAPTER 20

SCHOOL DAYS, CIVIL WAR, AND POLITICAL UNREST

THE BRITISH LEFT SUDAN IN 1956 after granting the country her independence. They left behind many graceful Victorian-style buildings, a functioning railroad system, and a good educational structure. But they also left Sudan after demarcating and establishing the borders between Northern and Southern Sudan. The Northern Sudanese are predominantly Muslim, with light- to dark-brown skin colors, and Arabic is the official language. On the other hand, the Southern Sudanese are mainly Christians and are originally sub-Saharan Africans.

After the British granted Sudan her independence and left for good, the war between the North and South intensified. Sadly, since her independence and for many decades thereafter, Sudan had been in a constant civil war between the North and the South. That finally ended in 2011 when the South gained its independence and formed a new country. In 2023, war erupted again! This time it was between the Sudanese army and a paramilitary group who transformed Khartoum and its suburbs into ruins and a deadly battlefield.

Besides the civil war, another highly predictable thing in Sudan were military coups d'état. Throughout my childhood and teenage years, I recall how a new military government seemed to take over the country every two years or less. All coups seemed to strategically start in Khartoum where the presidential palace and the TV and radio stations were located. The government ministries, the headquarters of the army, and Khartoum International Airport were also located there. That was just a few miles away from my childhood home by the Blue Nile.

Given their frequent occurrences, I became familiar with the predictable routine of military coups. The lone state-controlled TV channel would suddenly stop airing reruns of "I Love Lucy," "Lassie," and "The Invisible Man." Then martial music mixed with recitation of verses from the Koran in Arabic would play ceaselessly. Usually, at the early onset of the coups, the radio would stop broadcasting the public's favorite singers, Abdelhalim Hafez, Om Kolsom, and Mohammed Wardi, among others. Then martial music, readings from the Koran, and announcements regarding the new martial laws and curfews would hit the airwaves. Our family, much like others in Khartoum, would huddle around the radio and TV sets, anxious for news.

"Who is it this time? Who would finally be announced the president of Sudan: a new military coup leader who overthrew the current one, or did the president survive this last coup d'état? How many people died? Is there school tomorrow?" were questions I often pondered on as we waited.

After the new military leader was announced, his victory speech followed, and the martial music would resume. A rerun of the speech would continue most of the day as my parents worried whether it was safe to buy groceries and make it back home before the military curfew started. Unfortunately, the vicious repeating cycle of a coup, followed by a temporary period of peace, and then another coup was common in Sudan.

Military coups were not pleasant. Whether at school or the balcony of our home, I hated the smell of tear gas and the eerie sounds of distant machine guns. I shuddered at the strict military curfew that followed every coup and the military squads that shot anyone suspected of having anything to do with it.

"*What if someone is innocent?*" was what I mostly worried about.

As frequent as military coups were, no one could ever get used to them. Some of the scariest and most confusing moments of my childhood were related to them. I still remember the day Mom kept me hiding under a bed in one of our old houses to avoid the tear gas that was thrown in the surrounding neighborhood. I also remember the moment I was rushed with other young students to an enclosed space in my school where bicycles were parked. Our teacher wanted to save us from the stray bullets and tear gas that were within the vicinity of the school. You just never get used to or forget coups d'état! The instability, loss of peace, uncertainty, violence, and the fears that always came with them were especially hard if you were just a child. I still remember each one of them.

The Beautiful Days in Sudan
"Al-Ayam Al-Jamila"

The 1970s was a decade of joy and fun in Khartoum. We were at the time Christian, Muslim, Jewish, and Hindu Al-Comboni students of all races and colors who created a lifetime of beautiful memories together. We camped as Boy Scouts in Al-Sunut forest at the center of Khartoum by the banks of the White Nile. There we rested under the shadow of the forest's acacia trees near the waters of the Nile praying not to be stung by scorpions. I silently hoped as I swam in the Nile that I wouldn't be touched by an electric catfish that paralyzed swimmers or spotted by an alligator. The heat that easily topped 100° F in the summer felt to me like standing in front of a hot open oven. It was merciless even under the shade of the acacia trees.

But neither the heat, the venomous scorpions hiding under our blankets, or the malaria-causing mosquitoes could deter our fun and joy in the decade of the 1970s. Nor was my sense of bliss curtailed by the long lines of Khartoum's rich and poor waiting in their cars at gas stations or in bread lines during shortages. Even the frequent power outages and those occasions when the tap water looked like Coca Cola, made up from the rich muddy sediments of the great River Nile, did not steal my cheerfulness.

Our CCK school's motto, and Baden Powell's Boy Scouts' motto of "Be Prepared" made us all feel invincible, and unafraid. They made me feel passionate for more in life. I felt ready and prepared to face power outages, the long gasoline and bread lines, malaria, venomous scorpions, and snakes! In the 1970s and early 1980s life in Khartoum was great. Dad and Mom celebrated Christmas in Khartoum in the same Christ-focused way that their forefathers before them had done for centuries. Dad even managed to play with us his favorite childhood's family tradition, the upside-down coffee cup Christmas game. And just like his own dad used to do, he threw a big Christmas party where all the neighbors—Christians and Muslims—were invited.

In essence, all of us, family, and friends, seemed carefree and happy. But, mostly oblivious to the gradual wind of religious and political changes about to happen in Sudan.

Surviving Immunizations, Tropical Disease, and Circumcision in Sudan

Life in Khartoum during my childhood and teenage life in the 1970s was beautiful. Despite the power outages, occasional muddy Nile water in the tap water, and lines for necessities, it was still "the beautiful times." But then, there were tropical diseases, immunizations, and circumcision to survive. Growing up in the capital city Khartoum to a well-to-do family meant receiving good medical care and visits to Doctor Yahia Gamal, our skilled family medicine physician. But having a great family doctor didn't spare me from the dreaded travel vaccinations line. To me, the dreaded line that ended with receiving the painful shots, and getting a Yellow Card filled was one of Khartoum's worst lines. It was long and filled with the dread and worry of what lay ahead. Yellow fever, hepatitis, meningitis, tetanus, and other shots were usually given by a male or female nurse holding a long needle. After a brief sterilization in a watery solution between the shots, the same nondisposable needle seemed to be used on everyone in the line.

That dreaded line and the needle were two necessary evils needed before traveling. Yet, there was another line even worse than the travel vaccination line. The absolute worst of all lines in Khartoum in my view was the short but painfully unforgettable *Al- tahour* (circumcision) line. Fulfilling the unpleasant vaccination requirement of the Yellow Card was easy compared to what awaited me at the front of *Al-tahour* line. I must have been about eight years old when I cluelessly stood in line for that haunting, torturing moment of agony and pain. I walked confidently in my white *jellabiya* (Sudanese traditional dress that I remember wearing just once) not knowing what awaited me. A man with what looked like a sharp deadly blade greeted me as I tensely looked at him. Moments later he finished the agonizing procedure that everyone called *Al-tahour* returning me back to my dad minus a foreskin.

Decades later, I still remember the torturous drive back home. Every bump in Khartoum's Street multiplied my tears and agony as I stood inside the car desperately trying to pull my *jellabiya* away from my bruised body part. Circumcision, an important milestone for Christian, Muslim, and Jewish Sudanese boys was celebrated by some families in a grand style. Newspaper ads announced the solemn occasion, and families felt proud and overjoyed. But my only joy and solace at that time was that I never had to do it again. Never again!

I have no idea how I survived my own *Al-tahour*. But then, I do not know either how I survived the many tropical diseases: cholera, bacterial meningitis, and African sleeping sickness. In many ways, I was truly blessed to only get a few bouts of malaria and ameboid dysentery. Thankfully, Dr. Yahia Gamal and his male nurse diagnosed and treated me after miserable days of fever and untold gastrointestinal suffering. But to me, all the tropical diseases, the power outages, coups, Khartoum's waiting lines, and even the memory of my agonizing *Al-tahour* could never quench the joy of the beautiful times and memories of the 1970s in Khartoum.

CHAPTER 21

FINALLY MEETING DAD'S FAMILY IN EGYPT!

Egypt, only two hours away, always felt like a million miles away. Dad's decision to take Mom, my siblings, and me to Egypt was not an easy one for him. The potential risk of us being rejected or subjected to any skin-color-related bias was always on his mind. He just was not sure how his family in Egypt would treat us. Once he felt reassured enough that we wouldn't be treated by his family inferiorly because of our skin colors, he took me and my siblings in a Cairo-bound plane to meet them. I was nearly a teenager when I met Dad's sister, Rose, and her family in Egypt for the very first time.

Dad's change of heart took some time. I guess, one can say that God transformed his heart in such a way to make him feel peaceful about introducing us to his family.

"*Gobran, the children need to meet your side of the family in Egypt. They don't have any relatives in Sudan,*" Mom used to tell him.

A Change of Heart

Uncertainty about how well we would be received by his family, and worries about whether Mom, my siblings, and me would be rejected, permeated his mind for a long time. Before our first trip to Egypt, he thought for years about Mom's words and considered the benefits of uniting us with his family. But then, he reflected on what he viewed as potential risks of any racial biases we might face. He decided to wait until an opportune time or perhaps a confirmation from God.

Dad's decision to reconsider Mom's suggestion to introduce us to his family happened after what I would consider as divine intervention. According to my Egyptian cousin whom I met years later, no one in Dad's family in Egypt knew that he had a wife and children in Sudan. It was only through a set of unexpected circumstances that his family in Egypt knew about us. Dad's young niece accidentally found out in the early 1960s that Dad was a happily married man in Khartoum. In one of his trips to Europe, he took a plane ride to Italy where his niece lived with her deceased mom's Italian family. He offered to take her with him to Egypt after discerning that she was not happy there and needed to leave. It was during that Egypt-bound trip from Europe that she saw Dad's Sudanese passport. It listed Mom as his wife and their children's names.

"You have a family in Sudan? Why didn't you tell us? Why did you keep them away from us?" she said in utter surprise.

His niece's surprise and dismay that he kept his family in Khartoum away from them was the confirmation and assurance from heaven that he needed. Dad wanted some kind of guarantee that none of us would be discriminated against or made to feel less. His young niece's genuine and caring reaction to her accidental discovery of his family appeared to ease those worries. I can only imagine her surprise and that of Dad's family in Egypt of that unintended discovery. Dad had a large, beautiful, and dark family in Khartoum that he deeply cared about, and they had no idea!

Finally Meeting Dad's Family in Egypt!

Dad was a true pioneer. He did what he believed was right at whatever cost, including having a biracial family of his own in Sudan.

A couple of years after his niece's discovery, my olive-skinned sister was the first to meet Dad's side of the family. She traveled with him for a tonsillectomy surgery in Cairo and met his family there for the very first time. Thankfully, that went well. Dad shared with Mom his sister Rose's reaction when she met my sister for the first time in Cairo.

"She looks like us, Gobran. Why did you keep her from us for so long?" said my aunt Rose.

That was quite reassuring to Dad and Mom. But given my sister's light skin color (she was viewed by some as "the whitest" in the family after Dad!), my dad began to wonder. Would Mom and the rest of the family, all darker in color, be received and accepted just as well as my sister was?

In his society and world where he saw how one's human value was determined by the shade of his or her skin color, Dad worried. But eventually, he decided to take a step of faith and introduce Mom and the rest of the family to his family in Cairo. That was a major milestone for Dad. He believed his role as a loving husband and father included protecting Mom, my siblings, and me from the confusion of prejudice and skin color biases.

Dad's love and deep instinct to protect our family must have touched his sister and other siblings' hearts. To Dad and Mom, it was great that Dad's sister Rose and the rest of his living siblings warmly embraced our family. In a world, culture, and a society with centuries of color barriers, biases, and colorism, Dad and Mom were pioneers, and a breath of fresh air. Aunt Rose, who was Dad's closest sibling, became a pioneer in her own culture and society as well. She and her family fully embraced Mom, the rest of our family, and treated us like family.

For the first time, I was introduced to words that I have never heard or used before.

"Meet your aunt Rose, her husband Kamal, and here are their children: your cousins, Haney, and Magda, your other cousin Ramiz is not here. And here are your uncles George and Mousa."

Aunt, uncles, cousins, "blood relatives" and other terms and descriptions sounded so foreign but so good to me. But what we had in common was more than just "blood." We were all minority Christian families in Sudan and Egypt trying to preserve our faith in predominantly Muslim Sudan and Egypt. Just like us, they were all trying to live in peace and be good friends to their Muslim neighbors. The difference of our skin shades and complexion paled and vanished as I reflected on what was great and common between us.

Many years later as a practicing physician in America, I had similar feelings and reflections whenever I treated patients of a different skin color or race than mine. Biases seemed to always cease when we appreciated the common good between us. My patients' forts and walls of reservation and biases always fell when they knew that I genuinely cared for them. We all have this in common: a desire to be cared for and to be close to those who care for us. Years ago in Cairo, our families, "blood relatives," saw what was common between us: human challenges, hopes, dreams, and yearning to be cared for. And for a moment intergenerational biases began to fade, just as it still does in my medical exam rooms in America.

Dad and Mom saw each other as equal no matter what biases, racism, and colorism they encountered. And that was one wonderful thing I have learned from them in my own journey as a multiracial teenager in Sudan. Their belief in each other's equal value and worth helped me navigate years later America's minefields of racial tension and confusion. Witnessing how they valued, loved, and respected each other taught me to see myself as the final outcome of two beautiful God-created races and cultures that gracefully merged. Much like the equally amazing but different waters of the Blue and the White Niles merging to form the unique River Nile! God knows how much I needed to remind myself of that in my own immigrant journey in America many years later.

My high school Boy Scouts troop in a camp near the Nile.

Same high school friends enjoying the waters of the Nile (or just all of us just showing off).

Swimming in the Nile and jumping with joy with my high school friends. Those were the Beautiful Days.

The last painting I drew in Sudan about a couple of months before coming to America.

CHAPTER 22

THE DAY THE MUSIC STOPPED IN SUDAN: THE DEATH OF WILLIAM ANDREA: THE BEGINNING OF THE END OF THE "BEAUTIFUL DAYS"

> "To everything there is a season, and a time to every purpose under the heaven . . . A time to weep, and a time to laugh; a time to mourn, and a time to dance . . . A time to love, and a time to hate; a time of war, and a time of peace."
>
> Ecclesiastes 3:1,3, 8 KJV

As the writer of Ecclesiastes said, there is a season for everything under heaven. In Khartoum, the beautiful peaceful days of the 1970s, a time to laugh, dance, and love was suddenly interrupted in July 1976. It was replaced by a time to weep, mourn, and hate when Sudan's top basketball star and renowned musician William Andrea was killed.

That was the year the music stopped in Sudan. William Andrea, a Christian Sudanese of *Habasha* and Lebanese heritage, was mourned by Christians and many Muslims alike. Government soldiers armed with loaded Kalashnikov machine guns came to his family's home in Khartoum following a deadly coup d'état in Khartoum. They shot him dead at the doorstep of his home.

William Andrea, known to Sudanese as *Al-gazal al-asmar* (the brown gazelle) wasn't just a well-known basketball star who won top competitions for Sudan. He was an accomplished singer in one of the best-known jazz and pop bands in Sudan. That talented and gifted young man was a source of immense pride and inspiration to all young Sudanese. But particularly young Sudanese Christians, and those with *Habasha* heritage. He was one of us.

To me and my family, William was even more than that. He and his family were more than just friends. We shared common Christian, Ethiopian, Eritrean (*Habasha*), and Levantine roots that bonded us together. We felt like one large family. He would sometimes play for Dad some of his best tunes on his acoustic guitar whenever we visited his family's home or he visited ours. I remember watching with some of my family members William and his band playing on live TV. That was during the opening night of the full-color TV studios of "Sudan TV." We watched him perform on his family's TV his classic song *"Kifaia Misah"* during that big event in Sudan. A few months later, he would be shot dead a few feet away from that TV by the house door.

I will never forget the day I heard of William's death. I was with Mom, Dad, and my siblings in a busy restaurant in Cairo. A close family friend from Sudan visiting Egypt at the time broke the news to us. She didn't know how close we were to him and his family.

"Do you know William Andrea just died? He was killed by soldiers in the coup," she said.

We were all in a state of shock and disbelief. I still recall Mom's deep grief and anguish as she tried to figure out a way to return to Khartoum to be with William's mom and family. Khartoum was at that time in a state of emergency because of the military coup. We had to wait in Cairo until we could get a flight back home.

His execution by the soldiers occurred during one of Sudan's endless coups. The coup against Nimeiri, the military ruler at the time, was blamed on *mourtazaga* (mercenaries). Inexplicably, Eritreans, Ethiopians, and people with William's heritage, known in Sudan as *Habash*, a term often used in a derogatory fashion, were blamed. In retrospect, the killing of twenty-five-year-old William Andrea was emblematic of subtle underlying ethnic and religious generational biases. And that was the condition of the hearts of those who decided to fire their machine guns and kill him.

As soldiers loyal to the military ruler fought against the organizers of the coup, they decided to round up people in Khartoum who looked like "*Habash*." They went to their homes in the city looking for *mourtazaga*. Stories abound from eyewitnesses, friends, and family regarding what exactly happened on July 2, 1976, leading to the death of William, the "brown gazelle."

"*Da bait Habash* (this is the home of Ethiopians and Eritreans)," said a bystander to the soldiers pointing his finger to William Andrea's home according to one account.

The soldiers stopped their truck and with Kalashnikovs in hands knocked on his home door to search for mercenaries. He answered the door and courageously told them that there were women including his sisters in the house and that he did not want them to enter. They mercilessly shot and killed him at the doorstep of his home. William, a natural-born Sudanese citizen who loved Sudan and won top basketball competitions for his country, was gunned down. The beloved young man who happened to be a Christian of Ethiopian, Eritrean, Southern Sudanese, and Lebanese heritage died in the arms of his family. All he wanted to do was to protect his sisters, mother, and family. He died from multiple rounds of machine gun fire without committing any crime. His Christian and *Habasha* heritage seemed to be the only reason the soldiers knocked on his home door, and eventually shot him and silenced his talent, beautiful voice, and music.

The news of his murder that ended the "beautiful days" of the 1970s was not made known to the public after it happened. Nor was it fully investigated. Grievously, the story of his life, contributions to Sudanese music and sports, and the circumstances of his death were silenced and hushed for a long time.

His funeral and burial were done quietly during the coup. A close family friend recalled those events many years later.

"William's funeral and burial was at the Christian Saint Francisco Cemetery. They were only attended by his immediate family and his godfather. The large number of people who wanted to attend his burial couldn't get out of their homes because of the ongoing shooting taking place at the time in the streets of Khartoum. There was no option but to bury him during the coup. We drove on the 'Horia' bridge as the constant piercing sounds of gunshots were heard all around us during the ride and at the burial ground."

Losing William: The Aftermath

The murder of William Andrea affected the psyche of many of my friends irrespective of their religion, culture, or color. The fun, freedom, and general tolerance enjoyed by Sudanese of different religions and skin colors were suddenly interrupted in 1976. To me, and to many of the younger generation in 1970s Sudan, William was the equivalent of Michael Jackson, Elvis Presley, and Michael Jordan combined! He was also "family" who shared with me the same Christian and *Habasha* heritage, the likely reason the soldiers shot him dead at his home.

Following his death, life in Sudan didn't feel as safe and secure as before. It was never the same again. To me, a sixteen-year-old teenager, his killing was akin to the killing of the beautiful days in Khartoum by a weapon called hate. It felt to me like an ominous sign of probable future ethnic and religious suppression and of worse things to come. Seven years after William Andrea's killing, the Islamic Sharia law was instituted in Sudan.

CHAPTER 23

AMERICA: THE INTRIGUING AND PUZZLING LAND

M<small>Y EARLY IMPRESSION OF AMERICA</small> and Americans wasn't just shaped by the Saturday night movies at my Roman Catholic school, CCK. I was also informed, or more accurately indoctrinated, about America from many of the Arabic newspapers sold in newsstands in Khartoum. Often, printed words like imperialism, Zionism, corruption, and immorality were used to describe the cultures and politics of America and other western countries. To add to the mix, a few of my good and more informed friends enlightened me further about this puzzling place called America.

"You know Americans think Africans live in trees like monkeys and eat bananas. They call people from Africa 'monkeys' and tell them to go back to Africa. But they like people who look like Michael Jackson who say things like 'hey man . . . hey baby . . . and get down.'"

Some of them resorted to creating imaginary stories of an older Sudanese student who moved to America years before and became something of a legend.

"Do you know Maeiz? He moved to America and bought a Chevrolet car. He drives American style and makes the sand blow from the rear tires. He even got an American job."

My own hypothesis of America at the time was that of a wild and vast country where American Christians donated food and money to help a country like Sudan. A country where Americans drove their Chevrolet cars like maniacs, and occasionally and randomly shot at each other. I also surmised (based on my movie analysis) that America is a country where all women were pretty; mostly skinny, blonde, and blue-eyed; easily fell in love; and always ready to be kissed by men.

By comparison to my teenage fanciful knowledge of America, I was clueless about the history of slavery in America and the racial problems there. I must have either been asleep or skipped my high school history lesson about that dark history in America. But perhaps that was not as emphasized as the region's more pertinent history of European colonization of Africa and Sudan.

The short film clips that I saw on the lone government-controlled TV channel were what opened my eyes to the deep racial divide between Blacks and whites in America. They showed troubling images and videos of racial riots from the mid-1960s. There were high-pressure water hoses aimed at Black Americans and snarling dogs chasing after them. I saw a side of America that I had never seen before and never thought existed.

What I saw looked so disturbing and awfully wrong. In the American movies that I saw in the 1970s, Black people in America were very cool like Sidney Poitier. The images of Black Americans blasted by high pressure water hoses and chased by vicious dogs looked so humiliating and undignified compared to the cool image of Sidney Poitier. It was after seeing those film clips that I began to read more about America's history of slavery. My reaction to that inexplicable history was utter disbelief. As a teenager, I could not comprehend the cruelty, ignorance, racism, and narcissism of slavery. What in the world could ever justify the evil abuse and enslavement of a fellow human by another in America, Africa, and throughout the world? Nothing but evil is what I could think of back then as a teenager, and now as an adult.

America's Fascination

Most Sudanese in the 1970s were generally fascinated by all things that sounded and looked American. The fascination with America extended to almost everything American but mostly music. My older brother and his childhood friend William Andrea grew sideburns just like Elvis Presley. On the other hand, my circle of friends and I loved the music of the Jackson 5, Michael Jackson, the Bee Gees, ABBA, John Denver, and some liked Isaac Hayes. Mr. Hayes, who was rumored to be coming to Khartoum for a concert, was awaited with great excitement and anticipation. But to everybody's dismay his concert got canceled. The reason given to the many folks who dreamt of experiencing a touch of America in Khartoum was something like: *"The electric power in the city couldn't handle his musical equipment."*

The American Marines guarding the American Embassy in Khartoum intrigued me with their uniforms and how Black and white marines seemed to get along amazingly well. That was so unlike the video images of white policemen chasing Black men and women with their dogs. That was encouraging and good to see.

"Could the relationship between Blacks and whites in America be better than what I saw on TV?" I wondered.

Dad and my older brother were also very fascinated by America. America to Dad was like an important person or entity to be liked, respected, and appreciated. Gradually, I learned to see America through my parents' and my older brother's eyes: a fascinating country of opportunities where people enjoy freedom and prosperity. After the killing of William Andrea, America's fascination to me was not just about the movies, colorful Marine's uniforms, music, Elvis Presley, the Jackson 5, or Michael Jackson. More important to me, the safety, peace, and security that America enjoyed suddenly became the most fascinating and alluring blessing that it could offer.

Missionary to America?

As I approached my thirteenth birthday, I recall going through a period of deep soul-searching. I began to reflect on my life's plan and purpose. I always had an inner deep sense that I was created to do something significant with my life, to help others, and perhaps to medically treat my family whenever they needed a doctor. But *"what plan does God have for my life?"* I wondered.

It was at that time of prayers and soul-searching that something quite unexpected happened. My prayers were answered in the most unusual way through a ship named *Logos* that arrived at Port Sudan harbor on the Red Sea. The year was 1973. Shortly after docking, its crew members set up a large book fair in the capital city of Khartoum. I remember standing next to my dad in line waiting to enter the book fairgrounds. I loved books and could not wait to buy a comic book translated to Arabic and nonfiction books that would not be found anywhere else in Khartoum.

At the time, I did not know much about the ship except that it was a Christian organization that transformed its ship into a floating bookstore and traveled to different ports in the world. They were selling at a cheap price great educational and Christian books including my favorite comic books that could not be found in the city. The *Logos* ship was operated by a Christian group called OM International, who believed in sharing the love of God to people of all races and cultures. They did that through selling great educational, wholesome, and Christian books they carried in their ship at bare minimum prices.

The staff and crew of the ship, made up of volunteers from multiple countries, lived for extended periods in the ship and traveled from one port to another. In 1973 in Khartoum, they transported thousands of books from Port Sudan where the ship *Logos* docked and opened the book fair to the Sudanese public. The crew of *Logos* also shared their Christian faith with songs and skits in one of Khartoum's large theaters. That was possible in Khartoum back in the 1970s when open-mindedness and religious tolerance prevailed.

Sadly, in 1988, the same *Logos* ship that came to Sudan in 1973 and to hundreds of other ports, ran aground and sank in extreme weather in South America. Miraculously all its crew were saved. The ship was replaced by the Christian charitable organization OM that operated it. A new ship continues to travel the world today, as a floating library, sharing the love of God to natives of many countries through religious and educational literature.

Being an avid reader, I would not have missed the book fair for the world. I had to be there. Dad, a fellow book lover, agreed and patiently waited in line with me and the thousands of Sudanese on the fair's opening day.

The moment the fair opened its doors, I rushed in. I was like a kid in a candy store running from one table of books to another. I was loading up with all the Arabic-translated comics (Superman, Batman, Tan Tan, and Mickey Mouse) that my small arms could carry. After picking up too many comics, I began looking at the science, geography, and other interesting books on display. It was at that moment that my eyes fell on a book that changed the course of my life.

That book was God's answer to the prayers of a nearly thirteen-year-old teenager desperately looking for a meaning and purpose for his life. It was a story about a Christian missionary doctor from America. He left the comfort of his suburban home in America and used his medical skills to help people in the remotest regions of the world. Driven by deep passion for his Christian faith, he faced countless dangers and hardships as he treated perfect strangers of a different race and culture than his.

I purchased the book and was captivated. Every page of the book absorbed me. As I held the book, there was an inexplicable conviction and an unfathomable certainty in my soul of my life purpose and plan. A deep sense of assurance that I could only describe as a divine inner, silent voice overwhelmed me. *"I will be a missionary doctor. In America,"* became my life's clear divine calling. That conviction became my new life direction at the conclusion of the *Logos* book fair and for the years to come.

After my encounter with the American missionary doctor's book, the sense of purpose and my life's mission to be a doctor in America continued. My parents were quite happy to hear about my dream of being a doctor. But going to America to be a physician was a totally different story.

As I got closer to finishing high school, Dad worried. His personal experience decades ago in Egypt where he was denied a promotion and a bonus because of his Christian faith made him worry. Dad was anxious that my Christian family name could be used to deny me admission into a university in Khartoum. He was pleased that I wanted to be a doctor and was ready to send me to a good school overseas to pursue that. But America! That was just too far away.

Mom, on the other hand, with her adventurous streak of crossing Sudan's border in her early teens, was much easier to convince. She was eventually able to convince Dad as well. After the death of William Andrea in 1976, it was overall easier for Dad to agree. He and Mom began to worry about the safety and security of their children, much like many other families in Sudan. They finally agreed together to send me to America, and I had their full blessing.

Many of my friends were shocked to hear about my decision to go to America for my college education. Most of them planned to go to Great Britain for their undergraduate and master's degrees. Others received scholarships from Eastern European communist countries at the time such as Poland, Romania, East Germany, and Russia. But America! It was back then like a movie, a fantasy, and a dream that was hard to come true. Being a doctor in America was just one of those impossible dreams that was hard for everyone to believe could come true.

Yet somehow, I could not waver from the path that I had started. It felt like I was immune to criticism, negative thinking, and any discouraging remarks about how "impossible" it was for me to be a doctor in America. I believed it was God's calling for my life to go to America and accomplish that dream. I was clueless as to how and what was needed to be a doctor in America. But at that time and season of my life, I just innocently believed and trusted, without knowing the "how?" that God would make that possible. In less than two decades after visiting the *Logos* ship book fair and purchasing a book that convinced me of my life mission, I graduated from an American medical school with an MD degree.

Undergraduate Education in America
"Goin' Back to Indiana," Michael Jackson & The Jackson 5

Soon after I convinced my parents of my plan to be a doctor in America, I ran into a dilemma. I knew from a geography class that there were fifty states in America. I had to choose an undergraduate college in one of those states, but how would I know which one to choose? Luckily, I knew one state well, or that's what I thought, thanks to Michael Jackson. As a child I often heard Michael Jackson singing my favorite song *"Goin' Back to Indiana."* I concluded that since Michael Jackson sang so fondly about it, Indiana must be one of the best states in America. I even wondered if it would be possible to spot him there. And so, Indiana it was! Once I made my decision, I went to the American cultural center in Khartoum, a short distance away from my high school, and asked for a list of undergraduate colleges in the state of Indiana.

"Here's the book that includes all the accredited colleges and universities in America. This is the section that lists the universities in Indiana," said the clerk as he placed a heavy, voluminous book on my table.

"What! A whole big book for colleges in America and all these pages just for colleges and universities in Indiana! You can't be serious," I wondered silently.

I was expecting one or perhaps a couple of universities, just like in Sudan at the time, to choose from. The book stated that all the universities listed were accredited which I assumed to mean all are good and reliable. *But which one should I pick? How do I know which one is the best for me?* The clerk was not offering me any solutions. There was no such thing as a high school academic counselor at the time, and definitely no one around me knew anything about American higher education. The American movies I saw on Saturdays were about cowboys, fast cars, and falling in love, but nothing about the colleges there. Personal computers, smartphones, Google, and school websites did not exist back then. I had to rely on word of mouth, but no one had any word to say about the American universities.

I felt lost, confused, and puzzled. I was not sure what to do next. I decided to pray. As I closed my eyes, a thought occurred to me. What if I ran my index finger down the long list of colleges and universities in Indiana and picked the university that my finger pointed at when I randomly reopened my eyes? I did exactly that, and my index finger landed on a private liberal arts college. The small college happened to be affiliated with one of the major Christian Protestant churches in America. I never heard of the name of the denomination before, but being part of a church must be a good thing, I concluded. I wrapped up my pre-Google era brief and limited research, and went home to tell Dad and Mom about my final decision. Of course, I did not tell them about my unconventional method of choosing the university in Indiana. But thankfully, they were relieved that it was affiliated with a major church in America and gave me their blessing.

Finally, Undergraduate Acceptance in Indiana!

It was a hot sunny afternoon at our home in the Khartoum suburb of Al-Manshia when Dad handed me an envelope with American stamps on it. It was from the small college in Indiana that I picked offering me admission to their freshman class. It was my acceptance letter! I remember jumping in the air a few times before I landed on the floor to read the acceptance letter for a few more times. But soon after the euphoric joy of reading my admission letter subsided, I began to feel mixed emotions. I felt fear, sadness for leaving home, and experienced what an American college student would call a "freaking out" moment.

The reality began to sink in. I was about to leave for good my bedroom, our family dog, turtle, pet monkey, cactus, mango, and guava trees. Pursuing my dream in America meant leaving behind my childhood home by the Blue Nile, my parents, siblings, friends, and Sudan, the country of my birth. I felt the heavy burden of abandoning forever all that was dear to me and wandering into the unknown awaiting me in America.

A few months after receiving my acceptance letter, I was surrounded by my family and a few large bags at Khartoum's main airport. I said goodbye to my parents, siblings, and friends fighting back the tears. I wondered as I boarded my long international flight to London and then America if I would ever see my family or return to Khartoum again.

That was my last time in Sudan. The Sharia law became the law in Sudan a few years after I took my first and last flight from Khartoum to America. As the conditions deteriorated in Sudan, many of my Christian, Muslim, and Jewish friends eventually began their own exodus to Western countries. Many Christians, especially women, felt like second-class citizens, and scores of Christians and Muslims migrated in search of peace and freedom.

During the long flight to America there was nothing but time to think, ponder, and reflect on my life, and those I left behind. Dad's wise words of advice and Mom's prayers before I left Khartoum came to mind.

"Ya Ebnee (my son), be careful and focus on your studies. Girls in America will come knocking on your door but don't open the door. I am sending you to America to be a doctor. Be diligent and don't let anything distract you from your school. Devote yourself to school like you devote yourself to God (but always put God first). Send us letters to assure us that you are doing well and if you need anything."

Many decades after Dad immigrated to Sudan from Egypt in search of a better life, and years after Mom crossed the borders of Sudan as a teenager in search of a job in Khartoum, I did something similar. I followed in their footsteps. It was my turn as a teenager to leave Sudan, the country of my birth, to go to America, the land of my childhood dreams. Much like my parents, grandparents, and ancestors, I was going to a new unknown land with nothing but faith, hope, and a dream.

At home. Ready for my American adventure.

PART FOUR

FINALLY, AMERICA

★ ★ ★

CHAPTER 24

COMING TO AMERICA: FEAR AND DIVINE INTERVENTION

It was early September morning when the British Airways transatlantic flight from England landed in New York. JFK International Airport looked busy and overwhelming! It didn't look at all like Khartoum International Airport with its one terminal. I felt lost and confused. As soon as I disembarked from the plane, I noticed policemen with handguns dangling from their belts. They reminded me of the revolvers that cowboys used in those western movies that I often watched at my Catholic high school. I have never seen one so close before. I wondered if it would be safe to walk close to them and if they would readily use those weapons like in the movies.

As I advanced on the "Only noncitizens" line leading to the U.S. Customs, I was anxious about what would happen next. My heart began to race as I held tightly to my Sudanese passport and the I-20 acceptance document from the university. That was the first time encountering Americans in America and not in the safety of the movie screen or my childhood home. I did not know what to expect. Worries and anxieties rushed through my mind.

"Are they going to tell me to go back to Africa? What if someone starts shooting? Are there any groups like the KKK at the airport? I miss my family and want to go back home."

But much to my surprise, the American customs officer gave me a warm welcoming smile, calming my fears. His friendly smile was the assurance that I desperately needed. I could not understand his foreign American accent and whether he was telling me to sit, stand, or go. But his smile as he began to stamp my passport was all that I needed.

Passing through customs was the last hurdle to overcome at JFK before claiming my many colorful pieces of luggage. That was it! I was finally in America, the land of fast Chevrolet cars, skyscrapers, cowboys, romance, Michael Jackson, and where my dream of being a doctor will come true. I felt like I was in a dream that was unfolding before my very own eyes.

There I was, with my Afro hair style at JFK. I worked hard using my African-designed Afro comb (some friends suggested using *"Abu Jamal"* Sudanese beer to transform my soft, curly hair to kinky hair for a better Afro) to make my hair look like Michael Jackson's. With an Afro as large as my head, I was ready to conquer America with big dreams, and lots of fears. I tried to hold on to faith even as worries and uncertainties filled my mind.

"What if I can't be a doctor? What if I fail? How would I be treated by whites in America who don't like my skin color?"

The only certainly I felt amid the fears was that I was in America to be a doctor. My only hope was to gather up courage and charge forward despite my doubts and fears. I had to believe that I wasn't alone, but that God was with me just as He was with my parents. I reasoned that everything great, like my dream, must have a long and scary road that needs courage to travel and accomplish; so, help me God!

Soon after I got through the U.S. Customs, I found myself aimlessly wandering in the mega airport. I was basically lost. It was about three in the morning by the time I claimed my baggage. I was starving, tired, sleepy, and desperately looking for a pay phone. Mercifully, I had a close family friend who lived with her American husband in Manhattan. I had her phone number with me, and all that I needed was to find a pay phone and call her to pick me up. But when I finally found one, all that I could do was to hold the receiver and ponder. I read the instructions and what coins were needed to make the call happen. But which one of the coins in my hand was a quarter, dime, or a nickel. I was holding on to the precious phone receiver but had no idea how to make it work.

Miraculously, just as I started to feel desperate, a young, attractive woman, whom I later learned is considered a Latina in America, approached me with a big friendly smile on her face. Two women accompanied her.

"Hi, my name is Olivia. This is my mother and here's my sister . . . Do you need any help?"

She must have assumed that I was a foreigner from Africa who just arrived by plane and was probably lost. She was right. Olivia walked in between the large suitcases surrounding me and got closer to me. God knows, I desperately needed help. Worn out and sleepy at 3:00 a.m. with a pay phone in my hand demanding to be fed American coins with strange names: quarters, dimes, and nickels; I needed a sign from above. That was when Olivia suddenly showed up like an angel from heaven.

"What's your name? Where are you from? I'm originally from Honduras. We were born there," she said pointing at her mom and sister.

"Let me show you. This a quarter . . . here's a nickel and the small one is a dime. So, what brings you to New York?"

"My name is Adel . . . pronounced 'Aadill.' I'm from Sudan. I came to America to go to college in Indiana . . . I am going to be a doctor."

Olivia told me how fascinated she was that I ventured to America to be a doctor. She helped me with the phone call and waited for my family friend to answer. After three attempts of calling without an answer, Olivia talked in Spanish to her mom, and then called a number. Shortly after that, a young man showed up and Olivia introduced him as her fiancé.

"It would be safer if he drives you to the address of your family friend in Manhattan. You wouldn't know where to go if a cab takes you there and you can't find your friend," she said in a tender, caring voice.

Her parting words to me as I left the airport with her fiancé were encouraging. They almost sounded divinely inspired and proved to be prophetic. I remembered Olivia's words, a beautiful soul who performed a random act of kindness to a total stranger, for many years to come. I believe they became a source of inspiration that God has used to encourage me. Years later, when my dream of becoming a doctor in America seemed so hard, and I wanted to give up, Olivia's words to me on my very first day in America consoled and energized me.

"Don't ever give up. Don't be discouraged. You will go to medical school in America and be a great doctor."

It was as if God was talking through her to assure me that my dream of becoming a doctor in America would one day come to pass. God knows, the road to be traveled between not knowing what coins to use to operate a pay phone in New York's JFK to being a doctor in America was a long one. I needed all the uplifting, cheering, and motivation to finish that journey.

Lost in America

Olivia's man did exactly what he promised her to do. He took me to my family friend's apartment in Manhattan by early dawn. My family friend, a soft-spoken Christian Sudanese with Lebanese and *Habasha* heritage, was shocked to know that I trusted a total stranger in New York to give me a ride so early in the morning. She lived in an expensive neighborhood in one of Manhattan's high-rise buildings and seemed overwhelmed by her life in the city.

"It's not like back home where I felt welcome in my neighborhood and knew all my neighbors well."

She shared with me her deep grief about the death of William Andrea that occurred nearly four years earlier. Her wounds were still so fresh and brought back the sad memories of William's tragic killing.

"Al-khouaf raba eialo (*the one who fears and is not courageous will live to nurture his own children*)," she repeated the phrase as she reflected on his gruesome death.

I could not grasp the depth of her words at the time, but as I processed William's life and sudden death in the years to come, I understood what she really meant. William Andrea lived courageously and unafraid. He did not live long enough to have children of his own because of his courage. How wrong was that? How sad we both felt.

She also talked about the loneliness that many felt in Manhattan.

"*The woman in the apartment facing mine has never visited me. She has lived here for years. We only say 'hi' to each other and go our way,*" she said.

America, Land of My Dreams, also was a place where people felt lonely, at least in Manhattan, where neighbors did not know each other.

"*Everyone is busy here and rushing all the time. All my neighbors see their therapists after work to help them cope with life,*" she said, sounding sad and overwhelmed.

I stayed for a few more days in Manhattan in the high-rise apartment that she shared with her American husband and took walks in the busy city praying not to be mugged. I was mostly in a daze as I walked the streets of New York. There was an endless flow of people of all colors and races that appeared to speedwalk all day long. I felt thankful to God that I miraculously chose an undergraduate university in Indiana and not in New York. In my brief stay in New York, I managed to suffer a cultural shock and to shock a frail, elderly white woman standing in a bus that I was riding. I got off my seat and offered it to her. She appeared shocked.

"*Thank you, young man. You must not be from New York,*" she said with a surprised look on her face as she sat down.

Following my brief stay in New York City, I took a plane to Jacksonville, North Carolina, to visit my sister who just moved there. My plan was to spend a couple of days before heading to Indiana to start college. Soon after the plane landed, I walked outside the airport and enjoyed the beauty of the palm trees and the sunny weather of Jacksonville, which reminded me of Khartoum. I patiently waited for my sister to pick me up. But after a long wait, I decided to return to the terminal to call my sister to remind her that she had forgotten about me. As soon as I entered the terminal, I heard my name called on the overhead intercom.

"Mr. Hanna, please see an airline ticket agent."

I walked to the airline ticket agent still not sure if it was my name that was just called.

"Excuse me. I am 'Aadill' Hanna did you just call my name?"

"Yes, I did. Someone called us from New York and told us you took the wrong plane to Jacksonville, Florida, instead of Jacksonville, North Carolina. We booked you on the next flight to Jacksonville, North Carolina," he said looking at my puzzled face. Before 9/11, oddities like that must have been possible by someone like me who wasn't used to cities in one country having the exact same name.

"Well, at least it wasn't my sister's fault. She didn't forget about me. I just went to the wrong state," I reasoned as I realized that she couldn't be blamed for failing to pick me up.

The sad reality that I couldn't figure out yet how to not get lost in America's streets, cities, and states bothered me. Somehow, someway, I needed to adapt quickly. I needed to find my way and learn how to survive in America if I ever wanted my dream of being a doctor to become a reality. Waiting for my sister in the wrong Jacksonville and in the wrong state seemed like a step (or a plane ride) in the wrong direction. To pursue and accomplish my God-given dream of being a doctor in America, I needed to do better. I figured out that I needed to start with these two baby steps: knowing the difference between nickels and dimes and the existence of at least two Jacksonville cities, one in Florida and the other in North Carolina.

Coming to America with an Afro hair like Michael Jackson and a dream.

My early days in America, reflecting on my future.

CHAPTER 25

UNDERGRADUATE YEARS: CULTURAL CHALLENGES AND CONFUSION

To MANY IN THE STUDENT BODY at my first university in America, I was an object of curiosity. A lot of the students in the small liberal arts college never ceased to wonder about *"how in the world did you know about this small college in Indiana all the way from Africa?"* I could not blame the students because most of them didn't hear about the college either, until their high school counselors told them about it. I decided not to tell them about how I ended choosing the school when my index finger landed on it. Nor did I tell them that I chose Indiana because of The Jackson 5's "Goin' Back to Indiana."

There were only three students from Africa in the university, including myself, each with a strange and fascinating story of how we ended up there. To our pleasure, we were all treated exceptionally well by the administration, including dinner invitations to the vice president and the biology professor's homes. The small liberal arts college made me and the other two African students feel like two kings and a queen. In retrospect, it turned out to be a God-sent place that provided me with an opportunity to know and experience America in a sheltered, caring, and safe environment. Even after moving out of the school dorms to an apartment off campus, the school librarian, Ms. Wilson, did not forget me.

"Oh dear, now that you are not eating in the school cafeteria make sure to eat balanced meals."

God knows how much I needed that outflow of love and compassion. I needed that to combat the sense of being lost, lonely, and the insecurity that engulfed my freshman year in America. Walking on campus and in downtown Indianapolis with an exaggerated version of Michael Jackson's Afro and bell bottom jeans earned me curious looks. I stuck out like a sore thumb, looked and sounded different, and felt like a true alien. Those were the days when folks like me coming to America from faraway countries were called aliens. That description probably fit me quite well, especially in my first year in college when I felt lost and very alienated.

But then, halfway through my freshman year, I became increasingly fascinated by the rights and freedoms that Americans enjoyed. To me, it was a new experience to live in a society where everyone can freely express his and her beliefs. Interestingly, students spoke and shouted their views without being threatened, jailed, or killed by some kind of government intelligence agency. Intrigued by these freedoms, I found myself seizing this opportunity and becoming a staff writer for the university's newspaper. I authored articles comparing the relationships between the sexes in Sudan and in America, and about race relations in America. I even wrote essays in the paper criticizing the apathy of the university students for not showing interest to vote in the American election of 1980. But, to my astonishment, I was not sanctioned. Nor was I harmed, threatened, or arrested. Freedom of expression was real and permissible without reprisals, at least in 1980 America, and that felt wonderful!

Surviving Campus Life and American Students 101

I remember how caring and friendly the school administrators were. But dealing with the students was not easy or predictable. Compared to the Americans who visited our family home in Sudan, many of the students behaved strangely on campus. The white American students on campus varied in their views and interactions when it came to me and the two other African students. Some fully embraced us, some were nice but chose to keep their distance, while a few others seemed to be overtly prejudiced. I was told by someone that those in the last group were considered *"rednecks who might belong to the Ku Klux Klan* aka KKK." Another person wanted me to be careful because a certain city in Indiana was supposedly where many of the KKK gathered. That turned out to be a bluff that kept me on my toes throughout my freshman year. I worried about the risk of meeting the KKK when I first came to America. The potential possibility that they existed nearby added an additional layer of worries to my American journey.

Despite the college's affiliation with a church, the students differed in their level of moral standards. Many seemed committed to schoolwork and Bible study groups. Meanwhile, a few others were in college to have sex and brag about it. At least that was what appeared to be my white roommate's primary motivation for pursuing higher education. Rick (not his real name) was a sandy-brown-haired, blue-eyed, overweight white student with a foul mouth. I was assigned to be his roommate by a nice college administrator who hoped to introduce me to American life and culture with a roommate like Rick.

But the cultural education about freedom in America and its greatness did not go too well with Rick. The only sense of freedom in America that he showed me was his liberal use of a barrage of foul language with an American accent, which I mostly could not understand. His celebration of sexual freedom in America was also quite pronounced. Rick's study desk in our dorm room was adorned with an assortment of women's underwear hanging on a string or wire that looked like a clothesline. That reminded me of our wet clothes drying line in the backyard of our home in Khartoum. All what I could think of was: *"Why in the world would he hang used underwear on his study desk?"* Noticing my confusion as I looked at his desk, he boastfully explained the significance of his women's underwear collection. The best I could understand from his American accent was his insinuation that those undergarments were from girls that he allegedly had sex with.

"Why would American girls give their underwear to someone like Rick? Why did he ask for them in the first place, and how would that help him to focus on his schoolwork and pass his exams?" I pondered.

Another student, Joe (name changed), a friendly, older, white roommate assigned to me during the summer of my first year, had his own idiosyncrasies. He shared with me how to easily own furniture on campus for free, plus a few other peculiarities.

"Why buy anything? These spoiled kids throw away at the end of the spring all the crap in their dorm rooms. They leave it in the basement floors of their dorms. You will find everything here, bookcases, desks, and textbooks, all in great shape. They even throw their dirty magazines there at the end of the school year. They don't want Mommy and Daddy to see their porno trash."

I thought Joe was joking until he showed me about what he was talking. I saw him running from one dorm basement to another. He was rummaging through piles that resembled some of the garbage piles in certain neighborhoods in Khartoum. Joe began digging deeper and deeper in the piles exposing what he viewed as treasures. There were old pictures, books, food barely eaten, furniture, and buried stacks of pornographic magazines that were no longer needed.

Equally interesting was another student who for some strange reason decided to scream at the top of his voice from the roof of his house dorm. He was screaming all types of American obscenities that could not be found in an English dictionary. His audience was the whole dorm occupants, armed police officers, and firemen watching from below. They all seemed to agree that "the kid is high." I agreed with them that the student was high up on the roof but why was he shouting from the high roof. Later, I came to understand that he was not just physically high on the roof. He was in a delirious, hallucinogenic bad trip, called a "high," caused by a psychedelic drug. *"He used LSD,"* said the firemen who were busy trying to convince him not to jump down.

Introduction to America's Racial Minefields, Football, and Music 101

My baptism by fire in America's messy race relations came during my first year in college. I was no longer watching on TV, from the safety of my childhood home in Khartoum, scary stories about racial prejudices in faraway America. I was now here!

In my first year at the university, I remember thinking about the unsettling notion that the ancestors of some of the white students on campus might have been slave owners. Some of their ancestors might have literally owned, much like owning properties, furniture, cars, or horses, some of the ancestors of the Black American students. It was a perplexing thought that led me to wonder, *"How would I feel if I were born in America as a Black American, and not as an African whose ancestors were not enslaved? How would I view the white students, and deal with them if that was the case? And how would the white students view me and interact with me?"*

In my first year in Indiana, questions and thoughts about race and slavery filled my mind. I reflected on the wounds, and the evil, destructive aftermath of one human race assuming superiority and enslaving another race. Wounds that are so hard to heal be it in America, Africa, or elsewhere. Why should any white or light-skinned person continue the centuries-old wrong and prideful belief of feeling superior because of his or her skin color? This destructive belief caused slavery in America and throughout the world. It caused racial injustice, apartheid, and human genocides for centuries and still destroys, wounds, and hurts today. I also wondered about how long should the old wounds, disrespect, and injustices, caused by any white students' ancestors, remain open in the hearts of the Black students? Would there be a new page where this past could no longer affect the future between Black people and white? The Black and white marines I knew in Khartoum got along together so well. Would that happen in America too?

In truth, those questions and reflections about the topic of race in America preoccupied my heart and mind for many years after coming here. The answers to my many introspections came from reflecting on my own parents' black-and-white, love-and-marriage story, and my own journey as a multiracial teenager. Dad and Mom individually left their home countries hoping and praying for a better life in Sudan. They met, fell in love, and got married because they saw the beauty of each other's soul and character. What their white and Black contemporaries or ancestors said, did, suffered, or caused others to suffer did not affect or hinder at all their personal love, companionship, and marriage.

Mom and Dad chose to be forgiving, and not to dwell on the past. They did not believe that either one of them should pay for the evil sins of their ancestors or contemporaries. Nor did they subscribe to living as wounded or enraged people because of any racial or religious wounds and hurts any of their ancestors had suffered, or their contemporaries were suffering from. As a Black-and-white couple, they believed in humility, new beginnings, letting go of the past, and offering forgiveness to those who wronged them. They were both determined to follow the way of Jesus in their lives, and live life to the fullest. Thankfully, they chose to be light and salt to each other, me, my siblings, and to those around us. Truthfully, I don't think I could have navigated America's complex and confusing racial issues and survived many of its battlefields without their good example.

It took me some time in Indiana to understand what the racial slurs and foul language exchanged between students or those targeted at me meant. In retrospect, my blissful ignorance kept me happy and peaceful on those occasions when I heard a racial slur directed at me. On one occasion, a white male student whom I did not know, decided to spontaneously give me the middle finger and call me the N-word. I was peacefully sitting in a study room at my dorm when he decided to stop by the door to offer his finger gesture combined with the N-word.

At the time, I had zero clue what either one of them meant. I assumed his gesture was an American peace sign and he was probably greeting me with his foreign American accent with words I could not comprehend. But he was not smiling, which made me a little suspicious of his intentions. I thanked him and wished him well too. Little that I knew, the student was probably what some Americans described as a "racist red redneck." It was very much later that I understood what the N-word meant and that his finger was not waving an American peace sign!

That combo of the middle finger and the N-word, plus the few occasions when young white men in speeding cars would hit the horn, shout, and imitate the sounds and gestures of a monkey as they drove past me, did not bother me when they happened. It took me some time to understand what they were doing and why they were doing it. Their words and gestures were meant to be degrading and to convey to me that I was less, inferior, and much like an African monkey. I always loved monkeys, played with my pet monkey in Khartoum, ate a lot of bananas, and never saw myself as a monkey or inferior to others. I did not care much about their words and gestures, which were meant to insult me. But how terribly hurtful and insulting, I thought, they would be to a Black American man or woman whose ancestors were once enslaved, bought, sold, and treated as inferior.

Thank God, most of the white students were not like that. They were curious, lacking knowledge about all things African, and with inner confusion and biases about race and color, much like most of us.

Soon after the N-word and the middle finger incident, I was told that my white roommate Rick wanted his friend, a white student, to move in with him. I was assigned to a different all-male dorm with Elijah (name changed), a Black American roommate. I figured out that someone in charge of moving students to different dorms must have rightly assumed that Rick was not yet ready for a dark African foreign student. I did not shed any tears for leaving Rick and his clothesline of hanging women's underwear. I thanked the one who rescued me, took my heavy bags, and ran to my new room.

Elijah, my new roommate, was friendly and very curious about my African heritage. He was on the school football team. American football didn't look at all like the football I used to play in Sudan, which Americans called "soccer." Seeing almost all of the student body going through the ritual of heading every weekend to the stadium to watch Elijah and his teammates play "football" was a unique experience. The strange-looking gear he and his teammates wore as they smashed into each other was one of my many reminders that I was no longer in Sudan. *But do they even play "soccer?"* I wondered.

My cluelessness about America was all encompassing. It included every sphere: American race relationships, culture, sports like American football and baseball, and stretched to music (excluding Michael Jackson).

"Oh my God! Oh my God! John Lennon was just shot. He died! He is dead!" shouted one of the students in my biology lab. Every experiment stopped and students began to shout, scream, and murmur.

"Excuse me . . . Excuse me please. Who is John Lennon?" I asked curiously. Everyone looked at me with disbelief. Some questions in America are better not asked. On December 8, 1980, my question was one of them.

Equally matched to my semitotal ignorance of American sports and culture was the American students' lack of knowledge of everything African.

"So where did you say you are from?" asked a white student.

"*From Sudan,*" I answered.
"*Sweden. OK.*"
"*No, it is S . . . U . . . D . . . A . . . N. Sudan.*"
"*So, do you drive sedans in Sudan.*"

These questions made me wonder if any of the white inquiring students have heard that Sweden was populated in the 1980s by white, blonde-haired Scandinavians, and not a dark-skinned, curly-haired guy like me. Either they were assuming that I was a very tanned Swedish Scandinavian male, or they have never laid eyes on a world map before! But who was I to declare them ignorant? I did not know much about America's history of slavery until it was time to come to Indiana.

Educated About All Things American
My African Student Mentor

Luckily for me, my freshman year ignorance about America, its culture, and many of the dos and don'ts was enlightened by Isaac (name changed), one of the African students on campus. He came from Africa a few years before me, and became a good friend and a God-sent mentor. His compassion, caring, and devotion to Jesus were contagious. He freely practiced his Christian faith, and prayed in public before starting his meals which was a fascinating sight for me to see. Isaac was well-liked by Black and white students alike and seemed to be everybody's best friend. God knows, I needed a cultural advisor about everything in America, and Isaac was the man.

"*You don't need to use your umbrella when it snows.*"
"*You can't just knock on a friend's door to visit. You must call first.*"
"*No, your student health insurance doesn't mean you get any medicine for free from any pharmacy,*" he once advised me when I walked with a prescribed medicine bottle without paying for it. I assumed I could get any medication for free in Indiana if I have a student health insurance.

"But the pharmacist just gave it to me and didn't ask me to pay for it," I argued.

His wise advice extended to love, relationships, and romance in America.

"On Valentine's Day, Americans send nice, friendly Valentine cards to each other," he said when I asked him "why is someone sending me a card with the name of Valentine on it?"

Isaac also kindly offered me his expert view on the status of interracial relationships in America.

"As an African, white girls will generally stay away from dating you. They like Black Americans because of the way they walk and talk. They have a certain style that makes the white girls like them."

"An American girl once assumed that I don't like women when I didn't want to go out with her," he once opined on the potential risk of not dating in America (that was at least how I interpreted his words).

Blessed with humility and integrity, my African friend was like a wise African chief who knew everything. He seemed to me like someone who mastered the knowledge of American culture, and the art of maintaining good relationships with both white and Black American students. His views on race relations based on his personal experiences in America and Africa were of particular interest to me. Isaac was fully aware of the reality of racial prejudice and biases in America. But he never let that stop him from building good relationships with the white students, especially Christians on campus.

"You know I have a good white Christian friend who is nice. I think he believes his white skin color is superior. But he's a good man."

"The white Europeans who colonized my country treated the native people inferiorly and expected to be treated superiorly. One of my friends back home who was standing in a line in front of the airport was told to move back in line by a white man so that he could take his place. My friend got mad, said 'NO!' and told him the country was now independent."

Isaac had a well-rehearsed and ready answer to the few curious American students who thought of Africa as one giant country. Or those who wondered if Africans in his country lived in trees.

"Yes, sure we live in trees. The American Ambassador lives in the tallest tree in the capital city. . . ."

The "Oreo Cookie" Experience

Witnessing how the Black and white American students interact (or more accurately do not interact) in the school cafeteria was one unique 1980s college experience. The Black students sat at a large, round table for breakfast, while the white students filled the other tables. I had no idea where to sit. I was invited to sit with the white students when I was still Rick's roommate. Then, when I became Elijah's roommate, I was invited to sit with the Black students. Elijah, and some of his friends, introduced me for the first time to the term "Oreo" as I joined them for breakfast at the cafeteria.

"See that Black guy over there, the one sitting with the white students. He is an "Oreo."

"Oreo?" I inquired as I wondered about this new American word.

"It's like when someone Black acts white. You know, like being Black on the outside but thinking and acting like a white on the inside. Like an Oreo cookie."

"What's an Oreo cookie?"

Well, it turned out that there was such a thing as an Oreo cookie in America. Apparently, the cookie's name was used by some of the Black American students to describe other Black American students in the cafeteria, not all the Black students but only those who associated a lot with the white students in the cafeteria. The way I understood it was that the brown and Black students who associated too closely with white students looked like the American Oreo cookie on the outside, but on the inside, represented by the white inner part of the Oreo, they behaved and acted like whites!

That made me wonder. "*Was I considered an 'Oreo' cookie when I was sitting for breakfast at my white roommate's table? Would they consider Mom an 'Oreo' because she married Dad?*"

I was perplexed. So pervasive were race issues in America's culture that even a delicious cookie was associated with race and ethnicity.

"*How will I ever eat an Oreo cookie in America now without thinking about its deep racial implications,*" I pondered.

Crossing the Racial Divide in the School Cafeteria

The cafeteria ritual of Black and white American students sitting separately, with few exceptions, made me feel uneasy. I had no idea where to sit to eat my American bacon and eggs for breakfast without offending someone in the student body. In my freshman year, I sat at the table with Rick, my first white roommate, and his white friends. In addition to sharing his limited knowledge about Sudan calling it Sweden, he also contributed his personal views about black skin color.

"*Hi 'Adoul (Adel)', Have you ever heard this before: 'if you're Black get back.' I tell you, Black may be beautiful, but tar is too far,*" he once declared as he started laughing.

Of course, I had no idea what he exactly meant or why he said that. But I figured out he meant that if a person's skin color is dark as "tar" then that would not be beautiful. Apparently, he considered shades of brown like mine as black and to him that might be beautiful, but if he ever saw my mom with a much darker skin tone than mine, he would consider her skin as ugly. That made me wonder about the many children in America, Africa, and elsewhere in the world who grew up feeling "ugly" and unattractive because of biased opinions like Rick's.

Because of her dark skin color, Mom grew up facing exactly that in colonized Africa! She fought and won against feeling unattractive and ugly throughout her childhood. I was glad that Rick was no longer my roommate. I could finally eat breakfast without the uneasiness and indigestion his biased words inflicted on me at the breakfast table.

In my second semester, I was introduced by my new roommate Elijah and my African friend Isaac to the few Black American students on campus. Isaac was a big star among the Black American students. The moment I was introduced, I was treated like a blood brother with a common African ancestry and heritage. The Black female students made me feel especially welcome: *"You're so cute. I love your hair. Are you sure you're from Africa? Come on, sit with us."* Feeling special, welcome, and embraced, I began to regularly sit down for breakfast at their table. That table just a few feet away from the tables where the white students sat felt like oceans apart.

I had no clue that crossing the short distance between the tables was akin to crossing an unseen racial line on the cafeteria ground. Unbeknown to me, there must have been an invisible line that divided the white from the Black American students. Inadvertently, I must have wandered over that line one of those mornings during breakfast. Apparently, I traversed that unseen racial divide in 1980 America totally unaware of what I did. As a foreign student, I felt pressured to decide during meals whether to sit with the white or the Black Americans. Sitting with the Black students who warmly welcomed me rendered me unwelcome by the white students that I once sat with. That was at least how it felt before saying grace and eating my American bacon and eggs.

It took me a while to realize that the racial divide in the cafeteria was the general state of racial relationships in America at the time. But fortunately, that was not the case with all the white students on campus. Many welcomed me in their small Bible groups, invited me to their churches, and did not seem to worry about which table I chose to sit at to eat my breakfast. They reminded me of the white missionaries from America who came to Khartoum. And of the Italian Catholic priests at my high school who enjoyed breaking bread with everybody and were always welcoming.

The subtle, unspoken biases and unwritten rules between Blacks and whites on campus reminded me of my own journey as a multiracial child in Sudan. I remember how some of my school childhood friends would react differently when my dad brought me to school versus when Mom did.

"THAT'S YOUR DAD!" some would say in a praising, complimentary voice.

The sense of WOW that exuded from their voices would change to that of a surprised, negative, or disappointed voice.

"Is she your mom!?"

The message back then and during my freshman year in an American university campus was somehow similar. It seemed that being accepted, wanted, and fully belonging in relationships, or to society was greatly influenced by one's skin color. My value, social status, and worth seemed to climb when I was somehow connected to someone or something white. But closely associating myself with someone or anything Black did the opposite! So ingrained were (and still are) such old, wrong, and confusing beliefs not only in Africa and throughout the world, but in a small liberal arts college cafeteria in Indiana.

The cultural and racial issues in America were too stressful and confusing for me to probe and dissect. So, I decided to write articles in the university newspaper sharing my two cents' worth of views, as a foreigner, about America. The white and Blacks students on campus who read my articles seemed to like them. Many thought they were a unique and enlightening perspective from a foreign student about relationships and politics in America. But one of my new Black American friends disagreed.

Gary (name changed) who adapted an African name and was fascinated with my African origin and all things African did not like what I wrote in one of my articles. He felt the race problem in America was too hurtful and deeply rooted for my simple solutions.

"Brother, I think you should stop writing about race relations in America."

My simplistic vision of seeing Black and white Americans getting along, united by love and common belief in God and country did not sit well with him. It was a vision that was much easier to imagine at my childhood home in Khartoum, than in America.

"It's Very Hard to Enter a Medical School in America"

The complexities of life choices and tensions in America that I experienced at my small college campus began to cloud my thinking. America was not all just bad or mysterious: a roommate commemorating his sexual conquests with women's underwear hanging on a clothesline, Rick's dirty magazines hunt, invisible cafeteria racial lines not to be crossed, humans nicknamed "Oreos," and a student in an LSD trip to add to the mix. But there was also a lot of good: school administrators, staff, professors, and students showing me kindness, love, and generosity. Most of all, there was limitless freedom. Everyone around me had the freedom to choose. Some chose to be biased, view other races as inferior, and to do bad and harmful things; while others chose to be welcoming of other races, focus on their schoolbooks, pray, and go to church. Nothing seemed like the American movies I saw in Sudan.

But then, there was my dream to be a doctor in America. Somehow, I needed to focus on the why. Why did I come to America? I realized that If I ever wanted to see my dream become a reality, I needed to steer away from what was bad and harmful. With my growing sense of loneliness and longing for the love and security of my home and family, my childhood dream felt impossible. Then as if I needed more doubts and uncertainties, my African friend Isaac offered me a commonsense piece of information. It was a forewarning and an alert that I have never considered in the pursuit of my dream.

"You know, it's very hard to enter a medical school in America. Even Americans, like one of my friends, can't get in. There's a lot of competition," he said drawing from his own personal experience and dream of becoming a doctor in America.

His words were sobering and discouraging. It made me question my lifelong precious dream.

"Maybe it's impossible to be a doctor in America. Would I ever be able to enter medical school? If a well-polished, well-groomed white American can't get into medical school, what about me? Do I stand a chance with my bell-bottom jeans, and Michael Jackson's Afro hairstyle? And if my African friend with his knowledge of all things American finds it hard to be a doctor in America, what hope is there for me?"

Self-doubts and negative thinking began to creep in. Then miraculously, Claudine (name changed), the African student from Zaire, overheard the conversation and chimed in. Her words offered me a glimpse of hope, and encouraged me to not give up on my dream.

"Adel, there is nothing impossible with God. My brother who lives in a different state wanted to be a doctor. He was told that he had no chance of becoming a doctor in America. But he prayed and God miraculously opened the doors for him. He was admitted to medical school," she said. I needed to hear that.

To me, Claudine's timely words were God-sent. Like her brother, it felt like I needed a miracle to be a doctor in America. What she said was like God's assurance that one day someway, somehow the dream that brought me to America will one day be a reality.

By the end of my freshman year, I started to realize that America was not exactly what the movies taught me. There were no fast cars speeding in Indianapolis, cowboys shooting each other, or beautiful girls who shared the common name "Baby." Nor was America all about colorism, racism, and sex-crazed people digging in the trash for dirty magazines or collecting women's underwear. I could also see white and Black students praying together; churches that talked about love, morality, and tolerance; and nice white students who wanted to be friends. *"There is hope for me in America,"* I assured myself as I reflected on the racial and moral chaos surrounding me.

After successfully finishing my first year in Indiana, I said farewell to my newfound friends and moved to an out-of-state public university. The scarcity of hard currencies, like the dollar, in Sudan meant less American dollars could be sent out of the country for my private education. It was time for me to transfer to a cheaper and much larger university. Hesitantly, I was leaving my small university in Indiana with its intimate and nurturing environment. After saying my final goodbyes to administrators, staff, and students who became my mentors and friends, I began to ruminate.

"How in the world will I ever survive in a large public university in America?"

Lost in a Big Public University: A Needle in a Haystack

After leaving my first undergraduate college in Indiana, I suddenly found myself lost in the large public undergraduate university. I was like a needle in a haystack. Gone was the personal attention I received at the private college in Indiana from faculty, staff, and the school administration. The difference between the church-affiliated university in Indiana and the large public university was obvious early on. On my first day of orientation at the public university (aka the party school), we were shown a cannon in the school. The student tour guide went into great length explaining the significance of the large cannon that was strategically placed at the main University Square.

"Ladies and gentlemen, the cannon you see here was placed by one of the fraternities many years ago. Legend had it, that the cannon would fire on its own if any virgin female student on our campus would pass in front of it. Of course, since the fraternity placed the cannon here it has never fired," explained the student.

As the students around me burst out laughing, I began to wonder. I heard of the word fraternities before in Indiana. But what exactly are fraternities?

"A cannon that never fired before! What did I really get myself into?" I contemplated.

It didn't take me long to know what fraternities and sororities exactly meant. Greek life, which I found out has nothing to do with foreigners from Greece, was all over campus. Whites and Blacks had their own separate fraternities and sororities, and each held their own wild parties. Foreign students who were not included in the Greek life formed their own home parties or went to bed early. The whole campus—citizens and foreigners alike—coalesced in the college town's main street for the mother of all parties: the big Halloween downtown party. The whole place felt like a resort with constant parties, alcohol, dating, and sex interrupted by classes and schoolwork.

"How in the world do students find time to study at the university library in between all that fun?" I often asked myself.

Black and white students for the most part kept to themselves except for "Sandy," my white, red-haired, Irish-American female classmate. She explained to me that her parents will never know about the Black American young man that she was dating.

"He's a big Black guy I met when he pumped gas in my car at a gas station. My dad will kill me if he ever finds out that I'm dating him."

But much like the small university in Indiana, there were still many student organizations that invited students to visit their Bible study groups and churches. Yet, the soft voices of Christian students trying to draw the attention of fellow partying students were hard to hear. Their voices calling others from the gods of pleasure, alcohol, and sex to Jesus often drowned in the noisy campus parties. The Jesus message of the Christian American missionaries who visited Sudan probably had more success of being heard by Muslims and other religions than in that public university.

Amid all the chaos and loud distractions of a large campus, I gradually began to feel lonely and insignificant. I was like a number, one of thousands of students in an impersonal campus wanting to belong. That was a dark time of wandering and being less anchored to the faith my parents had taught me. Like many others there, I was looking for acceptance, value, and worth that no campus life could provide. Yet, even during those days of feeling unwelcome, unloved, and away from home I was not alone. There was the still, calm, and inner voice of God assuring me that all would be well.

Then suddenly and unexpectedly a divine intervention happened. Dad, who financed my college education, suggested that I transfer to another Midwest university to be close to my sister. My sister just moved there, and he wanted us to live close to each other. But there was another reason that prompted him to send me to a new school. His decision was in part due to a photo that I had sent my parents in Khartoum from the school. In the colored photo, I wore a huge Afro, a maroon velvet jacket, and I held, like a professional, an electric guitar, which I did not know how to play.

He took a long hard look at the picture. Then he wisely discerned that I was probably too distracted at that school to carry out my mission of being a doctor in America. He and Mom sensed that I was going in the wrong direction and were concerned.

"Well, great. He's holding a guitar and not a book. I sent him to be a doctor in America but looks like he wants to be a musician now," he told Mom.

Thankfully, Dad decided to save me from self-sabotaging my own dream by sending me elsewhere. And that was the end of my exposure to the school with the cannon that never fired.

A Dream Fading
My Final Undergraduate Years in Another Public University

Moving closer to my sister and transferring to a reputable public university was what I needed. Thus far, I had quite a few trials, and enough distractions in my American journey to bury my dream. The enormity of the challenges and the loneliness of being away from home took a toll on me. I felt blessed for this new start, and the opportunity to reboot my faith, hope, and childhood dream.

The campus with its fascinating old and modern architectural designs was occupied with students of every skin color and race. It was the early 1980s and Michael Jackson, and new names I had never heard of before—Prince, Bruce Springsteen, Billy Joel, and Van Halen—ruled the airwaves. They fiercely competed with college biology, chemistry, and calculus. In general, the pattern of campus life was somehow like the other universities. The students studied intensely in the school library on weekdays and partied with vengeance on weekends and spring breaks. Everyone had total freedom to say and do whatever he or she wanted, assuming no written laws were broken. *"But, what about those who are too drunk or intoxicated to know if a law existed, or to know if a law is even broken?"* I often wondered. I figured out that this is when a student loses his freedom in America, goes to jail, and gets a police record. What that entails is the risk of a messed-up resume with a police record, no medical school, and giving up on my dream. I stayed far away from alcohol and drugs.

For sure, America was clearly not Sudan, and I needed to stop analyzing and reflecting on the drastic differences between them. It was time for me to get serious, focus on my pre-med major, and meet other pre-med students.

"Pre-meds are aggressive backstabbers. They are usually cutthroat," one of the students told me.

I could not fully understand the meaning of his descriptive words, but it did not sound good. I took them to mean that there are potentially very competitive American students who might ironically resort to doing harmful things to get into medical schools where they would train to be knowledgeable, kind, and caring doctors.

But then I met a friendly white American pre-med student who was too sweet and gentle to be a "cutthroat," harmful or hurtful. That was yet another reminder to me about the folly of generalizing and quick conclusions in America. In the years to come, I experienced some of the hurt and unfairness of the above when quick conclusions were drawn about me because of my looks, accent, color, faith, or African heritage. I learned to stop drawing quick conclusions based on generalizations, because of how hurt and bad I felt when the same was done to me.

The level of fierce competitiveness to enter through the gate of a medical school worried me. So, I decided to add biology, then chemistry majors to my premed major. And just to be safe, I included a business minor on top of that. That was certainly a time in my life when I was living by sight and not by faith. In essence, I was trying to figure out how to humanly accomplish a dream that started with nothing but faith. I always believed that my childhood dream to be a doctor was from God, and He would make it possible. But as the years passed in America, I was starting to lose touch with God's love and presence. Consequently, to enter medical school and be a doctor in America felt scary and impossible.

Meanwhile, my parents' letters from Sudan with Dad's handwriting became my reminders of why I came to America.

"My dear son Adel, our neighbor Banouna across the street from us, is asking about how our son 'the doctor' is doing in America."

Dad and Mom's letters made me aware that my dream of being a doctor in America was no longer just mine. It belonged to Mom, Dad, family friends, Banouna, her son Mohammed, and the rest of our neighbors and friends in Khartoum. They all seemed to cherish living their own hopes and dreams vicariously through me. My dream became theirs, and they, too, wanted it to become a reality.

A Taste of Racial and Other Biases at My New Campus

Unlike my first college campus in Indiana, this campus had many more foreign students. They mostly kept to themselves doing their own things: a mixture of international festivals, ethnic parties, and being involved in a group called the INTERNAT. The International-American campus group hosted a weekly coffee hour and entertaining events. American students curious about us or eager to practice their language skills would often come and join us.

Generally, the white male American students tended to not interact much with male foreign students unless someone was seen with a white female student. That happened to me and my dark-skinned Indian roommate. A couple of white males, as far as we could tell, spotted us chatting and giggling with female white students. And so, they decided to place a plastic container packed with small snakes in front of our apartment door. Neither of us had seen an American garden snake before and so we panicked. The message to both of us at that time seemed to be: stay away from white girls if you don't like snakes. Thankfully, the Black and white American students who embraced me and other foreign students, and frequented our international events made me feel welcome. Many of them invited me to their churches and potluck dinners and made up for the sins of those who left the "slimy" snakes at my door.

Terrible as it was, my snake encounter paled in comparison to what I experienced next. As the "executive vice president" of the INTERNAT group, I found myself embroiled in a major controversy. I was dragged with the group into one ugly racist incident involving a white fraternity on campus. The fraternity organized a party, named it after a revered Black American civil rights icon, and labeled it a trash party. Then adding insult to injury, they advertised it on flyers that stereotyped Black Americans by offering free access to the party to anyone who brought a watermelon and food stamps as admission tickets! A very unthinkable occurrence in twentieth-century America. Thankfully, a lot has changed in America since then!

Understandably, the administration wisely sanctioned the fraternity and did the right thing. Part of their long list of punishments was to sponsor and attend a minority group's campus event. They chose to sponsor one of our International-American student organization's "coffee hour." As the executive vice president of the organization, I found myself in the front line of America's deep-rooted racial problems. I had to decide with a couple of other group leaders if we should allow the guilty fraternity to sponsor our "coffee hour" or not. I doubted the fraternity's true intentions for hosting our minority group. I did not believe that they were truly repentant, and so I decided to apply my newly found American freedom of expression.

"No, I don't think we should let them sponsor us. I don't think they are sincere," I said to the other officers as I cast my vote.

Many years later after my decision to say no, I ran into many people in high positions of power and leadership who reminded me of that incident. They would say and do token words and deeds of diversity and racial equality, but without sincerity, just like that fraternity.

The rest of the INTERNAT leadership, which included a Black American female student and an Asian American, agreed with me wholeheartedly. But a couple of days after our group declined the fraternity's sponsorship, I learned another lesson about freedom in America. Our organization was not sanctioned, nor were any of the officers threatened or beaten for our opposing view, which was refreshing to me. Instead, our small organization and the officers, including me, were mentioned in a series of articles in the campus newspaper. A caricature about our organization depicting it as a bridge burner said it all. It was perplexing to see how the object of harsh criticism and scorn was no longer the fraternity's prejudice action. It was our obscure group, officers included, who became the object of scorn for refusing to let the fraternity host our "coffee hour"!

Yet, that was another lesson for me about freedom in America. I was granted full freedom to voice my opinion, to express my views, and freely make a choice. But the officers, me, and our small organization were caricatured as bridge burners when we did. That was a lesson that I learned back then and for many years to come. Freedom to express my opinion, faith, or moral beliefs are wonderfully granted and protected in America. But taking moral stands and voicing your beliefs would come with harsh consequences, even in America.

I ventured to voice my opinion about the white fraternity's intentions and that came with adverse consequences. That was when I figured out that there is always a price to pay, even in America, for expressing my two cents' worth of peaceful ideas and views. It might get me bad press or cost me a relationship, a promotion or a job in America, Land of My Dreams. But thankfully, not a jail, or death sentence without trial: a reality in many nations in the world.

Biases and Prejudices in America

Sometime after being exposed to the plastic container with curled-up garden snakes and dealing with the white fraternity racial incident, I felt more mature. Somehow, I became more perceptive and wiser to the various forms of biases that some students inflicted on others. I heard people from Kentucky ridiculed for their accents, overweight students being shunned and rejected, and peaceful, friendly Christians on campus called fanatics. Then there was a female Jewish student who told me that she was labeled a "JAP." It turned out that "JAP" has nothing to do with the white, sandy-blonde-haired Jewish student having any Japanese ancestry. It was a hurtful pejorative stereotype that she was cruelly subjected to. Prejudice and biases seemed to spare no one: Blacks, minorities, dark-skinned people, white Christians, Jewish, overweight students, and Kentuckians with nice foreign accents labeled "Southern." America, Land of My Dreams was suddenly not perfect. Not perfect, but a place where I could still see God's goodness flowing through many caring ordinary Americans to strangers, including a stranger from overseas like me.

Undergraduate Life: Romance, Partying, and Getting Hurt

Thus far, undergraduate life in America seemed to be, for some students, like a resort experience where they silenced their inhibitions and partied endlessly. To some, the campus was like a giant meeting place, away from parental supervision, where free love, fun, and casual relationships could be found. To me, the whole campus scene was like a powerful MRI magnetic field pulling me away from my dream.

"How in the world can anyone stay focused with so many campus temptations, and still manage to get a college degree?" I often wondered, as I tried to revive and hold tightly to my own vision and reason for coming to America.

Ultimately, surviving my undergraduate college years with my dream still intact was nothing but an act of God. College challenges, random biases, tempting campus life, and the emotional challenges of all of the above felt overwhelming. But thankfully, they ultimately could not doom the mission that brought me to America. Instead, many years later, I believe God used those challenging days and all my mistakes to shape me into a more caring and empathic physician.

CHAPTER 26

MY DAD'S PASSING: AN "IMPOSSIBLE DREAM" RESURRECTED

It was a sizzling summer day in August when Mom called me from Sudan crying. Dad passed. He died from complications of malaria with Mom by his bedside to the very end.

"He was calling your name . . . all the children's names," she said in a mournful voice.

He was not only Dad who loved me but my hero, teacher, and provider who believed in me. He sacrificed time, energy, and money to see my dream of being a doctor in America become a reality. As a teenager, I never thought the cost of leaving Sudan to pursue my dream would include never seeing Dad again in this life.

Yet, it was his death that brought me down to my knees and much closer to God. Looking back, God used my grief to work out something good in my life, and to redirect my path. After his unexpected passing, I reflected on the brevity of life, and on "Why." Why did I sign on to be a doctor in the first place? And why did I choose America to fulfill my dream? I reminded myself of how certain I once was of that higher calling to help in healing and mending broken bodies and hearts. That was why I came to America. And once more, I felt determined and passionate about my mission of being a doctor in America: my dad's deepest desire before dying in Khartoum. It was time to recommit. It was my time to carry the baton of faith and the pursuit of a better life that Dad and Mom passed on to me. Life felt so fleeting and unpredictable, and I was finally ready to be serious about what truly mattered.

Then God Moved!

Shortly after my dad passed, I was determined to run and finish my race to be a doctor in America. Things suddenly and miraculously began to happen when I was no longer dabbling but totally committed to be all in! Closed back doors leading to new opportunities began to divinely open for me in America. That was like what my parents experienced in Khartoum when they began their adventurous immigrant journey in Sudan.

In a miraculous twist of fate, I ran into an elderly Sudanese man on the university campus. He did not speak English and seemed lost. We were pleasantly surprised that we were both from Sudan and began to converse. The pleasant elderly gentleman, from one of the ethnic Muslim tribes in Sudan, reminded me of my close Muslim neighbors and friends back in Khartoum.

"*Al-salam alikom. Inta min Al-Sudan? (Peace upon you. Are you from Sudan?)*" he asked.

We talked about memories from back home, and the sickness that brought him to an American hospital for treatment. He desperately needed an interpreter and someone to teach him English.

Shortly after we met, he introduced me to others from various countries who came to America with him for long-term medical treatment. Then, he did something that miraculously got me closer to my dream of being a doctor in America. He gave my phone number to the coordinator of the medical treatment program where he and his friends were treated.

That, in turn, set a chain of unexpected future events starting with a call I received from the American coordinator.

"You are really an answer to my prayers. I hope you can help to interpret for them . . . and for the doctors?" she said over the phone with a deep sigh of relief.

I am convinced that was the time when God suddenly moved and brought me closer to my dream. After the call, I found myself surrounded by a top-notch team of world-renowned American physicians and surgeons. They worked as a team that genuinely appreciated my interpreting skills and treated me as one of their own.

The A team was made up of naturalized and native-born Americans of every race, color, religion, and ethnic background. It included Black, white, Hispanic, Asian (Indian, Korean, and Filipino), nurses, nurse practitioners, physicians, and surgeons, including two world-renowned Jewish specialists.

The American medical team was led by a white Jewish American physician, an immigrant, who was at the top of his medical specialty. Mercifully, he took me under his wing once he and the team knew about my dream of being a doctor. Not only did they become a tremendous source of teaching and encouragement, but they also showed me America at its best! They cared about my well-being, health, love life, the apartment I moved to, and my beat-up red 1973 Chevrolet car. It was fascinating to see how my dream to be a doctor in America mattered to them. They were all rooting for me and led by their renowned physician leader, they all wanted me to succeed. To me, it felt like one big, amazing conspiracy of kindness orchestrated by God!

Owning My Dream

God only knows how I needed that sudden and unforeseen mentorship that Americans from every background began to give me. As a pre-med foreign student in the battlefields of America's undergraduate college life, I was far away from home. I needed the loving, caring, and nurturing environment that they generously offered. To me, that was a hidden, back door that God miraculously opened in my American immigrant journey. I wholeheartedly walked through that door onto a path that I hoped would lead to my lifetime dream.

Through their mentorship, I was exposed to patient care for the very first time. I learned about the art of medicine in exam rooms, during medical procedures, and in operating rooms. Witnessing the physical challenges and the emotional cries from human hearts who yearned for rest, health, and a better life transformed me. I could see how a smile, a kind word, a gentle, caring touch healed, and gave hope amid suffering. That God-sent opportunity to be directly exposed to patient care ignited my passion to be a doctor in America. It reminded me of my calling. I was not just called to be a doctor equipped with America's best medical knowledge. More important, I was entrusted with a God-given dream to genuinely care for the whole person: body, mind, and spirit.

"One day, I want to offer God's words of hope, love, and encouragement to people suffering physical, mental, and emotional illnesses," became my prayer, and in a way my personal mission statement.

I was no longer just a teenager from Sudan who believed in a distant dream in America. Nor was I a soul lost and wandering in the maze of America's undergraduate wilderness. I was finally a young man in America who decided to fully embrace my God-given dream as my own. I finally owned it and fully accepted it as my calling.

Mom and dad visiting me in America.

Undergraduate years in America.

Undergraduate college graduation.

CHAPTER 27

MEDICAL SCHOOL: THE JOURNEY

Once I walked through the incredible back door that was just opened for me, there was no turning back! I hit the books, finally signed up for all the advanced science classes that I once dreaded, and studied for my Medical College Admission Test (MCAT). More important, I stayed focused, prayed hard, and felt heartened by all the encouragement I received. There is something supernatural and empowering that happens when someone is encouraged. I felt that encouragement from family and friends back in Sudan and from strangers in America.

Soon, letters of recommendation to medical schools from the team of American physicians and nurses who mentored me began to pour in. The Jewish-American specialist and team leader wrote a powerful letter of recommendation on my behalf and regularly checked on my progress. He even followed that with a second strong letter listing additional positive things that he noticed about me! Everyone's letter was incredibly supportive and described every quality in me that they believed would make me an exceptional physician. They all believed that I could do it and wrote that they were "looking forward to calling me a doctor in the future." The impact of their investment of time to mentor me, care, and write outstanding recommendation letters touched me. It greatly blessed my life for many years to come.

The kindness of those Americans to a total stranger from Sudan taught me a principal life lesson beyond medicine. I learned to not miss an opportunity to help a young man or woman in need, just as I once was. Listening and offering encouragement that would help someone fulfill her or his worthy dream became part of my life mission. And how could I think otherwise! My family, friends, Americans including Olivia, the lovely Latina from Honduras, and Christian students on campus, motivated, encouraged, and helped me. When I was young, a stranger to some, and hopelessly in need of help and encouragement from all, they were there for me.

Diligence, Sweat, and Prayers

Dad used to often encourage me with an Arabic proverb to motivate me to be diligent and to accomplish my important life goals:

"*Mann talab al oula, sahar al-lialee.*"

Translated, it means that whoever is seeking higher goals in life must persevere, be diligent, and stay many late nights! He taught me that arduous work, even if it meant little sleep at night, is needed if I were to accomplish any worthwhile goal in life. Both he and Mom worked extremely hard to attain their high hopes and dreams as immigrants in Sudan. It was time for me to do the same in America even in the face of all setbacks and rejections.

But accomplishing my big dream of being a doctor in America did not come easily. Two university transfers, and early setbacks as I scrambled to figure out my way in America nearly discouraged me. But it was time to look forward to a brand-new chapter in the storybook of my life. Any past negative paragraph in a past chapter of my life story was over and no longer here. I resolved that my only path in life was moving forward and not backward, toward tomorrow, and into my calling. I still believed that God who gave me that vision and dream will make it a reality; someway, somehow. I just had to do my part, run the race, and make it to the finish line for the reward!

Thankfully, my renewed mindset and belief that with God nothing is impossible kept me in the race. It kept me sane and resilient as I read rejection letters, and hopeful when placed on a waiting list, or offered an interview. Years later, as an American board-certified physician, I still draw a lot of inspiration, strength, and encouragement from those days. A good dream is a heavenly gift. It is too precious to let go of, waste or throw away. I still recall how I finally decided to fight hard for it, and I am so glad that I did. In retrospect, I felt so cheered up at that time. Not just by my family, caring friends, and an exceptional American medical team, but by something more. I was buoyed and sustained by a great cloud of heavenly witnesses cheering me up from above, including Dad. I could envision the thunderous applause and cheers from heaven to run a race, that seemed so hard and impossible to me at the time, to the finish line!

The End of The Beginning
The Start of the Dream: Medical School!

Receiving my medical school acceptance letter reminded me of that day in Khartoum when I read my undergraduate acceptance letter. I jumped for joy, thanked God, called my family, friends, American mentors, and then finished reading the letter.

The significance and lifetime implications of the words I read in that acceptance letter began to dawn on me as soon as I calmed down from my euphoric joy.

"I am pleased to inform you of your admission to the freshman class . . . The faculty joins me in welcoming you."

My God-inspired dream that started at the age of thirteen with a book that I read in Khartoum was about to launch. It felt like a God-orchestrated plan for my life that started where I once lived by the Blue Nile in Khartoum. It was about to be fulfilled in America!

Fulfilling the Dream: Becoming A Doctor

There I was in medical school, a once clueless teenager with huge Afro hair who only knew of Michael Jackson's state of Indiana. A young man who once could not tell a dime from a nickel, who trusted total strangers to take him to Manhattan at 3:00 a.m., and took the wrong plane to Jacksonville, Florida, instead of Jacksonville, North Carolina, was on a path to be a doctor in America! If that was not a miracle from God, then I don't know what miracles are! The journey to accomplish my mission of being a doctor in America, Land of My Dreams just began!

What followed next for me were endless battlefields of rigorous medical education, dealing with the grief and loss of my dad, national medical exams that had to be passed, residency training in one of the top five family medicine programs in the country, and being a Family Practice Board Certified physician, the crown of the profession. I am by no means the only one who started and completed a dream of being a doctor in America, or any other worthy dream. Thankfully, there are many who can do just that and inspire others to do the same. But I still marvel at the miracle of being led as a teenager to come to America. Much like my parents who came to Sudan with nothing but their dreams, I came to America with nothing but a dream. It was God's love, mercy, and goodness that made our inspired dreams become realities, against all odds.

My immigrant story in America, much like my parents' immigrant stories in Sudan, is filled with appreciation. As I put down my pen, I can only think of gratitude. A deep gratitude to God, my parents, America, Land of My Dreams, and to Americans who welcomed, mentored, and invested in a total stranger like me.

The End

Adel G. Hanna (Khouri), MD
America, Land of My Dreams

True love does not fail. Mom and Dad growing old together.

Dad, my brother, and me during Dad's last visit to the U.S. He died in Sudan three years later.

Medical School Graduation. Adel G. Hanna, MD. Inspired dreams do come true with God's help.

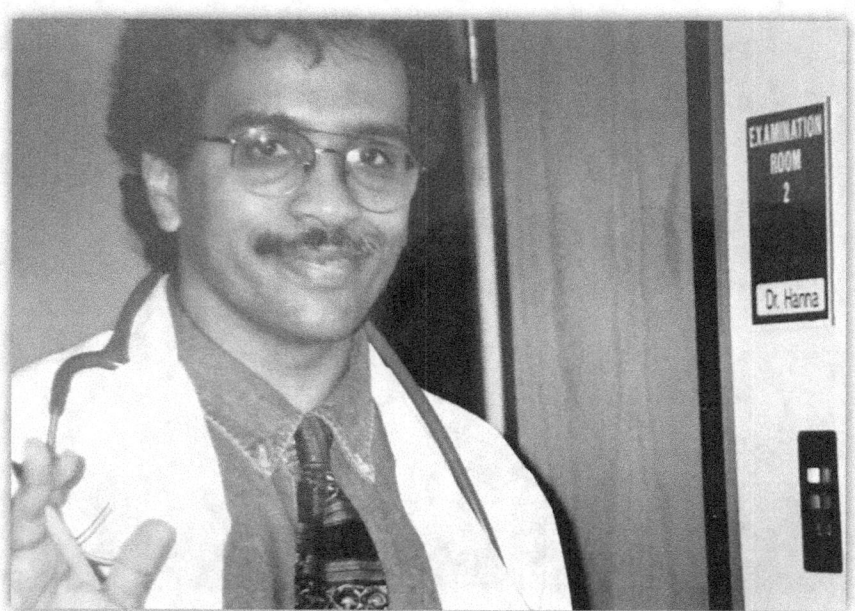

Starting my career in medicine, so help me God.

A cookout with some patriotic soldiers.

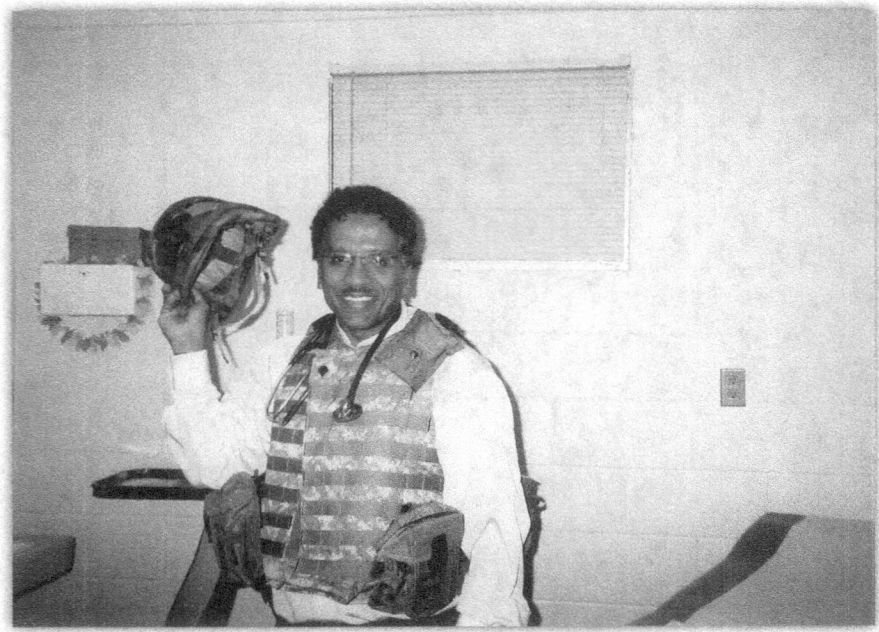

Me, offering medical care to deploying soldiers.

The joy of serving the country where God gave wings to my dream of being a doctor.

Dr. Hanna.

Experiencing my childhood dream and the gift of serving and caring.

IN BRIEF

JIM WITMER/DAYTON DAILY NEWS

A good citizen
Adel Gobran Hanna, originally of Sudan, holds a flag as he is naturalized as a citizen of the United States in ceremonies Monday at Sinclair Community College. He was among 62 people from 33 countries seeking citizenship. And it was a fitting day, Flag Day.

A proud naturalized citizen of the United States holding tightly to my U.S. flag.

Not the River Nile but plenty of fun in America at the beach. Mom and my son.

Blessed with my two boys who are Americans with a rich heritage to always be proud of.

My daughter and my blessing who is now taller than me.

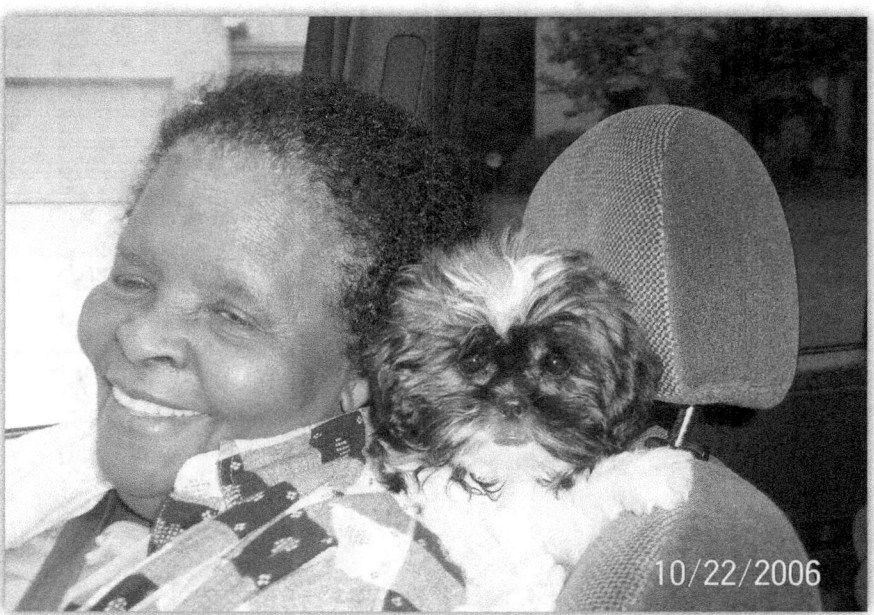

Mom in America with a native-born American dog.

Mom, my older brother, and me.

Mom (on the left) and a relative in her Tigrinya Zuria dress at her birthplace, the Highlands of Ethiopia.

✶ ✶ ✶

AFTERWORD

Mom's incredible journey from the Highlands of Ethiopia to Sudan as a teenager, and her miraculous encounter with Dad there, has always inspired me. As I reflect on my own immigrant journey in America from a wide-eyed teenager with a big Afro hair to a board-certified family medicine physician, I often think about them. They were a brave Black-and-white couple who got married at the time of the Anglo-Egyptian colonization of Sudan when such unions were shunned. The only common bond that united them, and all that kept them devoted to each other, was faith and love. They believed in Jesus Christ, loved God and one another. Otherwise, they had very little in common. They came from different races, educational levels, socioeconomic classes, and did not even speak each other's language!

My parents left their families, friends, and possessions, and moved to their new home in Sudan. They never looked back or returned to their old homes except to visit their loved ones. There is something about moving forward and running our life race without constantly looking back onto our past. They left behind past good and bad relationships, old successes and failures, and many cherished and painful memories. To them glancing at the past was only meant to help them learn from old mistakes, and to be encouraged by previous victories. They grieved and forgave the past when needed but they never dwelt there. To them, the past was all gone and forgotten.

When I came to America, I followed their example and ran the race for my dream to be a doctor. I left my room, books, fun days, old hurts, sad memories, and the past behind. Thankfully, they taught me the wisdom of asking God to forgive my past mistakes, and to forgive myself and others. I learned by their example to change my old ways, to move forward, and to not keep looking back. To grieve, forgive, learn, reflect, but not to dwell on the past. The past is over and long gone, and all that I have is today, and God willing, tomorrow in America, Land of My Dreams.

Throughout my medical career, I have treated thousands of native-born American patients. They were not immigrants from faraway lands like me, but nevertheless still immigrants in heart and soul. Many of them left, or were ready to leave, their past behind in search of a better life. Some of them made bad choices in the past but decided to do a complete 180 and start all over again. At heart, we all are immigrants with dreams and unquenchable zeal for a new beginning and a better life.

I am so glad that my parents never gave up on their dreams in Sudan. Mom saved her family in Tigray's Highlands from starvation with domestic jobs she held as a child. She brought up her own six children in Khartoum but continued to help her family up to her old age. That was her dream. Dad became a renowned, highly sought-after architect in Sudan. He accomplished his dream of a distinguished career, a loving wife, and a large family. Most of all, their dream of finding a Christian partner and having a Christian marriage came true even in a world dominated by racial biases. They met and got married against all odds.

My dream of being a doctor in America, much like my parents' personal dreams in Sudan, was worthy and life changing. But to us, those dreams were unreachable, faraway, and humanly impossible to attain without help from above. In my immigrant's journey in America, I finally learned what my parents personally saw and experienced: with God's help nothing is impossible. We all did what was possible for us to do, and God did the impossible that we could not do.

The stories of my ancestors, parents, and mine found in this book remind me that with God's help all things are possible. Even in the face of overwhelming situations and impossibilities, failure, injustice, or prejudice, we can all rise from the ashes and finish our life race well. Like my parents, I believe, God authors our most challenging and beautiful dreams. He gave me the dream in Sudan and helped me to achieve it in America!

Never waste a good dream.
Never give up.

"What is impossible with man is possible with God."
Luke 18:27 (NIV)

★ ★ ★
ENDNOTES

Chapter 1: The Khouri Family: My Levantine Heritage

1. Anon, Khoury surname origin, meaning & last name history—forebears. https://forebears.io/surnames/khoury (Accessed August 21, 2022).
2. Anon, Levant, https://en.wikipedia.org/wiki/Levant (Accessed January 26, 2023).
3. Zeidan, Adam, 2022. Levant, https://www.britannica.com/place/Levant (Accessed January 26, 2023).
4. Anon, 2022. Khouri. *Wikipedia.* https://en.wikipedia.org/wiki/Khouri (Accessed August 21, 2022).

Chapter 2: Gabal Lebnan (Mount Lebanon): The Khouris' Ancestral Home?

5. Anon, 2022. Mount Lebanon. *Wikipedia.* https://en.wikipedia.org/wiki/Mount_Lebanon (Accessed August 23, 2022).
6. Anon, 2022. Kahlil Gibran. *Wikipedia.* https://en.wikipedia.org/wiki/Kahlil_Gibran (Accessed August 23, 2022).

War and Migration

7. Mansel, P., 2011. *Levant: Splendour and catastrophe on the Mediterranean,* New Haven: Yale University Press.
8. Ibid.

9. Ibid.
10. Ibid.

Christians Escaping the Levant and the Ottoman Empire
11. Mansel, P., 2011. *Levant: Splendour and catastrophe on the Mediterranean*, New Haven: Yale University Press.
12. Anon, 2014. Six unexpected WWI battlegrounds. *BBC News*. https://www.bbc.com/news/magazine-30098000 (Accessed August 28, 2022).

A Ray of Hope in the Darkness
13. Anon, 2022. American University of Beirut. *Wikipedia*. https://en.wikipedia.org/wiki/American_University_of_Beirut (Accessed August 28, 2022).
14. Anon, 2022. Great famine of Mount Lebanon. *Wikipedia*. https://en.wikipedia.org/wiki/Great_Famine_of_Mount_Lebanon (Accessed August 28, 2022).
15. Anon, 2022. History of Gaza. *Wikipedia*. https://en.wikipedia.org/wiki/History_of_Gaza (Accessed August 28, 2022).

Chapter 3: Gaza: Grandpa's birthplace

16. Anon, 2022. History of Gaza. *Wikipedia*. https://en.wikipedia.org/wiki?curid=21567020 (Accessed September 2, 2022).
17. Filiu, J.P., and J. King. 2014. *Gaza: A history*, New York: Oxford University Press.
18. Ibid.

Chapter 4: Egypt: The Gift of the Nile

19. Anon, 2022. Nile. *Wikipedia*. https://en.wikipedia.org/wiki/Nile#cite_note-: 1–59 (Accessed September 6, 2022).

20. Anon, United Nations Development Programme. *UNDP*. https://www.undp.org/ (Accessed September 6, 2022).
21. Holmes, M. *et al.* (2004) *Nile*. London: BBC Worldwide.

Chapter 5: Al-Khouris' New Life and Challenges in Egypt

22. Anon, 2019. Egypt Profile—Timeline. *BBC News*. Available at: https://www.bbc.com/news/world-africa-13315719#:~:text=1859%2D69%20%2D%20Suez%20Canal%20built,formally%20becomes%20a%20British%20protectorate (Accessed September 6, 2022).

Levantines in Al-Zagazig, Egypt
23. Fahmy, Z., 2011. *Ordinary Egyptians: Creating the modern nation through popular culture*, Stanford, CA: Stanford University Press.
24. Ibid.

Music and Culture in Nineteenth and Early Twentieth Centuries Egypt
25. Fahmy, Z., 2011. *Ordinary Egyptians: Creating the modern nation through popular culture*, Stanford, CA: Stanford University Press.

Religious Tensions in Their New Home, Egypt
26. Fahmy, Z., 2011. *Ordinary Egyptians: Creating the modern nation through popular culture*, Stanford, CA: Stanford University Press.
27. Ibid.
28. Ibid.
29. Ibid.

Chapter 6: Slavery and Racial Biases in Paradise

30. T., and K. M. Cuno. 2011. *Race and slavery in the Middle East: Histories of trans-Saharan Africans in nineteenth-century Egypt,*

Sudan, and the Ottoman Mediterranean, the American University in Cairo.
31. Ibid.
32. Arsenault, N., C. Rose, and T. Lozano. Africa enslaved—minio.la.utexas.edu. *slavery_in_ottoman_egypt.pdf.* https://minio.la.utexas.edu/webeditor-files/hemispheres/pdf/slavery_in_ottoman_egypt.pdf (Accessed September 12, 2022).
33. Walz. Op cit.
34. Anon, 2022. Slavery in Egypt. *Wikipedia.* https://en.wikipedia.org/wiki/Slavery_in_Egypt (Accessed September 11, 2022).
35. Mak, L., 2012. The British in Egypt: Community, crime and crises 1822–1922, I.B. Tauris.
36. Ibid.
37. Anon, 2022. Anti-slavery Society (1823–1838). *Wikipedia.* https://en.wikipedia.org/wiki/Anti-Slavery_Society_(1823%E2%80%931838) (Accessed September 18, 2022).
38. Walz, T. and K. M. Cuno. 2011. *Race and slavery in the Middle East: Histories of trans-Saharan Africans in nineteenth-century Egypt, Sudan, and the Ottoman Mediterranean,* the American University in Cairo.
39. Baron, B., 1970. [pdf] liberated bodies and saved souls: Freed African slave girls and missionaries in Egypt: Semantic scholar. *undefined.* https://www.semanticscholar.org/paper/Liberated-Bodies-and-Saved-Souls%3A-Freed-African-and-Baron/228da49a0aa13e0bc03a1a38598b0df27e066f87 (Accessed September 29, 2022).
40. Fahmy, Z., 2011. *Ordinary Egyptians: Creating the modern nation through popular culture,* Stanford, CA: Stanford University Press.

Chapter 7: Dad's Early Childhood During World War I

41. Mak, L., 2012. The British in Egypt: Community, crime and crises 1822–1922, I.B. Tauris.

42. Ibid.
43. Wikipedia (2022) *Oswald Chambers, Wikipedia*. Wikimedia Foundation. https://en.wikipedia.org/wiki/Oswald_Chambers#cite_note-21 (Accessed: September 30, 2022).
44. Falls (2022) *Raid on the Suez Canal, Wikipedia*. Wikimedia Foundation. https://en.wikipedia.org/wiki/Raid_on_the_Suez_Canal (Accessed: October 1, 2022).
45. Strachan, H. (2003) *The First World War (Volume I): To Arms*. New York: Oxford University Press.
46. Fahmy, Z., 2011. *Ordinary Egyptians: Creating the modern nation through popular culture*, Stanford, CA: Stanford University Press.
47. Mak, L., 2012. The British in Egypt: Community, crime and crises 1822–1922, I.B. Tauris.

Post WWI Egypt: Life and Historical Discoveries

48. Mosleh, M. (2018) *Sham El-Nessim: Egypt's oldest celebration, EgyptToday*. https://www.egypttoday.com/Article/4/47334/Sham-El-Nessim-Egypt's-oldest-celebration (Accessed: December 5, 2022).
49. Hichens, R. (1910) *The spell of Egypt*. Leipzig: B. Tauchnitz.
50. Taylor, B. (1856) *A journey to Central Africa; Egypt and Soudan 1851*. New York: Big Byte Books.

Surviving WWII in Egypt

51. Gilbert, A. (2021) *Battles of el-alamein, Encyclopædia Britannica*. Encyclopædia Britannica, inc. https://www.britannica.com/event/battles-of-El-Alamein (Accessed: October 11, 2022).
52. Gilbert, M. (1992) *Churchill: A life*. London: Minerva.
53. Churchill, Winston S., (2000) *The Second World War: Volume IV The Hinge of Fate*. London: Folio Society.
54. Goldsmith *et al.* (no date) *World War II and its aftermath, Encyclopædia Britannica*. Encyclopædia Britannica, Inc. https:

//www.britannica.com/place/Egypt/World-War-II-and-its-aftermath (Accessed: October 11, 2022).

Chapter 8: The Khouri Family's Riches to Rags Story: Life in Hayy El-Sakakini

55. Buzz, E.S. (2020) *Sakakini Palace: The story behind one of Cairo's architectural gems, Egyptian Streets.* https://egyptianstreets.com/2020/02/10/sakakini-palace-the-story-behind-one-of-cairos-architectural-gems/ (Accessed: November 2, 2022).
56. Raafat, S. (1997) *Adopt A Monument, Sakakini Palace: How about the palace that turns a hundred years old this year? April 5, 1997.* http://www.egy.com/landmarks/97-04-05.php (Accessed: November 2, 2022).

Chapter 9: Egypt's Black-White Color Divide

57. Salih, Z. (2020) *Viewpoint from Sudan—where black people are called slaves, BBC News.* BBC. https://www.bbc.com/news/world-africa-53147864 (Accessed: November 2, 2022).
58. Aida (2022) Wikipedia. Wikimedia Foundation. https://en.wikipedia.org/wiki/Aida#CITEREFGreene1985 (Accessed: November 13, 2022).
59. Green, A. (2019) *Synopsis of Verdi's opera, Aida, LiveAbout.* LiveAbout. https://www.liveabout.com/verdis-aida-synopsis-723733 (Accessed: November 13, 2022).

King Farouk's Architectural Marvel Completed and Dad's New Life in Sudan

60. Zaatari, A. (2002) *The third citizen—JSTOR.* https://www.jstor.org/stable/3172454 (Accessed: December 6, 2022).

61. *Cairo fire* (2022) *Wikipedia.* Wikimedia Foundation. https://en.wikipedia.org/wiki/Cairo_fire#Gol04 (Accessed: November 13, 2022).
62. Corgnati, M. (no date) *Van Leo from Turkey to Egypt.* http://www.contemporarypractices.net/artistessay/Van%20Leo.pdf (Accessed: November 13, 2022).

Al-Sudan: Dad's New Home

63. "Sudanese Civil Wars," Encyclopedia of the Modern Middle East and North Africa (2022). *Encyclopedia of the Modern Middle East and North Africa.* Encyclopedia.com. November 16, 2022, Encyclopedia.com. https://www.encyclopedia.com/humanities/encyclopedias-almanacs-transcripts-and-maps/sudanese-civil-wars (Accessed: November 25, 2022).
64. Specia, M. (2018) *383,000: Estimated death toll in South Sudan's war, The New York Times.* The New York Times. https://www.nytimes.com/2018/09/26/world/africa/south-sudan-civil-war-deaths.html (Accessed: November 25, 2022).

The Kingdom of Kush

65. *Kingdom of Kush—History of Africa with Zeinab Badawi [Episode 4]* (2020) *YouTube.* YouTube. https://www.youtube.com/watch?v=CwaP1kyAqqo (Accessed: November 25, 2022).
66. Kessler, P.L. (1999) *African Kingdoms, The History Files.* https://www.historyfiles.co.uk/KingListsAfrica/AfricaSudan.htm (Accessed: November 25, 2022).
67. The Editors of Encyclopaedia Britannica (no date) *Islamic encroachments, Encyclopædia Britannica.* Encyclopædia Britannica, inc. https://www.britannica.com/place/Sudan/Islamic-encroachments (Accessed: November 25, 2022).

Part Two: Mom's Story

Chapter 10: Mom's Birthplace

68. National Geographic Society (no date) *The Kingdom of Aksum, National Geographic Society*. https://education.nationalgeographic.org/resource/kingdom-aksum (Accessed: November 25, 2022).
69. Zeratsyon, H. (2019) *Ethiopia mosque ban: 'our sacred city of Aksum must be protected,' BBC News*. BBC. https://www.bbc.com/news/world-africa-48634427 (Accessed: November 25, 2022).
70. Ofcansky, T.P. and L.V.B. Berry. (1993) *Ethiopia: A country study*: United States Government Printing Office.
71. Zewde, B. (2002) *A history of modern Ethiopia, 1855–1991*. Athens, Ohio: Ohio University Press.
72. Hansberry, W.L. (1974) *Pillars in Ethiopian history*. Washington, DC: Howard University.
73. Britannica, T.E.of E. (2020) *Haile Selassie summary, Encyclopædia Britannica*. Encyclopædia Britannica, inc. https://www.britannica.com/biography/Haile-Selassie-I (Accessed: November 25, 2022).

Mom's Christian Ancestors

74. Hansberry, W.L. (1974) *Pillars in Ethiopian history*. Washington, DC: Howard University.
75. Shinn, D.H. and T.P. Ofcansky. (2004) in *Historical Dictionary of Ethiopia*. Lanham (Md.): Scarecrow Press.

The Italian Invasion of Ethiopia & WWII in Mom's Neck of the Woods

76. Getahun, S.A., W.T. Kassu and H. I. Tijani. (2014) "INTRODUCTION," in *Culture and customs of Ethiopia*. ABC-CLIO, LLC.

77. Editors, C.R. (no date) *The Scramble for Africa: The History and Legacy of the Colonization of Africa by European Nations during the New Imperialism Era Kindle Edition.* CreateSpace Publishing.

Early Childhood in Tigray's Highlands of Ethiopia

78. *Beta Israel* (2022) *Encyclopædia Britannica.* Encyclopædia Britannica, inc. https://www.britannica.com/topic/Beta-Israel (Accessed: December 27, 2022).
79. Ofcansky & Berry, Op. Cit.

Chapter 11: On the Brink of Starvation

80. *Audio version of the Wikipedia Article: East African Campaign (World War II)* (2018) *YouTube.* YouTube. https://www.youtube.com/watch?v=V1ryfdHvh0g (Accessed: November 26, 2022).

Child Labor in Little Rome: Asmara

81. Britannica, T.E.of E. (2019) *Asmara, Encyclopædia Britannica.* Encyclopædia Britannica, inc. https://www.britannica.com/place/Asmara (Accessed: November 26, 2022).
82. *Africa's "Little Rome," the Eritrean city frozen in time by war and secrecy* (2015) *The Guardian.* Guardian News and Media. https://www.theguardian.com/world/2015/aug/18/eritrea-asmara-frozen-in-time-africas-little-rome?msclkid=2a2796a7c36311ec96a4650fe83c231e (Accessed: November 27, 2022).

Chapter 12: Agordat: Mom's Last Train Stop

83. *Battle of Agordat (1941)* (2022) *Wikipedia.* Wikimedia Foundation. https://en.wikipedia.org/wiki/Battle_of_Agordat_(1941). (Accessed: November 27, 2022).

84. Splinter, H.van der (no date) *Agordat (Akordat), Eritrea*. http://www.eritrea.be/old/eritrea-agordat.htm (Accessed: November 27, 2022).
85. Wikipedia (2021) *Barka River, Wikipedia*. Wikimedia Foundation. https://en.wikipedia.org/wiki/Barka_River (Accessed: November 27, 2022).

The Bus Trip to Barentu: Mom's Cultural Shock

86. Project, J. (2022) *Kunama in Eritrea, Joshua Project: People Groups of the World*. https://joshuaproject.net/people_groups/12850/er (Accessed: November 27, 2022).
87. Victor, R.K. (2018) *Who are the Kunama people? WorldAtlas*. WorldAtlas. https://www.worldatlas.com/articles/who-are-the-kunama-people.html (Accessed: November 30, 2022).

Chapter 13: Early Morning Journey from Teseney to Kassala

88. Mustvisitplace.com, (2019) *Beautiful tourist places to visit in Teseney, Eritrea, Africa, MustVisitPlace.com*. https://www.mustvisitplace.com/beautiful-tourist-places-to-visit-in-teseney-eritrea-africa/ (Accessed: November 30, 2022).
89. *Teseney* (2022) *Wikipedia*. Wikimedia Foundation. https://en.wikipedia.org/wiki/Teseney (Accessed: November 30, 2022).

Chapter 14: Making It to Kassala

90. Voyages, J.A.- A. (2022) *A visit to Kassala, Sudan, Medium*. Globetrotters. https://medium.com/globetrotters/a-visit-to-kassala-sudan-6c1c95410e1c (Accessed: December 6, 2022).
91. Britannica, the Editors of Encyclopaedia. (2018) *Kassala, Encyclopædia Britannica*. Encyclopædia Britannica, Inc. https://www.britannica.com/place/Kassala-province-the-Sudan (Accessed: November 30, 2022).

92. Wikipedia (2022) *Kassala, Wikipedia*. Wikimedia Foundation. https://en.wikipedia.org/wiki/Kassala (Accessed: November 30, 2022).

Chapter 16: Khartoum: Mom's New Home: The "Holy War" Against Britain and Ethiopia

93. Lohnes, K. (2022) *Al-Mahdī, Encyclopædia Britannica*. Encyclopædia Britannica, inc. https://www.britannica.com/biography/al-Mahdi-Sudanese-religious-leader (Accessed: December 4, 2022).
94. Britannica, the Editors of Encyclopaedia (2018) *Kassala, Encyclopædia Britannica*. Encyclopædia Britannica, inc. https://www.britannica.com/place/Kassala-province-the-Sudan (Accessed: December 4, 2022).
95. Holt, P.M. and M. W. Daly. (2014) *A history of the Sudan from the coming of Islam to the present day*. Oxfordshire, England: Routledge.
96. Zewde, B. (2002) A history of modern Ethiopia, 1855–1991. Athens, Ohio: Ohio University Press.

Khartoum

97. Anacker, C. (2020) *Khartoum, Sudan (1821-) BlackPast.org* https://www.blackpast.org/global-african-history/khartoum-sudan-1821/ (Accessed: December 4, 2022).
98. Britannica, the Editors of Encyclopaedia. (2022) *Battle of omdurman, Encyclopædia Britannica*. Encyclopædia Britannica, inc. https://www.britannica.com/event/Battle-of-Omdurman (Accessed: December 4, 2022).
99. Collins, R.O. (2012) *A history of modern Sudan*. Cambridge: Cambridge University Press.
100. Metz, H.C. (1992) *Sudan: A country study*. Washington, DC: Federal Research Division, Library of Congress.

Mom and Dad's unlikely meeting in Khartoum

101. Aga, M.T. (no date) *Allaboutethio.* https://allaboutethio.com/hwegypt.html (Accessed: December 4, 2022).

My Godmother Zanabesh

102. Getahun, S.A., W. T. Kassu and H. I. Tijani. (2014) "INTRODUCTION," in Culture and customs of Ethiopia. ABC-CLIO, LLC.

★ ★ ★

REFERENCES

Africa's "Little Rome," the Eritrean city frozen in time by war and secrecy (2015) The Guardian. Guardian News and Media. https://www.theguardian.com/world/2015/aug/18/eritrea-asmara-frozen-in-time-africas-little-rome?msclkid=2a2796a7c36311ec96a4650fe83c231e (Accessed: November 27, 2022).

Aga, M.T. (no date) Allaboutethio. https://allaboutethio.com/hwegypt.html (Accessed: December 4, 2022).

Aida (2022) Wikipedia. Wikimedia Foundation. https://en.wikipedia.org/wiki/Aida#CITEREFGreene1985 (Accessed: November 13, 2022).

Anacker, C. (2020) Khartoum, Sudan (1821-) BlackPast.org https://www.blackpast.org/global-african-history/khartoum-sudan-1821/ (Accessed: December 4, 2022).

Anon, 2014. Six unexpected WWI battlegrounds. BBC News. https://www.bbc.com/news/magazine-30098000 (Accessed August 28, 2022).

Anon, 2019. Egypt Profile—Timeline. BBC News. https://www.bbc.com/news/world-africa-13315719#:~:text=1859%2D69%20%2D%20Suez%20Canal%20built,formally%20becomes%20a%20British%20protectorate (Accessed September 6, 2022).

Anon, 2022. American University of Beirut. Wikipedia. https://en.wikipedia.org/wiki/American_University_of_Beirut (Accessed August 28, 2022).

Anon, 2022. Antislavery Society (1823–1838). Wikipedia. https://en.wikipedia.org/wiki/Anti-Slavery_Society_(1823%E2%80%931838) (Accessed September 18, 2022).

Anon, 2022. Great famine of mount Lebanon. Wikipedia. https://en.wikipedia.org/wiki/Great_Famine_of_Mount_Lebanon (Accessed August 28, 2022).

Anon, 2022. History of Gaza. Wikipedia. https://en.wikipedia.org/wiki/History_of_Gaza (Accessed August 28, 2022).

Anon, 2022. History of Gaza. Wikipedia. https://en.wikipedia.org/wiki?curid=21567020 (Accessed September 2, 2022).

Anon, 2022. Kahlil Gibran. Wikipedia. https://en.wikipedia.org/wiki/Kahlil_Gibran (Accessed August 23, 2022).

Anon, 2022. Khouri. Wikipedia. https://en.wikipedia.org/wiki/Khouri (Accessed August 21, 2022).

Anon, 2022. Mount Lebanon. Wikipedia. https://en.wikipedia.org/wiki/Mount_Lebanon (Accessed August 23, 2022).

Anon, 2022. Nile. Wikipedia. https://en.wikipedia.org/wiki/Nile#cite_note-:1-59 (Accessed September 6, 2022).

Anon, 2022. Slavery in Egypt. Wikipedia. https://en.wikipedia.org/wiki/Slavery_in_Egypt (Accessed September 11, 2022).

Anon, Khoury surname origin, meaning & last name history—forebears. Forebears. https://forebears.io/surnames/khoury (Accessed August 21, 2022).

Anon, United Nations Development Programme. UNDP. https://www.undp.org/ (Accessed September 6, 2022).

Arsenault, N., C. Rose and T. Lozano. Africa enslaved—minio.la.utexas.edu. slavery_in_ottoman_egypt.pdf. https://minio.la.utexas.edu

/webeditor-files/hemispheres/pdf/slavery_in_ottoman_egypt.pdf (Accessed September 12, 2022).

Audio version of the Wikipedia Article: East African Campaign (World War II) (2018) YouTube. YouTube. https://www.youtube.com/watch?v=V1ryfdHvh0g (Accessed: November 26, 2022).

Baron, B., 1970. [pdf] liberated bodies and saved souls: Freed African slave girls and missionaries in Egypt: Semantic scholar. undefined. https://www.semanticscholar.org/paper/Liberated-Bodies-and-Saved-Souls%3A-Freed-African-and-Baron/228da49a0aa13e0bc03a1a38598b0df27e066f87 (Accessed September 29, 2022).

Battle of Agordat (1941) (2022) Wikipedia. Wikimedia Foundation. https://en.wikipedia.org/wiki/Battle_of_Agordat_(1941)#:~:text=The%20Battle%20of%20Agordat%20was,of%20the%20Second%20World%20War. (Accessed: November 27, 2022).

Beta Israel (2022) *Encyclopædia Britannica*. Encyclopædia Britannica, inc. https://www.britannica.com/topic/Beta-Israel (Accessed: December 27, 2022).

Britannica, T.E.of E. (2019) Asmara, Encyclopædia Britannica. Encyclopædia Britannica, inc. https://www.britannica.com/place/Asmara (Accessed: November 26, 2022).

Britannica, T.E.of E. (2020) Haile Selassie summary, Encyclopædia Britannica. Encyclopædia Britannica, inc. https://www.britannica.com/biography/Haile-Selassie-I (Accessed: November 25, 2022).

Britannica, the Editors of Encyclopaedia (2018) Kassala, Encyclopædia Britannica. Encyclopædia Britannica, inc. https://www.britannica.com/place/Kassala-province-the-Sudan (Accessed: December 4, 2022).

Britannica, the Editors of Encyclopaedia. (2022) Battle of omdurman, Encyclopædia Britannica. Encyclopædia Britannica, inc. https://www

.britannica.com/event/Battle-of-Omdurman (Accessed: December 4, 2022).

Buzz, E.S. (2020) Sakakini Palace: The story behind one of Cairo's architectural gems, Egyptian Streets. https://egyptianstreets.com/2020/02/10/sakakini-palace-the-story-behind-one-of-cairos-architectural-gems/ (Accessed: November 2, 2022).

Cairo fire (2022) Wikipedia. Wikimedia Foundation. https://en.wikipedia.org/wiki/Cairo_fire#Gol04 (Accessed: November 13, 2022).

Collins, R.O. (2012) A history of modern Sudan. Cambridge: Cambridge University Press.

Corgnati, M. (no date) Van Leo from Turkey to Egypt. http://www.contemporarypractices.net/artistessay/Van%20Leo.pdf (Accessed: November 13, 2022).

Editors, C.R. (no date) The Scramble for Africa: The History and Legacy of the Colonization of Africa by European Nations during the New Imperialism Era Kindle Edition. CreateSpace Publishing.

Egypt: The Gift of the Nile

Egypt's Black-White Color Divide

Encyclopedia of the Modern Middle East and North Africa (2022). encyclopedia of the modern middle east and North Africa. encyclopedia.com. 16 Nov. 2022, Encyclopedia.com. Encyclopedia.com. https://www.encyclopedia.com/humanities/encyclopedias-almanacs-transcripts-and-maps/sudanese-civil-wars (Accessed: November 25, 2022).

Fahmy, Z., 2011. Ordinary Egyptians: Creating the modern nation through popular culture, Stanford, CA: Stanford University Press.

Falls (2022) Raid on the Suez Canal, Wikipedia. Wikimedia Foundation. https://en.wikipedia.org/wiki/Raid_on_the_Suez_Canal (Accessed: October 1, 2022).

Filiu, J.-P. & J. King, 2014. Gaza: A history, New York: Oxford University Press.

Getahun, S.A., W. T. Kassu and H. I. Tijani, (2014) "INTRODUCTION," in Culture and customs of Ethiopia. ABC-CLIO, LLC.

Gilbert, A. (2021) Battles of el-alamein, Encyclopædia Britannica. Encyclopædia Britannica, inc. https://www.britannica.com/event/battles-of-El-Alamein (Accessed: October 11, 2022).

Gilbert, M. (1992) Churchill: A life. London: Minerva.

Goldsmith et al. (no date) World War II and its aftermath, Encyclopædia Britannica. Encyclopædia Britannica, inc. https://www.britannica.com/place/Egypt/World-War-II-and-its-aftermath (Accessed: October 11, 2022).

Green, A. (2019) Synopsis of Verdi's opera, Aida, LiveAbout. LiveAbout. https://www.liveabout.com/verdis-aida-synopsis-723733 (Accessed: November 13, 2022).

Hansberry, W.L. (1974) Pillars in Ethiopian history. Washington, DC: Howard University.

Hichens, R. (1910) The spell of Egypt. Leipzig: B. Tauchnitz.

Holmes, M. et al. (2004) Nile. London: BBC Worldwide.

Holt, P.M. and M. W. Daly, (2014) A history of the Sudan from the coming of Islam to the present day. Oxfordshire, England: Routledge.

Kessler, P.L. (1999) African Kingdoms, The History Files. https://www.historyfiles.co.uk/KingListsAfrica/AfricaSudan.htm (Accessed: November 25, 2022).

Kingdom of Kush—History Of Africa with Zeinab Badawi [Episode 4] (2020) YouTube. YouTube. https://www.youtube.com/watch?v=CwaP1kyAqqo (Accessed: November 25, 2022).

Lohnes, K. (2022) Al-Mahdī, Encyclopædia Britannica. Encyclopædia Britannica, inc. https://www.britannica.com/biography/al-Mahdi-Sudanese-religious-leader (Accessed: December 4, 2022).

Mak, L., 2012. The British in Egypt: Community, crime and crises 1822–1922, I.B. Tauris.

Mansel, P., 2011. Levant: Splendour and catastrophe on the Mediterranean, New Haven: Yale University Press.

Metz, H.C. (1992) Sudan: A country study. Washington, D.C.: Federal Research Division, Library of Congress.

Mosleh, M. (2018) Sham El-Nessim: Egypt's oldest celebration, EgyptToday. https://www.egypttoday.com/Article/4/47334/Sham-El-Nessim-Egypt%E2%80%99s-oldest-celebration (Accessed: December 5, 2022).

Mustvisitplace.com, (2019) Beautiful tourist places to visit in Teseney, Eritrea, Africa, MustVisitPlace.com. https://www.mustvisitplace.com/beautiful-tourist-places-to-visit-in-teseney-eritrea-africa/ (Accessed: November 30, 2022).

National Geographic Society (no date) The Kingdom of Aksum, National Geographic Society. https://education.nationalgeographic.org/resource/kingdom-aksum (Accessed: November 25, 2022).

Ofcansky, T.P. and L. V. B. Berry, (1993) Ethiopia: A country study.: United States Government Printing Office.

Project, J. (2022) Kunama in Eritrea, Joshua Project: People Groups of the World. https://joshuaproject.net/people_groups/12850/er (Accessed: November 27, 2022).

Raafat, S. (1997) Adopt A Monument, Sakakini Palace: How about the palace that turns a hundred years old this year? April 5, 1997. http://www.egy.com/landmarks/97-04-05.php (Accessed: November 2, 2022).

Raid on the Suez Canal (2022) Wikipedia. Wikimedia Foundation. https://en.wikipedia.org/wiki/Raid_on_the_Suez_Canal (Accessed: October 1, 2022).

Salih, Z. (2020) Viewpoint from Sudan—where black people are called slaves, BBC News. BBC. https://www.bbc.com/news/world-africa-53147864 (Accessed: November 2, 2022).

Shinn, D.H. and T. P. Ofcansky, (2004) in Historical Dictionary of Ethiopia. Lanham (Md.): Scarecrow Press.

Sir, C.W.L.S. (2000) The Second World War: Volume IV The Hinge of Fate. London: Folio Society.

Specia, M. (2018) 383,000: Estimated death toll in South Sudan's war, The New York Times. The New York Times. https://www.nytimes.com/2018/09/26/world/africa/south-sudan-civil-war-deaths.html (Accessed: November 25, 2022).

Splinter, H.van der (no date) Agordat (Akordat), Eritrea. http://www.eritrea.be/old/eritrea-agordat.htm (Accessed: November 27, 2022).

Strachan, H. (2003) The First World War (Volume I): To Arms. New York: Oxford University Press.

Taylor, B. (1856) A journey to Central Africa; Egypt and Soudan 1851. New York: Big Byte Books.

Teseney (2022) Wikipedia. Wikimedia Foundation. https://en.wikipedia.org/wiki/Teseney (Accessed: November 30, 2022).

The Editors of Encyclopaedia Britannica (no date) Islamic encroachments, Encyclopædia Britannica. Encyclopædia Britannica, inc. https://www.britannica.com/place/Sudan/Islamic-encroachments (Accessed: November 25, 2022).

Victor, R.K. (2018) Who are the Kunama people? WorldAtlas. WorldAtlas. https://www.worldatlas.com/articles/who-are-the-kunama-people.html (Accessed: November 30, 2022).

Voyages, J.A.- A. (2022) A visit to Kassala, Sudan, Medium. Globetrotters. https://medium.com/globetrotters/a-visit-to-kassala-sudan-6c1c95410e1c (Accessed: December 6, 2022).

Walz, T. & K. M. Cuno. 2011. Race and slavery in the Middle East: Histories of trans-Saharan Africans in nineteenth-century Egypt, Sudan, and the Ottoman Mediterranean, the American University in Cairo.

Walz, T. & K. M. Cuno, 2011. Race and slavery in the Middle East: Histories of trans-Saharan Africans in nineteenth-century Egypt, Sudan, and the Ottoman Mediterranean, the American University in Cairo.

Wikipedia (2021) Barka River, Wikipedia. Wikimedia Foundation. https://en.wikipedia.org/wiki/Barka_River (Accessed: November 27, 2022).

Wikipedia (2022) Kassala, Wikipedia. Wikimedia Foundation. https://en.wikipedia.org/wiki/Kassala (Accessed: November 30, 2022).

Wikipedia (2022) Oswald Chambers, Wikipedia. Wikimedia Foundation. https://en.wikipedia.org/wiki/Oswald_Chambers#cite_note-21 (Accessed: September 30, 2022).

Zaatari, A. (2002) The third citizen—JSTOR. https://www.jstor.org/stable/3172454 (Accessed: December 6, 2022).

Zeratsyon, H. (2019) Ethiopia mosque ban: 'our sacred city of Aksum must be protected', BBC News. BBC. https://www.bbc.com/news/world-africa-48634427 (Accessed: November 25, 2022).

Zewde, B. (2002) A history of modern Ethiopia, 1855–1991. Athens, Ohio: Ohio University Press.

★ ★ ★
ABOUT THE AUTHOR

Born in Khartoum, Sudan, a few blocks from the River Nile, Adel Gobran Hanna (Khouri) moved to the United States after high school. He came to America with a goal and a God-given dream to become a doctor. He earned his undergraduate degree and graduated from medical school in Ohio. Dr. Hanna completed his Family Practice residency training and is Board Certified in Family Medicine. Over the past 25 years, he has treated thousands of patients, including many years of treating college students with various medical and mental health illnesses. His approach to medicine is treating the whole person: Body, mind, and spirit. Not just with pills but with good listening ears, skills, love, and compassion. He is the author of Soldier to Soldier, Heart to Heart, A Doctor's Stories from a Military Camp. Dr. Hanna lives and practices medicine in Ohio and a few other states.

INDEX

A
"Adia," 58–59
Al-Khouri ancestors, Mount Lebanon origins, 7–9
Al-Khouri family
  Egypt, 17–19
  loss of home, 53–55
Al-Khouri name, 3–4
Al-Mahdi in Khartoum, 139
Al-Sudan. *See* Sudan
Al-tahour, 201–202
Al-Zagazig (Egypt), 17
  coffee houses, 23–24
  culture, 23–24
  family assimilation, 22–23
  father's life, 34
America
  arrival, 225–228
  college plans, 218–221
  friend's help, 227–228
  hope in, 248–249
  Indiana, 219–221, 235
  Jacksonville mistake, 229–230
  KKK (Ku Klux Klan), 235
  newspaper's influence, 213–214
  Olivia and phone call help, 227–228
  pop culture interests, 215
  racial divide, 214–215
American Embassy in Khartoum, 215
American movies at CCK, 183–184
American University of Beirut, 11
Andrea, William, 209–212
  legacy, 229
Arabic proverb for motivation, 266
architectural design competition, 59–60
Axum/Aksum, 74–75

B
Beirut, Switzerland of the Middle East, 12
Bliss, Daniel, 11
British Anti-Slavery Society, 29–30
British Army in Khartoum, 139

C

Cairo
  violence, 60–61
  YMCA, 36–37
CCK (Comboni College Khartoum), 181
  American movies, 183–184
  Islamic Sharia Law and, 182–183
  Muslim prayers, 186
childhood
  circumcision, 201–202
  healthcare, 200–201
  travel vaccinations, 200–201
childhood home, 172
  shelter for refugees, 173
Christians
  ancestors, 4–5
  Ethiopia, 75–76
  Lebanese Christian massacres, 7–12
  move to Egypt, 5
  religious tension in Egypt, 24–26
Christmas celebrations, in Khartoum, 189
circumcision, 201–202
college
  liberal arts
    African friend, 241–243
    Black American students, 245–246
    cafeteria experiences, 244–247
    cultural education, 235–236
    early days, 233–234
    friends and acquaintances, 236–237
    Oreo, 243–244
    racial issues, 235, 237–241
    racial slang and gestures, 239–240
    skin color prejudices, 244–246
  medical school
    acceptance, 267–268
    letters of recommendation, 265–266
  public university, 249–251
    INTERNAT group, 254–256
    letters from home, 253
    medical school, 247–249
    prejudices on campus, 256–257
    pre-med students, 252–253
    transfer, 251–253
colonization, racial bias and, 106–108
cultural education in early days, 235–236

D

Dad
  architectural design competition, 59–60
  brothers, relationships, 42–47
  career advice from Mom, 171–172
  childhood memories, 34–35
  courthouse wedding, 156
  death of, 259–260
  death of son George, 170
  discouraged from marrying, 155–156
  early dates with white women, 153
  family, first meeting, 203–207
  family's wealth, 42–47
  first meeting of Mom, 143
  inclusiveness, 151–152

Khawaja, 152
meeting Mom, 60–61
move to Sudan, 57–64
proposal to Mom, 144–145
protectiveness of, 156
reputation, spread of, 160–161
sisters, 47–48
socioeconomic status in youth, 42
WWI years, 35–38
WWII years, 41–42
YMCA, 36–37
"Dukul al-Hamam Mish Zay Khuruguh," 26

E

Egypt, 17–18
  Abu Serga (St. Sergius), 40
  Al-Zagazig, 17, 21–23
  Christians, religious tension, 24–25
  Dad's family, first meeting, 203–207
  family's arrival, 21
  King Tutankhamun's tomb discovery, 39
  move to in 1865, 5
  Nile Valley Delta Region, 19
  racial bias, 27–28, 30–31
  Sham El-Nessim Day, 39
  slavery, 27–30
El-Sakakini Pasha Palace, 53–54
Ethiopia
  Mom's childhood, 82
  WWII Italian invasion, 77–78

G

Gaza, grandfather's birthplace, 13–15
George (brother), death, 170–172
Gibran, Khalil Gibran, 7
Grandfather Hanna
  Al-Zagazig culture, 23–24
  early years in Egypt, 33–34
  Egypt arrival, 21
grandparents love story, Grandma Mislal and Grandpa Tesfi, 78–80

H

Hanna. *See also* Grandfather Hanna
  name change, 4
hope in America, 248–249

I

Indiana, 219–221
  KKK (Ku Klux Klan), 235
INTERNAT group on campus, 254–256
interpreter job, 260–261

J

Jehovah's Witnesses, 186–188
jihad (holy war) declaration, Turkish Sultan, 37–38

K

Kassala, history, 124–125
Khartoum
  Al-Mahdi in, 139
  American Embassy, 215
  Anglo-Egyptian colonization, 141
  British Army, 139
  Christmas celebrations, 189

Dad's move to Sudan, 64
Mom's bus trip, 131–138
Mom's new job, 141–142
Syrian club, 161
treatment of Mom and Dad, 151–163
Khouri name, 3
   change in Khartoum, 4
   variations, 5
King Farouk, architectural design competition and, 59–60
King Farouk Mosque building process, 65–68
King Tutankhamun's tomb discovery, 39
Kingdom of Kush (Sudan), 62–63

L

L' Ebat Al fanagean, 35
Lebanese Christian massacres, 7–12
letters
   from home during college, 253
   of recommendation to medical school, 265–266
Levants (Shaouam), 35
Logos ship, 216–219

M

Mahdists' control in Khartoum, 139
Makeda/Queen of Sheba, 74–75
marriage, parents
   challenges after George's death, 170–172
   racially fueled issues, 159–161
medical school, 247–249
mentorships, 261–262

military coups in Sudan, 197–199
Mom
   Abda, 152
   Abeba and trip to Khartoum, 136–137
   Agordat, 104–105
   Aunt Azieb, 101–102
   Aunt Sahitea, 83–84
   aunt's return and death, 91–92
   Barentu, 105–106
   beatings by female relative, 92–93
   birth, 80–81
   birthplace, 73–75
   car rides, 143–144
   childhood in Ethiopia, 82
   children passing gas, 91
   Christian ancestors, 75–76
   Christian Orthodox Church, 74–75
   courthouse wedding, 156
   as Dad's "Aida," 60–61
   Dad's proposal, 144–145
   Dad's status, 153
   death of son George, 170
   derogatory terms about, 152
   discouraged from marrying, 155–156
   domestic work, 85
   domestic work for Italian families, 95–97
   Egyptian biases, 143–145
   first meeting of Dad, 143
   Habasha family, 110–111
   Habashia, 152
   Hassan's help with job, 111–112
   Italian families leaving, 101–102

jealousy from other women, 162–163
Khadama, 152
Khartoum
   bus trip to, 131–138
   new job, 141–142
leaving childhood home, 102–103
Mislal (Mother) death, 157–158
mother's cooking, 93–94
oxen at home, 93
parents' love story, 78–80
return to parents' home, 88–91, 93–95
sending money home, 144–145
sham paper marriage, 126–127, 134–138
Shashou the chicken, 91
starvation, 86–88
Sudan
   border crossing, 121–129
   coyote helper, 115–116
   decision to move, 112–114
Tadalish, 109–110
Teru and border crossing, 118, 122–128
Teru and trip to Khartoum, 131–133, 137–138
Teseney, 108–111
visits with parents in Adwa, 84
WWII years, 77–78, 86–87
Zanabesh, 143, 146–148
motivational Arabic proverb, 266
Mount Lebanon, Al-Khouri ancestors, 7–12
Muslims in Sudan
  as Christians among, 176–178
  prayer at CCK, 186

O
Oreo, 243–244

P
prejudices on campus, 256–257

Q
Queen of Sheba/Makeda, 74–75

R
racial issues
  America, 214–215
  childhood problems, 174–176
  college cafeteria, 244–247
  college campus, 235, 237–241
  colonization and, 106–108
  commonalities and, 206–207
  derogatory terms, Mom and, 152
  in Egypt, 27–28, 30–31
  marriage challenges, 159–161
  Mom's treatment in Khartoum, 154–155
  in Sudan, 57–58
  whites only places, 161–162
Ras Atula, 140–141
religious tension in Egypt, 24–26

S
Sham El-Nessim Day, 39
Shaouam (Levants), 35
Sharia law
  CCK (Comboni College Khartoum) and, 182–183
  in Sudan, 62
skin color prejudices

as child, 174–176
      Dad's family, 205–206
      college, 244–246
slavery
   British Anti-Slavery Society, 29–30
   considerations during college, 237
   in Egypt, 27–30
stone on one's back, 128
Sudan
   1970s, 199–200
   civil war, 197–198
   courthouse wedding, 156
   Dad's move to, 57–64
   father's move to, 26
   independence granted, 197
   Khartoum, 64
   Kingdom of Kush, 62–63
   living as Christians, 176–178
   Mahdists' control, 139–140
   military coups in, 198–199
   Mom's border crossing, 121–129
   North and South differences, 169–170
   racial bias, 57–58
   Sharia law, 62
Switzerland of the Middle East (Beirut), 12
Syrian Club in Khartoum, 161

T

Teru, Mom's border crossing and, 118, 122–128
the Levant, Islamic conquests, 4
travel vaccinations, 200–201

U

USAID (U.S. Agency for International Development) humanitarian aid, 184–185

W

wedding (parents)
   in Christian church, 158
   reception in Adwa, 159
   in Sudan courthouse, 156
whites only places, 161–162
WWI years, 35–38
   post war years, 39–40
WWII years, 41–42
   Italian invasion of Ethiopia, 77–78
   Mom's food situation, 87–88

X-Y-Z

YMCA in Cairo, 36–37

Zanabesh, 146–148

www.ingramcontent.com/pod-product-compliance
Lightning Source LLC
Chambersburg PA
CBHW070531010526
44118CB00012B/1099